STANDING OUT, STANDING' TOGETHER

The Social and Political Impact of Gay–Straight Alliances

MELINDA MICELI

Foreword by Steven Seidman

Routledge
Taylor & Francis Group

New York London

Published in 2005 by
Routledge
Taylor & Francis Group
270 Madison Avenue
New York, NY 10016

Published in Great Britain by
Routledge
Taylor & Francis Group
2 Park Square
Milton Park, Abingdon
Oxon OX14 4RN

International Standard Book Number-10: 0-415-95091-0 (Hardcover) 0-415-95092-9 (Softcover)
International Standard Book Number-13: 978-0-415-95091-6 (Hardcover) 978-0-415-95092-3 (Softcover)
Library of Congress Card Number 2005006116

Library of Congress Cataloging-in-Publication Data

Miceli, Melinda.
    Standing out, standing together : the social and political impact of gay-straight alliances / Melinda Miceli.
        p. cm.
    Includes bibliographical references and index.
    ISBN 0-415-95091-0 (hb : alk. paper) -- ISBN 0-415-95092-9 (pb : alk. paper)
    1. Gay youth--United States. 2. Gay students--United States. 3. Gay-straight alliances in schools--United States. I. Title.

HQ76.3.U5M49 2005
306.76'6'0835--dc22

2005006116

Taylor & Francis Group
is the Academic Division of T&F Informa plc.

Visit the Taylor & Francis Web site at
http://www.taylorandfrancis.com

and the Routledge Web site at
http://www.routledge-ny.com

DEDICATION

*For my mother Donna. She is the true writer in the family,
and a constant source of comfort, love, and wisdom
and
for Molly and Rene, for letting me into their lives and
inspiring me to write this book*

CONTENTS

FOREWORD

Lesbian and gay life in America has changed considerably since the Stonewall rebellion in 1969. Just 10 years ago, gays were either not represented in popular culture or stereotyped in disrespectful and hurtful ways. Today, lesbian and gay characters are routinely present on television, in the movies, in magazines and newspaper reporting, and so on. The struggle for gay rights has also witnessed remarkable progress. For example, although the right to marry has so far been denied to gays, domestic-partnership rights have been recognized in many towns, cities, states, businesses, professions, and unions across the country. And, while a segment of the Christian fundamentalist community steadfastly resists lesbian and gay equality, these anti-gay activists are today challenged not only by a well-organized gay movement but by many allies and institutions in straight America.

As I have argued elsewhere, the era of the closet is passing. From the 1950s through at least the early 1990s, the state, along with other social and cultural institutions, deliberately and aggressively sought to purge any traces of homosexuality from public life. Through repressive laws, a public culture of homophobia, pervasive institutional discrimination, and everyday violence, the homosexual was persecuted, and survived by a life of hiding or pretending to be heterosexual.

However, not all homosexuals retreated into the closet. Lesbians and gay men also responded by creating communities and political organizations that resisted an America seemingly at war with homosexuals. Between the 1960s and 2005, the lesbian and gay movement has achieved much. Today, many individuals are able to choose to organize lives as lesbians and gay men outside the framework of the closet. However, the expanded personal freedom and social tolerance many gays experience is not the same as winning social equality. Lesbians and gay men may be visible, socially integrated, and recognized as Americans, but heterosexuality is still enforced as the preferable and ideal way to organize personal and social life.

Perhaps no other group or segment of America has better known the contradictory status of being gay in America today, experiencing both expanded personal freedom and continued second-class citizenship, than have lesbian and gay youth. In contrast to gay youth who came of age in the sixties, seventies, or eighties, today's youth do not feel so alone or isolated, and do not necessarily believe that they are somehow abnormal or perverted. Many gay youth today know that there are lesbians and gay men everywhere in America; they know that many Americans, including straight Americans, value and respect them. Moreover, many lesbian and gay youth today can turn to organizations in their own communities for direct personal, legal, and social support. Many of these youths understand that they are part of a larger community and movement and one that increasingly has considerable mainstream support.

These youths may have unprecedented resources to fight back against prejudice and disrespect, but their struggle for self- and social acceptance is made considerably more difficult by their dependency on two of the most homophobic institutions in America: the family and the public school. With the exception perhaps of the military, the family and our public schools have been arguably the most resistant institutions to accommodating to the changing status of lesbians and gay men in America. Families have been relatively immune to legal and social policy-based reform. Still, there is growing evidence that more and more families in America are learning to accommodate to their gay kin as a condition of maintaining strong family bonds. Schools, however, are more directly vulnerable to legal and social reform, but until recently have resisted such efforts. Sadly, many of our public schools remained repressive, openly homophobic environments with little pressure from teachers, administrators, or parents to bring about social change.

Lesbian and gay youth experience the contradictory status of being homosexual in perhaps the most intense, personally dramatic way. Coming of age earlier than previous generations, quicker to self awareness and self acceptance because of the broader normalizing currents in America, and increasingly choosing to refuse the closet as a social accommodation, today's gay youth face the difficult task of fashioning a life of integrity while navigating their daily lives in institutions that are often aggressively hostile and rarely supportive.

Sadly, many youths succumb to these tensions by choosing to isolate themselves, to live double lives, or worse, to end their lives. But, as Miceli forcefully argues, many gay youths today refuse to be victims. Some individuals bravely engage in acts of great personal risk as they try to forge manageable lives. Many gay youths have come to understand anti-gay prejudice as a social problem that requires a political solution. These young people have organized to demand respect and justice.

Standing Out, Standing Together documents the growth of organizations representing our lesbian and gay youth. These young adults are being transformed from victims into prideful political agents. In this regard, Miceli sounds a theme that all Americans should hear: gay youth and our public schools are today a key battleground not only for lesbians and gays but for Americans in general. Melinda Miceli's book is, to date, the most empirically based and reliable guide to understanding the contradictory status of being young and gay in America.

Steven Seidman
Author of Beyond the Closet: The Transformation of Gay and Lesbian Life

ACKNOWLEDGMENTS

This book would not have been possible without the assistance of a diverse team of people. My most sincere appreciation to everyone who shared their stories, experiences, knowledge, and insights with me as I conducted the research for this book. None of this could have happened without the willingness of students, teachers, and activists to take time out of their very busy lives to assist me in my endeavor. I hope they all feel that the book has done justice to the work they all do on a daily basis.

Completing this project on time was made possible by the professional support of Woody Doane, Jane Horvath, David Goldenberg, and Steve Misovich. Thank you to Lindsey Thatcher for the hours she spent transcribing. Thank you to Kassia Wosick-Correa and Amanda Tompkins for their assistant organizing and formatting hundreds of newspaper articles over the years I spent collecting them. Thank you to Terri Schroeder for connecting me to the ACLU, and to Joe Kosciw at GLSEN for his research assistance.

The discussions I have had with my students inside and outside of the classroom over the years have contributed invaluable insight and inspiration. I thank them all. I particularly want to thank all the students in my "Political Sociology: Identity and Culture" seminar at the University of Wisconsin-Eau Claire, especially Chrissy Smith, Trever Hagen, and Amanda Tompkins, for pushing my thinking on identity issues in new directions. All of them are destined to be great sociologists one day. I also want to thank all of the young women in my "Forces that Change Society" course—Ashley, Jessica, Laura, Rachel, Shaina, LeShea, Cheryl, Cathryn, and Julie—for their patience and for keeping me motivated as I finished writing the book.

My family provided me with a tremendous amount of support through the process. A special thank you to my parents for nurturing me, emotionally and physically, through the final stages of writing. I thank my sister Stacey for the hours she spent on the phone letting me vent my stresses and frustrations and always encouraging me to continue on.

I cannot thank my mother enough for the lifetime of writing lessons she has given me and for the countless hours of editorial work she lovingly donated to me and this book.

THE PERSONAL
AND THE POLITICAL

Two of the things that most frustrate my students are the pace and complexity of social change. Students arrive in my introductory sociology class generally believing either that the social world is their oyster (with all inequalities and injustices in the distant past) or that the world is stacked against them (stuck in generations of prejudice). Much of this perception is shaped by their short life experience—an amalgamation of what they have witnessed and what they have been promised. As we go through the course together, the students come to realize that neither perception is entirely correct. Social change does happen, but usually not quickly, and almost never completely. When I talk to my students about my research, I always ask how many of them had a gay–straight alliance group (GSA) in their school. Each year the number who had such a group gets larger. Some students view GSAs as just a normal part of their past high school life, while, for others, it is a foreign and uneasy concept. That I can discuss the issue with my students in an intelligible and thoughtful way (but not completely free of tension and emotion) is remarkable evidence of how quickly social change has happened, and at the same time, a reminder of how much is still incomplete.

When I think back to the starting point of my research on lesbian, gay, bisexual, and transgender (LGBT)[1] youth I find the speed of the change is almost incomprehensible. Perhaps this is because I do not want to acknowledge how much older I am now than when I started the research in 1994. In my personal world, it seems like only yesterday. More objectively, however, in the scientific measurement of social change, a decade is a rather short period of time, and, in this case, a good deal has happened very quickly. Back in 1994, I was sitting in a Sociology of Sexuality class as a graduate student listening to a guest speaker talk about his work as a facilitator for a support group of LGBT teenagers. I sat and listened in utter amazement as he spoke about the fourteen-, fifteen-, and sixteen-year-old kids who not only knew that they were LGBT, but were brave enough to acknowledge that to others. My shock was both personal and professional. On a personal level, as a twenty-four-year-old woman who did not privately or publicly identify as a lesbian until the age of 21, I could not comprehend that these kids were so self aware at such a young age. As someone who had been through high

---

[1]   I use the acronym LGBT throughout the book for consistency. Many organizations, academics, and individuals use a variety of different configurations of, and additions to, this acronym to refer to the same population. GLBT, GLB, GLBTQ or LGBTQ (questioning), GLBTQQ or LGBTQQ (queer and questioning) are just a few examples of alternatives. My use of LGBT should not be interpreted as a political statement or a value judgment, but rather one conditioned only by a need for consistency and relative simplicity. Occasionally throughout the book, I also refer to "gay youth" or "gay students" to break up the monotony of LGBT. My use of the term gay is always intended to be inclusive rather than exclusive. My original inclination was to use LGB instead of LGBT, for two reasons. First, there were no transgender individuals included in my own qualitative research. This was not because I intentionally excluded them, but rather because none were present in the case studies and none responded to my call for interviews. For this reason, it seemed factually inaccurate to use the "T" as part of my reference to the youth I studied. Second, it is my opinion that while those who write about and work with these students almost always include the transgender "T," it is done more as a politically correct gesture than as a true reflection of their understanding or inclusion of transgender youth and the unique issues they face in schools. (As I discuss in chapter four, The GSA Network in California is a notable and important exception to this rule.) As a result, I feel that, much of the time, it is factually incorrect to include transgender in referring to the research on and advocacy for this population. This is particularly true of work done before the late 1990s. However, I realized that if I were to use this criterion, I would also have to exclude bisexual from most of my references, because this group is similarly treated in research and advocacy. Although I think those who work with gay youth and the gay rights movement need to seriously address the lack of true inclusion and understanding of bisexual and transgender people, I decided that giving this issue the attention it deserves fell outside of the scope and goals of this book. In the end, I decided to use the more inclusive LGBT, despite my uneasiness with its accuracy, rather that furthering the feeling of exclusion for these groups of young people.

school, I was terrified for these kids, sick to my stomach with thoughts of what they would have to endure at the hands and from the mouths of status-seeking, norm-enforcing teenagers. As a professional sociologist in training, what this man was reporting to us about his work with gay youth contradicted much of what I had been studying about sexual identity.

I had learned from the existing [in the early 1990s] literature on the topic that people generally do not come to recognize their sexual orientation until they are in their late teens and early twenties. The research indicated that my personal experience was the "normal" one. These kids he spoke about seemed to me, at first, to be an interesting research anomaly. I had also been taught that it was common for gay people to react to their sexuality with shame and secrecy. However, these kids left their homes, traveled downtown, and entered a gay and lesbian community center to tell a group of strangers they were LGBT and find companionship. In terms of what I had learned up to that point in my life, this phenomenon made little sense.

Fortunately, doctoral students in sociology are in the business of seeking out nonsensical elements of the social world. I needed to know more, so read anything I could find (which wasn't much) on LGBT youth, and attended a meeting of this gay youth support group. Although I continued attending these meetings for three years, the first was unforgettable. As I sat in the circle of young adults I was profoundly aware that I could have been one of these kids, and at the same time, I knew I never could have been like them less than a decade earlier when I was in high school. Immediately I felt that some type of serious social change was under way. When these kids spoke about their experiences, thoughts, and hopes for the future, there was something about the situation that was distinctly different from both my academic knowledge of, and personal experience with, gay and lesbian communities. Even though much of what they spoke about was painful rejection and abuse from their families and peers, there was an underlying attitude of pride in their sexual identity and a resolve that they would spend their energies trying to change the attitudes of others, but they would not waste their energy feeling bad about themselves. Again, clearly, some things remained the same, but it seemed something had profoundly changed. When I asked the group if they would allow me to come to their meetings as part of my research, they were shocked and excited that someone was interested in their lives and they welcomed me into their group. During the following three years, I was fortunate to meet over a hundred unique kids as they came in and out of this group. Each of them left an imprint on me in some way.

During this period, from 1994 to 1997, there was only a vague sense of what a GSA was. At the very beginning of my research, the only resource for these youths was the support group run through the local gay and lesbian community center. About six months into my field research, a few of the kids in the community support group decided they wanted to start a LGBT-related student activist club in their school to educate the student body and staff about homophobia and related issues. The controversy that this sparked in the school was shocking to them, but not to me, and it was fascinating to watch how the events played out. As this was unfolding, some other members of the support group decided to try to start a similar club at their own school. This time, the controversy was even more intense. I began researching these controversies, interviewing teachers, school administrators, students, and community members, trying to understand their positions on the issue. The students working on these clubs were truly making it up as they went along, and in the process of gathering information discovered that other students in the surrounding communities were attempting to start clubs as well. They began networking, sharing experiences, and giving advice and support to one another. Through all of this, none of us was aware of the gay–straight alliance as a solidified concept. Late in 1996, this changed, when some local teachers began a chapter of GLSTN, the gay, lesbian, straight teachers network. It was in connection with this organization that I learned the extent to which LGBT school clubs like the ones I was researching were appearing in small but growing numbers across the country. Gay–straight alliance club had become the term used to refer to groups established by students for the purpose of uniting with those who shared their interest in discussing gay rights issues, educating their school community about these issues and the extent and effect of homophobia in their school, and making school policy more supportive of LGBT students' rights. The extent to which the meaning of this term and the goals of these locally scattered clubs were shared by a growing number of people indicated that more than just local change was happening.

I was nearing the end of the data-gathering portion of my dissertation by this point and had begun to write. I finished and defended the dissertation in 1998, arguing in the conclusion that what I had found was the beginning of significant change. My dissertation research was largely focused on the changes LGBT youth were making to our academic, cultural, and social conceptualizations and understandings of sexual identity. At the time I, truthfully, had no real sense of the potential institutional, political, and social impact of this burgeoning youth activism and social networking or how soon change would come. There has been so much change since 1998 that I needed to conduct an entirely new research project to be able to now speak meaningfully about LGBT high school students' lives and the impact of their activism. This book is the result of that research.

THE GROWTH OF COLLECTIVE ACTION

While I was immersed in the local case studies that became my dissertation, and in the years since, rapidly growing groups of LGBT teenagers have emerged into the public arena in the United States. Individual acts of coming-out by youth solidified, in many ways, into a political act of "coming-out" for this population, which was once thought of as either nonexistent or rightfully hidden. These students spoke out about their identity and experiences, and asked that their local schools tolerate, include, and protect them in the same ways they do other students. What began as the actions of individuals or small groups of students in local schools became community-wide discussion and debate over the origins and morality of homosexuality, the rights of students, and the responsibilities of America's public schools.

As these localized debates increased in frequency and entered national headlines, their scope and reach broadened. National gay rights and conservative Christian groups became interested in these struggles as arenas in which important gains or losses could be made for their larger social, cultural, and political goals. For gay rights groups, the struggles of these students spoke to the larger political issue of the civil rights of LGBT citizens. For conservative Christian groups, these local debates were symptomatic of the threat of the "gay agenda" to American culture and family values. These interests led established national organizations and newly formed groups to become involved in local battles. This brought their views on the importance of these issues into the national political spotlight.

What began as isolated school battles over various related issues—establishing a GSA, adding "sexual orientation" to schools' antidiscrimination and harassment policies, adding books on LGBT issues to school curriculums or libraries, or allowing same-sex couples to attend the prom—eventually coalesced into a movement for larger social change. Some of those fighting to change their school's policy or curriculum are interested only in changing this one element of their school that they see as unfair, with little or no concern for furthering LGBT rights in general. Others, however, do view their school battles within the context of these larger social, cultural, and political issues. The same could be said of those who oppose such school changes. To students who just want an after-school group with which to discuss their experiences and concerns (naive to the power of these forces of history), the uproar that their proposed GSA causes is often more than they are prepared to handle. Organizations like the American Civil Liberties Union (ACLU) and Gay Lesbian Straight Education Network (GLSEN) mobilized to help students navigate the political, legal, and emotional waters into which their request for a GSA plunges them.

The Conceptualization of Gay–straight alliances as a New Social Movement

Throughout this book I refer to and examine gay–straight alliance groups as a social movement. However, I do not intend this book to be an intricate analysis of all the complex technical social movement factors that made the GSA movement[1] possible and are playing a part in its successes or failures. This is not to say that it is not a subject worthy of such analysis; it is, but that is the stuff of academic journal articles. I sincerely hope that experts in the field of social movements will be inspired sufficiently by this book or other accountings of the activism of LGBT youth and their allies to subject it to such technical analysis suitable for scholarly journals. I am confident that many additional insights could be gained from such a pursuit. I use some of the academic terminology of social movements throughout the book, in an attempt to connect the events and activities associated with LGBT student activism over the past two decades into the sum of its parts, which is a larger movement toward social change.

At the most basic level, social movements consist of groups of people utilizing similar practices and discourses in attempts to bring change to some aspect of society. As I illustrate throughout the book, although everyone puts his or her own unique stamp on it, students, teachers, organizational leaders, and supportive community members all share a common discourse in advocating for GSAs. Part of the dialogue of every social movement is to speak about what is wrong with the current state of affairs, to speak about suffering and injustice, and to be critical of those deemed responsible. Those in the GSA movement define the negative in terms of the suicide rates, dropout rates, rates of harassment and experiences of isolation suffered by LGBT students. Blame is generally spoken of as resting in a culture of intolerance and in educational institutions that not only fail to protect but also actively foster these negative outcomes. Although dispersed across schools, communities, and states, the majority of those involved in GSAs share this general language, which has evolved into the discourse of a social movement.

These individuals, groups, and organizations also share common practices or strategies for improving these negative circumstances. These practices involve forming alliances to construct strength in numbers out of scattered marginalized individuals. This strategy to get those who have been teased, harassed, or silenced for standing out and being different to stand together and be counted has proved to be a powerful one. It has bolstered the efforts to educate schools, communities, and the nation about the sources and effects of discrimination suffered by LGBT students and the fundamental principles that should guide us toward rectifying the situation. As we will see, students "speaking truth to power," is the GSA movement's most compelling practice. The personal testimonies of these teenagers expose the blatant discrimination and climate of homophobia in schools that everyone knew was there but no one was doing anything about. Supporting these students' voices, helping to network their efforts, using the law to define their rights, conducting research, and consolidating information to provide more weight to student testimony are all practices shared by the various organizations involved in the social movement. All of these strategies are of the type social scientists refer to as *empirical rational* or *normative re-educative* tactics. In simpler terms, empirical rational strategies seek to change the way people think about an issue or a group of people by conducting research and gathering evidence that refutes commonly held beliefs and understandings. The assumption behind this tactic is that most people are rational thinkers who can be persuaded by the weight of empirical evidence. In contrast, normative re-educative strategies look to change people's attitudes, values, feelings, and beliefs about an issue or a group on a more personal level. This method seeks to break down myths, stereotypes, and fears that impede efforts at creating social change through workshops, diversity training, panel discussions, and stories shared by those directly impacted by the issue.

The individuals and groups that make up the GSA movement are conditioned by social and political reality to employ these basic tactics.

Most of the barriers to winning support for the movement and the rights of LGBT students have been constructed out of deeply entrenched scientific claims, religious beliefs, and cultural stereotypes about homosexuality. Surmounting these barriers is made easier if the elements that built them can be at least partially deconstructed. Assisted by the GSA movement, LGBT students began the process of deconstruction when they asserted identities for themselves that transcended some or all of these entrenched notions. The continuation of this disassembling process through the discourse and practices of the GSA movement qualify it as a "new social movement" in the arena of identity politics.

New social movements like the GSA movement have complicated traditional strategies of identity politics. Throughout American history, minority groups have struggled for control over the descriptions and meanings that are institutionally and culturally applied to them, because these meanings define their rights and shape the qualities of their lives.[2] The issue of identity may not be new to American politics, but the manifestations of these political struggles changed in some significant ways over the past three decades. New social movements go beyond asserting the rights of their group in the public sphere. They also actively critique the power relations involved in the construction of these social meanings that have fashioned their experiences and assert their ability to create new identities of their own control.[3] In this way, groups engaged in identity politics seek to understand and combat the institutional, political, social, and cultural forces that define, shape, and impose identity categories. These movements, and individual activists, challenge the division between the private world of identity formation and the public sphere of politics and cultural power.[4] Throughout this book, I demonstrate that the GSA movement and its participants exemplify these goals and challenges. In doing so, it has begun to create significant change in the lives of LGBT students, and in the social and political struggle for the rights of all LGBT people.

It is important to emphasize that, although the GSA movement may share some of the same discourse, practices, and goals as the gay rights movement, it is distinctively its own movement, which, significantly, was started by independent students and not as an offshoot of some existing organization. The actions of LGBT students and their straight allies brought issues of gay rights into a "new arena." Early on, the civil rights and women's rights movement targeted educational institutions for change because they recognized that schools, as major institutions through which every developing young person passes, have tremendous socializing influence and, therefore, are crucial to social change efforts. The gay rights movement, for a variety of reasons discussed later in the book, did not work in a similar way to change the entrenched heterosexism passed on by schools. The GSA movement has made this its primary goal. It seeks to reverse the influence of educational institutions from institutions that help to instill prejudice and condone the discrimination, harassment, and abuse of gay people into institutions that instill ideas of tolerance and respect for social diversity.

THE COMPLEX DYNAMICS OF SOCIAL CHANGE

I was teaching a class on social change for a group of honors students as I wrote the bulk of this book. This was fortuitous for me because it allowed me to be more fully conscious of how wonderfully complex the change around GSAs has been. The course covered the diversity of complex factors that play a role in creating social change and resistance to change. My students and I spent the semester immersed in the intricacies of struggles over civil rights, women's rights, worker's rights, gay rights, environmental protections, and war protests, among other things. It became clear to all of us that it was not just one person, one organization, one event, or even a handful of events that created change in any of these areas. It was actually multiple factors connected in a beautifully intricate tapestry. As I taught my students about these other struggles for change, I realized this was also true of the GSA movement.

The emergence of movements for social change are almost always partially correlated to cultural and political shifts, which suggests to potential activists that there are small or large openings for the improvement they are seeking. In the case of the GSA movement, by the early 1990s, lesbian and gay subcultures and politics had become more mainstreamed in America, and more visible gay and lesbian public figures, media images, and narratives had emerged.[5] The early 1990s also ushered in a more liberal political climate. After twelve years of a Republican administration sympathetic to, if not fully accommodating of, conservative Christian concerns, Bill Clinton's overt efforts to gain, and acknowledge, the support of gay and lesbian communities for the Democratic party at least gave the impression that gay rights issues had a place at the larger political table.[6] From 1992 through the end of the decade, public opinion polls showed an increase in positive attitudes toward homosexuality. This more tolerant social and political atmosphere, and the access to information and role models, rendered it more possible for groups of LGBT teenagers to emerge into the public arena and ask for change.

Another basic principle of social change is that all social movements are met with resistance from groups that oppose their efforts. This makes the journey toward their goals for improvement fraught with tension, conflict, roadblocks, steps forward and steps back. In the case of the GSA movement, these same cultural and political shifts that organizers saw as an opportunity to advocate for the rights of LGBT students signaled to some conservative Christian groups that the "gay agenda" had reached dangerous heights. In reaction to this, they increased their efforts to seek out and oppose every move made (or that they perceived had been made) by gay rights groups in any social arena, including schools. Now, with the twice-elected George W. Bush presidential administration, which more openly sympathizes with their concerns about the declining morality of American culture, Christian groups are stepping up the aggressiveness by which they seek to counter the efforts of the GSA movement.

Most formal organizations of social movements emerge out of the grassroots activities undertaken by small and localized groups of motivated citizens who wish to improve some element of their community. The GSA movement began as students and teachers tried to figure out how to get their individual schools to offer some services and support to LGBT students, figuring out what discourse and practices worked best as they went along. These grassroots efforts expanded as individuals networked with one another to share the lessons they learned with the next group that endeavored to start a GSA. Progress was made, not only from this collective action, but also from individual acts of altruism, courageous behavior, and resistance. The history of the GSA movement, to this point in time, would not have been possible if individual students had not risked their personal safety and the support of their family; and teachers had not risked rumor, scandal and the loss of their jobs to take a public stand against the social injustices they feel are being imposed on LGBT students.

Movements often gain attention and support as a result of tragic events. For example, the violent treatment, or even murder, of social protestors, or an environmental or industrial hazard that injures, sickens, or kills may bring attention and sympathy to the concerns of a group in more powerful ways than activist efforts were able to do. In the case of the GSA movement, one of the strongest elements drawing people to support and advocate for LGBT students is their vulnerability. Published reports of high rates of suicide and other risk behaviors, cases of severe abuse of LGBT students that ended in publicized lawsuits, and cases of hate crimes directed at gay youth, such as the Matthew Shepard case, were able to bring attention and concern for the rights of gay youth in more meaningful ways than grassroots activism had. The vulnerability of these *children* brought sympathy and a sense of injustice to a level that is generally not extended to the adult gay and lesbian population.

The grassroots activism in response to these tragic events, and the more formal organizing of groups like the ACLU and GLSEN, helped attract diverse groups to the GSA movement. Alliances such as these are necessary to all successful lasting movements for change. Several factors have played a part in the GSA movement's ability to forge coalitions with a rather wide diversity of groups. Straight students who also felt like outsiders and victims at school could empathize with LGBT student sufferings and realized they had a vested interest in their cause. Parents who may not have been motivated to become activists to support their adult gay or lesbian children were motivated to take action to ensure the safety and educational success of their teenage son or daughter. Teachers who were committed to their professional calling to educate, protect, and promote the growth of all their students were able to overcome their own homophobia or fear of losing their jobs to fulfill this dedication to students. If vulnerability was one of the keys to their success at making alliances, the other key was their strength. One of the activists I interviewed pointed out that students' courage and bold leadership unintentionally stirred up feelings of shame in some adults—both gay and straight—for not taking action on their own to help these kids.

Although youth has been an asset to building these alliances, it has, at times, also been a liability. Resistance to the GSA movement, largely led by conservative Christian organizations, has capitalized on LGBT students' status as "children" to evoke stereotypes of homosexuals as sexual predators or recruiters who have a "gay agenda" to influence impressionable young minds into choosing a deviant and dangerous lifestyle. Opposition groups have used these techniques to attract allies who might be moved to take action to protect children, not from suicide or harassment, but from the threat of the gay agenda.

This brings me to the final theme from my social change class that kept haunting me as I wrote this book. During just about every class meeting, my students wrestled with the seemingly contradictory reality that, although collective action has resulted in tremendous change over time, it often seems like nothing has changed at all. Our intense study of social change had put us all on an emotional roller coaster ride. At one moment we were amazed and energized by the incredible degree of progress that individuals and organizations were able to bring about, often in the face of seemingly unbeatable odds. In the next moment, one or all of us would find ourselves crushed by the reality of how much prejudice, inequality, and injustice still exist today. Sometimes out of frustration a student would exclaim, "What's the point of trying!"

We talked about all the work and the sacrifices made by participants in the civil rights, women's rights, and gay rights movements, and, in the next breath, we talked about current inequalities faced by these same groups. The realization of what a long hard road is still left to travel caused some to feel that nothing accomplished before really mattered. I continually had to try to lift the students' spirits and get them to focus on, and find inspiration in, the progress that *has* been made. Although equality has not been achieved, and resistance will always exist, historically we have come a long way out of very oppressive conditions. The possibilities of the change their generation might be able to create in this less constrained environment are endless, not hopeless.

Today, LBGT and straight ally students are in a position to imagine the possibilities of change that they can accomplish by capitalizing on the progress made by the gay rights movement. Leading gay rights movement historian and social analyst John D'Emilio argues that, through the history of the movement:

> "Coming out and community-building have had enormous staying power
> as core strategic impulses. Both seem to speak directly to what is perhaps
> the defining feature of gay experience, the fact that almost all gay men
> and lesbians are neither raised nor socialized at an early age into a gay
> community. The imprint of those critical years of isolation, especially
> compounded by the historic invisibility of homosexuality in everyday life
> and in popular culture, creates an insistent need for the alternative—for
> visibility and the connection that community provides."[7]

This is the first generation in which a sizeable portion of LGBT are in some real ways being socialized from a relatively young age into a gay community, and more broadly, into a community of gay and straight people of all ages who provide the visibility and connection of community. Political activism, alliances, and community building are now becoming the defining developmental experiences in the lives of a significant portion of gay teens. What impact will this have on the future personal experiences of these students and young adults as they take their places in America's other major social institutions? How will these institutions respond to a sizeable cohort of LGBT people who desire to live their lives in ways that are, as Steven Seidman phrases it, "beyond the closet."?[8] What will be the political and social impact of this newly empowered group, who never bought into the idea that there is any shame in being gay or any rational justification for denying them their rights?

A BRIEF STATEMENT ABOUT THE ORGANIZATION OF THE BOOK

The organization of the book chapters are meant to document the progress of LGBT youth from an invisible population; to an "at risk" youth population; to pockets of youth across the nation asserting a positive, proud, and unapologetic self-image; to agents of change claiming a space and a voice in schools; to catalysts for a social movement. In an effort to understand what it took to reach this point in time, I examine the strategies employed by some of the major organizational leaders in this movement, look at how and why religious conservative organizations oppose the GSA movement, and analyze the impact their resistance has had on both public opinion and the tactics employed by the GSA organizers.

I analyze news coverage, the demographic characteristics of the areas where GSAs have been most successful, and the experiences and perceptions of student leaders and faculty advisors from around the country as a way to understand the political, social, cultural, and individual factors that have had an impact on local efforts to start a GSA. I then provide an assessment of the movement's current status, including the impact it has had on public opinion, school policies, and the school experiences of LGBT students. Finally, I take a critical look at the movement's successes and failures to date. Has it fulfilled its potential to empower students, to build alliances across social categories of age, sexual orientation, gender, race, and ethnicity? Has it made an impact on the larger movement for gay and lesbian rights? Has it effectively advocated for the rights of *all* students to be educated in social institutions that respect, value and nurture them, rather than merely tolerate them?

ONE

GAY–STRAIGHT ALLIANCES
From an Idea to a Social Movement

In this first chapter, I offer a chronological historical account of the development and spread of GSAs throughout the United States. I do not claim that the historical account I provide is unabridged. Thousands of events that are important and significant to individual lives, local communities, state policies, and social change have taken place over the past twenty years. An account of all these events could fill a sizeable volume, or several volumes, and still not document everything. What I hope to provide in this chapter is an overview of the major events that have had a specific and direct influence on propelling the movement of LGBT student rights and GSAs forward. Included in this category are legislative decisions that set precedents for the rights of LGBT students and GSAs, the founding of state or national organizations that advocate for LGBT students' rights or coordinate student leadership, the passage of statewide legislation that protects LGBT students from harassment and discrimination or provides services to meet their needs, and stories about LGBT students that made national news headlines.[1]

COLLEGIATE LGBT STUDENT GROUPS:
A TESTING GROUND FOR ORGANIZATION AND RIGHTS

Although the focus of this book is specifically on students organizing in high schools, it is historically significant to note that gay and lesbian college students were the first to challenge educational institutions for a place, a voice, and protection from harassment. Lesbian and gay college students began forming officially recognized student organizations in the early 1970s.[2] The emergence of such groups at that time was not random or spontaneous, but was clearly connected to changes in the larger political climate. The 1969 Stonewall Riots in New York City, which protested police harassment of patrons of lesbian and gay bars, is regarded by most activists and scholars as the beginning of contemporary lesbian and gay rights activism. Lesbian and gay individuals had formed communities and organizations before this date, but the general *modus operandi* of these earlier groups was to use quieter, more secretive tactics for affecting social change—changing the medical classification of homosexuality and sodomy laws, for example.[3] One of the substantial changes that occurred with the Stonewall Protests, and a main reason they are designated as the event marking the start of the modern gay rights movement, is that resistance to oppression and the call for equality became loud and visible. The public acknowledgement of a homosexual identity and the collective demand to be treated humanely and justly by governmental authorities and, later, by social institutions, was in many ways revolutionary to the way the public perceived homosexuals, and the way lesbian and gay individuals viewed themselves.

There is not space in this book to fully document the thirty-five-year history of lesbian and gay rights activism since Stonewall, and discuss its relationship to the current GSA movement in high schools.[4] However, I highlight many of the significant connections throughout the book. My point in mentioning Stonewall here is to suggest it is not coincidental that, in the climate of increased visibility and emphasis on freedoms of speech and assembly, college students scattered throughout the country began to form student organizations and fight for their right to exist and to have a voice on their campus.

The dynamics involved in establishing lesbian and gay college student organizations were, and still are, different from high school student organizations in some significant ways. First, college students are adults, which gives them more power to advocate for their own interests. Second, because the college student population consists of adults rather than minors, their curriculum, policies, and decisions are considerably (although by no means completely) less under the influence of parental concerns and demands. Third, colleges are free of the political influence of school boards and the financial tie to their local community. All of these things help to mitigate, to some extent, the potential for resistance to or conflict over lesbian and gay college students organizing on their campuses. Despite all of these factors, collegiate groups sometimes found (and still find today) themselves surrounded by controversy. Some of the controversies over collegiate lesbian and gay organizations that made national headlines foreshadowed some of the issues with which high school groups would struggle.

In 1971, *The New York Times* ran a story with a headline declaring that "thousands of campus homosexuals are organizing openly to win community acceptance."[5] The story reported the existence of an organization called the National Gay Student Center, which formed the year before in Washington, D.C. for the purpose of networking the efforts of lesbian and gay college groups from around the country. This organization reported that there were 150 student groups on college campuses throughout the country. Although *The New York Times* spent a good deal of time discussing the psychological concerns surrounding homosexuality (at this time still categorized as a mental illness), it reported that lesbian and gay college students were engaged in a movement to shift the focus away from mental health. According to the story,

> At the root of the new movement is an assertion by gays that, contrary
> to prevailing medical opinion, homosexuality is not necessarily a mental
> disorder. For this reason, much of their effort goes into 'consciousness
> raising' among homosexuals to instill a sense of worth.... By organizing,
> the gay students hope to build a sense of community among gay
> young men and women and to disabuse their heterosexual classmates
> and the outside community of what they feel are damaging myths
> about homosexuality.

These goals and objectives very closely mirror the goals and objectives of the LGBT students who began the high school GSA movement twenty years later. There is a parallel between the stated purpose of both these 1970s collegiate groups and the 1990s high school GSAs, and a strong correlation in the students' explanation of why such groups were needed. This 1971 article about the new movement of gay college students, reported that, "The students say that their lives on these and other campuses are made difficult not necessarily by official harassment, but the personal hostility and indifference a student may encounter when his roommates or fraternity brothers learn of his homosexuality. The rate of suicide among homosexual students is said to be unusually high." The testimonies of high school students in the late 1980s mirrored these themes of social stigma and high risks of suicide, and became important elements in the call for social change. The controversy over these groups follows a similar pattern to high school groups today, centering largely around the issues of promoting a deviant lifestyle or protecting students from abuse and harm. Interestingly, in 1971, one of the college presidents interviewed for the *New York Times* story made this statement of support, "The colleges owe their homosexual students the full opportunity to learn and grow." This is the type of response that LGBT students and those who work within the GSA movement today hope to receive from school administrators.

There was a series of similar articles about "gay happenings" at college campuses around the country that ran in *The New York Times* and other major newspapers throughout the 1970s.[6] All of these articles spoke about the increasing visibility of homosexuals on campus, and the efforts of gay and lesbian students to form support groups or more politically minded clubs to educate the campus community and advocate for gay rights on campus and throughout the nation. All of these stories were, of course, set against the historical backdrop of a burgeoning gay liberation movement and the debate over the American Psychiatric Association's declassification of homosexuality as a mental illness. These articles are similar to the articles appearing throughout the 1990s and today about LGBT high school students (which are discussed in detail in Chapter 6) in that they focus on themes of the isolated, tortured, and victimized homosexual contrasted with a newly emerging, bolder, more positive, youth population. Of course, the youth population referred to in the 1970s was in its early twenties, and today the group spoken of is in its mid-teens. The controversy over the college groups then was over the exposure of impressionable young minds to a decadent and dangerous homosexual lifestyle, and whether colleges and universities were endorsing homosexuality by granting students protections and places to meet. Both of these concerns are at the forefront of opposition to high school GSAs.

In 1980, gay and lesbian students sued Georgetown University for discrimination in reaction to the University's refusal to provide their student organization with the same access to university resources as all other student groups. The University claimed that its Catholic foundations, which dictate the belief that homosexuality is a sin, exempted them from having to recognize a gay and lesbian student club. The University argued, and the court initially upheld, that their religious position on the group was protected by the First Amendment. Lawyers for the students argued that Georgetown's use of federal funds made it a secular institution that could not impose a specific religious doctrine and was required by federal law to allow equal access to all student organizations. The students argued that failure to do so was analogous to racial discrimination on religious grounds. In an earlier case filed against Bob Jones University, the Supreme Court had ruled that acts of racial discrimination on religious grounds are not protected by the constitution. In the Georgetown case, the court rejected this argument, ruling that "there is no similar national policy compelling government intervention in matters relating to sexual orientation."[7] This case highlights issues of religion, equal access, the first amendment, comparisons of LGBT people to racial ethnic minorities, and anti-discrimination policies that have become staples in the high school GSA movement since the mid-1990s.

All of this foreshadows what was to happen in the debates over, and media coverage of, the activism of LGBT high school students in the 1990s. In the intervening twenty years, some significant political and cultural strides were made for lesbian and gay communities. College students in particular have made great advances in establishing student clubs, so that now it is more the rule than the exception for a university to have such a club. However, the GSA movement exposed that many old notions, prejudices, and fears about LGBT people and the lesbian and gay rights movement were still simmering and ready to boil again when the next generation of younger students asserted its place in America's secondary schools.

RECOGNITION OF LGBT YOUTH: AN "AT RISK" POPULATION

Because research on, and public perception of, homosexual identity through the late 1980s concluded that it was first recognized in late adolescence for men and the early 20s for women, little thought was given to the idea of a population of LGBT youth. Before institutional advocacy or social activism by or for LGBT youth could take place, it first had to be established and acknowledged that they existed. The surfacing of LGBT youth as a population of interest and concern occurred through a complex combination of academic and governmental research, experiences and reports of various agencies who work with youth, the experiences of those in organizations that serve the gay and lesbian community, and the voices of the youth themselves. One of the first organizations to recognize and serve the needs of LGBT youth was the Hetrick-Martin Institute in New York City.

The Hetrick-Martin Institute [HMI], known as the Institute for Protection of Lesbian and Gay Youth until 1988, was founded in 1979 by psychiatrist Emery Hetrick and NYU professor A. Damien Martin. Hetrick and Martin were prompted to establish the institute after a fifteen-year-old boy living in a group home was beaten, sexually assaulted, and then evicted because he was gay. The goal of the institute was to provide social services, support, and advocacy for LGBT youth who had previously been ignored or discriminated against by other youth social service agencies. HMI offers a range of services to youth, including support services such as personal counseling, family counseling, medical and legal assistance and referrals, after-school activities such as arts programming, and school and career skills training, and the now widely publicized Harvey Milk High School.[8]

HMI founded the Harvey Milk High School in 1985 in conjunction with the Career Education Center of the New York City Department of Education.[9] The school, which is a fully accredited high school, was established to provide LGBT and heterosexual students who had experienced verbal harassment and physical violence in their previous schools with a safe learning environment. The school was established as an institutional reaction to the growing body of research on, and reported instances of, serious harassment faced by gay students, and students perceived to be LGBT, in schools in New York City and across the country. HMI argued that the school was needed not only to provide safety for these students but also to lower the drop out rate and academic failure rates of this population of students.

Over the past twenty-five years, the impact that HMI has had on thousands of youth in New York City who had no other source of support is immeasurable. Beyond this impact on the lives of individual adolescents, HMI and its founders played a significant role in the GSA movement by providing much needed research on, and recognition of, the needs of gay youth. HMI played a large role in defining and understanding LGBT youth as an at-risk population, and one that is largely put at risk by social and cultural prejudice and social organizations such as schools, which institutionalize this prejudice. Hetrick and Martin published the first scientific research that specifically dealt with the lives and developmental challenges of gay and lesbian youth.[10] This research helped to begin to fill a large gap in the academic knowledge of adolescence and homosexuality. It also provided much needed information to those who work with youth, and stimulated further research by academics and scientists (including me) from a variety of social science disciplines. All social movements require knowledge and evidence to inform and support their positions and actions. Hetrick and Martin provided LGBT youth and their advocates the knowledge they needed to begin their social movement.

Five years after HMI had its beginnings in New York City, an organization designed to provide services to gay and lesbian high school students began on the other side of the country. Project 10 Los Angeles was founded by Virginia Uribe in 1984. Her impetus to start Project 10 was not unlike the events that prompted the start of HMI. Uribe, a teacher and counselor at Fairfax High School in the Los Angeles Unified School District (LAUSD), was working on earning a doctorate degree in psychology. Through her research, which directed her to examine the support services offered to students in the ten largest school districts in the United States, she discovered that there were virtually no services offered to support LGBT students. During this same time period, a fourteen-year-old male student at Fairfax High School dropped out of school because of harassment by fellow students and the stress of being thrown out of his home when his parents learned he was gay. These events motivated Uribe to develop manuals of counseling advice to provide to those working with LGBT youth, and to establish Project 10 to manage, support, and disseminate services to this population.[11] Uribe also immediately began a counseling-based support group for LGBT and questioning students at Fairfax High School.[12] As far as I am able to document, this was the first ever in-school support group offered to LGBT students at a public high school.

When she began this project in 1984, the only information available to Uribe came from HMI. She used this information and consulted with Hetrick and Martin, but decided that their model was not the one she wanted to follow. Uribe had decided early on that it was important to work to get schools to provide services for LGBT and questioning students rather than to establish an organization to provide these services outside of schools, or in a separate school, as HMI did. As a teacher, Uribe felt strongly that public schools had a responsibility to protect and serve the needs of all of their students, and that they should, and could, be made to live up to this responsibility to

LGBT students.[13] Uribe was able to achieve this goal rather quickly in the Los Angeles Unified School District, at least on paper. Project 10 became the first district-wide school program to service the needs of LGBT students. In 1984, Project 10 established training programs for faculty, administration, and students, and established LGBT student support groups in public high schools throughout the LAUSD. Project 10 then became a model for other programs around the country and an inspiration for other organizations to advocate for the rights of LGBT students. Uribe's work and the significance of Project 10 are discussed in greater detail in Chapter 4.

LESBIAN AND GAY COMMUNITY CENTERS: PROVIDING SPACE FOR YOUTH TO SHARE EXPERIENCES

The history of the relationship between adult gay and lesbian communities and gay and lesbian youth is a complex, sometimes contentious, sometimes supportive one. It is a relationship that deserves to be more fully documented and analyzed than it has been. Youth, frequently college students, are often on the frontlines of activism and protest in social movements. This was certainly the case in the movement to end the war in Vietnam and in the struggle for black civil rights. Two of the most active organizations in these movements for change were the Students for a Democratic Society (SDS) and the Student Non-Violent Coordinating Committee (SNCC). Youths are often valued in social movements for their energy, their willingness to take risks, and their position in institutions of education. It is interesting to note that analogous organizations composed solely of LGBT youth or college students did not play such a pivotal visible role in the history of the gay and lesbian rights movement, although young adults surely have participated.

There are several possible explanations for this disparity. First, as I mentioned earlier and will expand on in the next chapter, through the 1980s it was widely accepted that homosexual identity development did not reach the stage of self-acceptance and public acknowledgement until the early twenties for men and mid twenties for women. Therefore, one explanation could be that there simply were not large numbers of self-identified LGBT youth or college students available to participate in social activism. Another possible explanation is that homophobia, the pervasive stereotype of homosexual men as pedophiles, and the popular myth of homosexuals as recruiters, pressured adult gay and lesbian rights activists to distance themselves from LGBT youth. I argue that both of these factors were very influential in making the gay rights movement less of a venue for youth activism than anti-war, civil rights, and women's rights movements.

The rise in youth activism throughout the 1990s and beyond reflects, among other things, both a drop in the age of self-identification as LGBT and the cultural changes that reduced, but by no means eliminated, some of the predatory stereotypes of LGBT people, thus producing the occasional positive healthy image. Both of these changes increased the possibility that youth would self-identify as LGBT and that they would want to take an active public role in advocating for their rights. At the same time, these changes influenced adult gay communities to become more inclusive and supportive of youth. As more and more teens self-identified as LGBT, they looked for places to support and assist them in dealing with all of the difficulties associated with this identification. The two primary institutions that youth are a part of, families and schools, were not only not equipped with the resources or knowledge to advise them, but were also quite often the main sources of problems these kids faced. This left them little alternative but to seek support from adult gay community centers in their local towns. The numbers of youth looking for support, the sympathy that gay adults had for the issues they faced, and the less homophobic culture made these adult gay community centers more welcoming to youth than they may have been in the past. In increasing numbers, beginning in the late 1980s and continuing throughout the 1990s, gay community centers in cities across the country began offering youth support groups, drop-in hours, and social events. I first became aware of the existence and experiences of this population through a gay community center in upstate New York in 1993. Although these youth groups within gay community centers proliferated in the 1990s, they did exist in some cities before this time frame.

Gilbert Herdt and Andrew Boxer brought national recognition to these community support groups, and to the growing population of LGBT youth with their book "Children of Horizons"[14] published in 1993. This book provides a case study of the Horizons Community Services, which was incorporated in Chicago in 1973 under the name "Gay Horizons." Established as a drop-in center for adults, the center began a gay youth support group in 1979. The book documents and analyzes the changes in the youth using the services of Horizons over the years as an indication of the beginnings of large social changes. According to the authors, through the early 1980s, members of the group were white middle- and working-class males in their late teens and early twenties. Over time, the group became increasingly diversified in terms of gender, class, race, and ethnicity, and the age of members dropped. By the late 80s, the group was limited to those between the ages of 14 and 21.[15] Throughout the book, the authors argue that LGBT youth are coming out earlier than the generations before and that they are also coming out differently. As beneficiaries of the activism of adults who came before them, LGBT youth were coming out more confident that they were not inherently ill or perverse, and that they could have a happy and "normal" future. In the end, the book focuses its attention largely on the psychological and sexual identity development of the youth who participated in the group from 1987 to 1988, rather than actually exploring the social and political significance of their experiences and actions. However, the book contributed to the understanding of the rise of LGBT youth activism in GSAs in two ways.

First, it provided an account of how an adult community could, and did, reach out to support youth, and it did so in a way that encouraged and gave permission for other gay and lesbian community centers to do the same. It demonstrated that the benefits gained from recognizing LGBT youth were worth the effort it took to overcome the fears perpetuated by stereotypes and false accusations. The impact of this, of course, can only be surmised. Second, the book provided both the first in-depth look at this population of youth and a framework for understanding them. It became a well-cited reference point for those in organizations working with youth and for those researching them. Although I was not particularly intrigued by the psychological analysis given in the book, its accounting of the lives of LGBT youth bolstered my interest in continuing my own research at a community center youth support group. What I found significant at the time, and argue now was an important contribution to the recent history of youth activism, was the book's positioning of LGBT youth not solely as a group suffering or at risk, although it did discuss these things, but also as a group that was becoming confident and self-assured.[16]

THE U.S. DEPARTMENT OF HEALTH AND HUMAN SERVICES REPORT ON YOUTH SUICIDE

As discussed previously, by the late 1970s at least some select individuals and organizations working with young people were aware that there was a growing population of LGBT youth, and that this group suffered from a disproportionate amount of discrimination and abuse than their hetero-sexual peers. This awareness increased at a slow but steady pace throughout the 1980s as youth went in search of support and assistance from their school counselors, social workers, teachers and local gay and lesbian community centers. Among those who had been working with these youth, there had developed an understanding that, as a group, they fit the definition of an "at risk population." Those working at HMI in New York City, Project 10 in Los Angeles, and in scattered gay community centers across the country, tried to educate social service providers, school districts, and community members about the perils faced by this population. In 1989, their efforts to convince others of these dangers and motivate them to take action were greatly bolstered by an unexpected source—an agency of the U.S. federal government. The United States Department of Health and Human Services [USDHHS] conducted research to try to better understand the high rate of suicide among the nation's adolescents. The rate of suicide for this age group had long been high and was increasing. In fact, it was the third lead-ing cause of death among teenagers. Among the findings of the USDHHS's report was that between twenty and thirty percent of the suicides in this population could be linked to conflict over sexual orientation.[17]

The impact of this report was far-reaching and long-lasting for several reasons. The report came from a national study conducted by an agency of the federal government commissioned to study the reasons that teenagers commit suicide and determine which groups were most at risk. The report's finding regarding sexual orientation was unexpected, but the researchers understood that it was significant to the understanding of the risk factors for suicide they sought, and they called attention to it in their published report. On its own, this report helped to call attention to the problems facing LGBT youth, and provided those involved in efforts like Project 10 and HMI with high-profile, unbiased, and dramatic evidence that they needed to back their efforts to get schools and social services agencies to define LGBT youth as a group "at risk" and in need of social supports. The fifteen-year-old USDHHS report is still one of the most cited pieces of evidence used by students and organizations advocating for student rights, and is routinely cited in media stories about LGBT students. Students and their advocates often summarize the findings of the report by stating that, "LGBT youth are three times as likely to commit suicide as their heterosexual peers." This statement is really an amalgam of the classic Kinsey study's[18] estimation that ten percent of people are homosexual, and the USDHHS study finding that up to thirty percent of teenage suicides are prompted by conflicts over sexual orientation. The logic behind the statement is that if ten percent of teens are homosexual and thirty percent of teen suicides are committed by LGBT youth, (rather than ten percent) then LGBT youth are three times more likely to kill themselves than heterosexual teens.

There are, of course, problems with the logic and math behind this statement, not to mention its reliance on the Kinsey study, which, while well cited, is a more complex conclusion than the simple statement that ten percent of the population is homosexual. At the most basic level, the statement takes the high end of two unrelated estimations—for two completely separate research projects done on different populations (one adult, one teen), and one done forty-plus years after the other—and puts them together in what sounds like a statement of fact. Regardless of this, the statement, backed by a government report, has proved to be a very powerful and effective way of bringing attention to, and sympathy for, LGBT youth as an at-risk population. Other data from social services providers working with teenagers, and the experiences of people like Virginia Uribe, Hetrick and Martin, and LGBT adults working with youth at community centers, all provided strong evidence to support this conclusion prior to the 1989 report (and have produced much more evidence since). However, none of this has had as great an impact on the activism surrounding LGBT student rights and the efforts to establish GSAs in high schools throughout the country as the statement that "Gay youth commit suicide at three times the rate of their heterosexual peers."[19]

One of the initial effects of this government report on the lives of LGBT students was that it was used by counselors and social workers in public schools to win their school administration's approval to start in-school support groups for students struggling with issues of sexual orientation. As discussed earlier, Project 10 began instituting such groups in the LAUSD in 1984. The USDHHS report not only expedited their efforts to convince schools to provide support groups, but it also influenced other school districts around the country to more seriously consider following Project 10's lead. As will be discussed in detail in Chapter 3, school support groups for LGBT students were an important precursor to the more social and political GSA clubs.

IT IS ALL IN THE NAME:
THE BIRTH OF THE FIRST GAY–STRAIGHT ALLIANCE CLUBS

Two private boarding schools in Massachusetts, Phillips Academy and Concord Academy, served as the birthing ground for the concept of high school gay–straight alliance clubs. Kevin Jennings, who later became the founder and national director of GLSEN (gay, lesbian, straight education network), claims to have been faculty advisor to the first GSA in the country at Concord Academy High School. From the very beginning, two major features made GSAs significantly different from the support groups for LGBT teenagers instituted by Project 10 in the Los Angeles area, and imitated by other schools around the country through the mid- to late-1980s. The support group model of Project 10, HMI, and local gay and lesbian community centers was focused on counseling and assistance with the emotional difficulties of being an LGBT teenager in a homophobic school and society. The groups were, therefore, generally composed solely of LGBT students, and the focus of the group was personal not political. The groups were, and continue to be, extremely important to those students who struggle with the personal emotional ramifications of social stigmatization, isolation, and harassment. However, these student support groups were not geared toward organizing and working to change the social conditions in the school that perpetuated their suffering. Gay–straight alliance clubs emerged in schools out of the desire of lesbian, gay, bisexual and straight students to create a more visible cultural and structural change that might improve the environment of fear, intolerance, and discrimination of LGBT people in which all students existed. The title "gay–straight alliance" marked these two very important shifts from the support group model.

The title of GSA, which became very significant to the direction and impact of the movement, had very simplistic beginnings. According to Jennings, the female student who initiated the group at Concord Academy came up with the GSA name. She was the straight daughter of lesbian parents, and Jennings was the gay male teacher she asked to help form a student club that would address LGBT issues at the school. As the two of them struggled to name the group, the student said to Jennings, "I've got it, you're gay and I'm straight, so why don't we call it the gay–straight alliance."[20] So, while the title gay–straight alliance seems so well conceived to symbolize the purpose and direction of a new social movement, according to Jennings, "there was no marketing group that chose the name. It was very much accidental."[21] The founding faculty advisor for the student group at neighboring Phillips Academy, Priscilla Bonney-Smith, reported to me that the choice of name for their group was much more conscious and strategic. The pairing at Phillips was reversed—a heterosexual faculty member and a lesbian student. According to Bonney-Smith, thoughts of potential reaction to the club factored into their decision, "We knew it would be too threatening to just have a gay organization, and we knew there were straight folks (like me) who supported gay rights … so we combined gay and straight."[22]

Although it was initially an unplanned alliance, bringing straight students and faculty together with gay, lesbian, and bisexual students and faculty quickly proved to be an effective partnership. The immediate and lasting impact of calling these student clubs gay–straight alliances was to communicate, just by their very existence, that lesbian and gay issues should be of interest to everyone, because they affect everyone. As I discuss in more detail later, the alliance of straight people with gay people gave the groups greater legitimacy and influence with school administrators, faculty, and the community at large. However, the visibility of the group, the use of "gay" in its name, and its desire to educate and involve its members with more political issues often made such groups less acceptable and more controversial than the support groups that preceded them. In Chapter 3, I take an in-depth look at these dynamics through the case studies of two schools in upstate New York that each first established a student support group and then a GSA student club.

It is significant to note that these original groups formed at the same time in two of the most prestigious independent boarding schools in the country. Phillips Academy Andover is the largest, second most selective, and fifth oldest boarding school in the United States. Many notables from the worlds of science, industry, literature, and politics, including George Bush Senior and Junior and Jeb Bush, are alumni of this well-endowed school. Concord Academy is the sixteenth most selective boarding school in the country, according to the *Boarding School Review,* and has a similarly prestigious and diverse list of alumni, although it lacks current and former presidents. It is interesting to ponder whether the climate and structure of these elite schools was at all causally related to the emergence of a GSA club there rather than in a public school. Based on interviews with some of the founding members of these first two GSAs and an examination of the "mission statements" of these schools, it would seem that there was a connection.

Not knowing anything about these schools other than their reputations, I had assumed that "elite" indicated conservative and, therefore, it was surprising that GSAs began there. According to those I spoke with, my assumption was very much incorrect. Everyone I spoke with felt strongly that the goals, climates, and structures of these independent boarding schools helped foster the emergence of GSAs. First, they all mentioned that even though the schools are "elite" in the quality of the education and students they produce, they are actually quite liberal in the educational philosophies of the school and of the faculty themselves. Critical thought about all topics, including social inequalities and social struggles of all types, are generally encouraged at these schools and the civic activity of students is nurtured. Those I spoke with also thought that, because these are boarding schools, they are used to, and need to be comfortable with, addressing the personal lives of students. Students live with each other and faculty, and these dynamics most likely increased the chance that discussions of sexual orientation and same-sex parents would arise at these schools. When these topics did come up, it was deemed appropriate for faculty and the school to address them. Once the idea surfaced, the administrative structures at these boarding schools made establishing a gay–straight alliance club much simpler than those at most public schools. There were no formal procedures for starting a student club at either school and there is no school board from which to seek approval. At both schools, the groups began simply and without any official request or approval, because none was required.[23]

Once the first GSAs were established at Concord and Phillips Academy in Massachusetts, word about them spread, and other students and teachers came looking for information and guidance. Through personal exchanges of information and some small-scale school workshops conducted by the faculty advisors of the first two groups, GSAs spread slowly through private and some public schools in Massachusetts. As I will discuss later, the nucleus for GLSEN began with networking among the faculty advisors for the clubs in these private schools. The gay–straight alliance concept and model gained in visibility and influence when it was used as a model for and incorporated into the Massachusetts Safe Schools program five years later. From that point on, GSAs shifted from what seemed to be a phenomenon of private schools to a public school trend. The major reason for this has been the passage of state or district policies and the use of federal laws to advocate for the rights of LGBT students. Ironically, the freedom from the politics and policy enforcement of public schools that once made these two boarding schools more open to student groups now allows private schools to escape these state and federal laws that have been used by the GSA movement to prompt public schools to allow these student clubs. The fact that public schools are bound to abide by wider policies and legislation has given the GSA movement access to influence over decisions about GSAs at public schools that it does not have over private schools, at least not on as large a scale. The first major large-scale influence on public school policy regarding harassment of LGBT students and the rights of GSA clubs came in Massachusetts.

THE MASSACHUSETTS SAFE SCHOOLS PROGRAM

The Massachusetts Safe Schools program was established in 1993 to provide a wide range of services targeted at improving the safety and educational outcomes for gay and lesbian students. The program emerged as a result of the 1989 USDHHS report on youth suicide, the activism of gay rights leaders in Massachusetts prompted by this report, and a close political race for governor. During the closely contested 1990 race for governor of Massachusetts, Republican candidate William Weld, in an attempt to win the votes of the gay and lesbian community, made a promise to community leaders that if he was elected he would establish a commission to investigate the problems of youth suicide and gay and lesbian students. Two years after winning the election, Governor Weld fulfilled his promise by creating the Governor's Commission on Gay and Lesbian Youth. The appointed members of this commission were given the task of developing a plan to lower the high rate of suicide for lesbian and gay youth, and to reduce the amount of violence and harassment they faced.[24]

The members of the Governor's Commission, who were already knowledgeable about the issue, assembled a total of five public hearings in locations throughout the state of Massachusetts. These hearings were open forums where parents, teachers, social service workers and, most significantly, students shared their experiences exposing the real, and often extremely painful and serious problems facing lesbian, gay, and bisexual teenagers. Several students and faculty members from Concord and Phillips Academies worked on this commission and testified at these hearings despite the fact that the target of the investigation was public school. The hearings resulted in a report entitled, "Making Schools Safe for Gay and Lesbian Youth," which was issued in February 1993. A major conclusion of the report was that the atmosphere within public schools was causally related to many, if not all, of the problems lesbian, gay, and bisexual youth faced within their walls. Therefore, the commission made the following four recommendations to the Massachusetts Board of education:

1. Schools should develop policies to protect LGBT students from harassment and discrimination.
2. Schools should institute support groups for all students dealing with issues of sexual orientation.
3. Schools should provide counseling services to families of LGBT students.
4. School faculty and staff should be trained in violence and suicide prevention.[25]

The board of education unanimously voted to adopt the Safe Schools Program for Gay and Lesbian Students in May of 1993 and it received funding by the fall of that year. Also during the fall of 1993, as the result of protests and lobbying by large numbers of students, the Massachusetts Board of Education added sexual orientation as a protected category in its anti-discrimination law. It was the second state to make this addition. Wisconsin had done so in 1991.

This rapid succession of achievements made Massachusetts the first state to develop a program to address the needs of LGBT students, and the second state to include sexual orientation in its anti-discrimination law. The program continues to be the most extensive and well-funded in the country, and has served as a model for those in other states seeking to establish protections and services for LGBT students in their community. Other states that have added protections for LGBT students to their anti-discrimination policies and established training for faculty and other supports for LGBT students at the state level include: Connecticut, Vermont, Minnesota, California, Washington, New Jersey, and the District of Columbia. This is progress, but it is rather sparse at the state level considering that more than a decade has passed since the ground breaking, comprehensive, and successful model established by the Massachusetts Safe Schools Program.

Nationwide, greater success has come at the local individual school level. Although statewide policies and programs can quickly have wide-reaching impact on large numbers of students, the political and bureaucratic environment of state legislation can make fighting for policy inclusion at this level prolonged and divisive. On the one hand, having a statewide anti-discrimination policy that includes sexual orientation can expedite the process of establishing a GSA at a local school. On the other hand, scores of GSAs can be established in the time that it takes a state department of education to add sexual orientation to its anti-discrimination policy. The work of students to start GSAs was gradually eased over the years by organized efforts to compile and share information and resources at the state and national level.

GLSEN: THE BIRTH OF AN ORGANIZATION AND A LEADER

The first organization to assist in this way was the Gay, Lesbian, Independent School Teachers Network [GLISTN], which began in 1990 with a conference of lesbian and gay independent-school teachers. The fledgling network, which was primarily one of support and information sharing among educators, cut its political teeth in 1992 and 1993 while assisting in the efforts to start the Massachusetts Department of Education Safe Schools Program.[26] The profile that GLISTN received through its work on this project resulted in increasing requests for information and assistance from teachers throughout the Northeast and beyond. The small group became strained in terms of resources and personnel as it tried to meet these requests. In 1994, Kevin Jennings published an edited collection of personal stories from LGBT teachers: "One Teacher in 10." The release of this book created even greater demand for him to travel to, speak to, and provide workshops for groups of teachers throughout the country. As a result, the group, then working under the name Gay, Lesbian and Straight Teachers Network [GLSTN], decided to solidify its structure and become an independent 501 c (3) national organization, and hired a small staff, with Jennings as the first paid member.[27]

Although GLSTN was officially a national organization, its main approach was to assist and coordinate the development of local chapters throughout the country. The focus on local chapters, was based on the belief that local educators know best what the needs of their schools are and what strategies for change would work best in their communities. The national organization, headquartered in New York City, was able to provide resources, workshops, and, eventually, funding to help establish local chapters and assist them in their efforts to impact the schools in their communities. Through the mid-1990s, GLSTN and its chapters focused on teachers by providing support for the rights of gay and lesbian teachers and for the role educators can play in improving the school climate for LGBT students. The strategies and goals at this time followed the model of the Massachusetts program: providing violence- and harassment-prevention programs, sensitivity and diversity training that included LGBT issues for faculty and administration, suicide education and prevention programs, and support for LGBT student groups on a school or school district level.[28]

As time went on, GLSTN expanded, and community members, parents, and students became involved. In 1997, the name was modified to the Gay, Lesbian, Straight Education Network [GLSEN] to reflect the change from its origins as a group of teachers supporting one another, to an organization helping communities to improve the lives and educational experiences of LGBT students. One of the most effective things that the organization was able to do to expedite the process of change in schools was to serve as an information clearinghouse. Staff members gathered all existing research and legal information related to gay youth and student rights; they conducted their own survey to measure the school climate for gay students, which is now distributed to schools across the country annually; and they developed their own "how to" guides for just about every possible situation in which a student or teacher might be involved (e.g., starting a GSA, dealing with the press, handling homophobic administrators). Anyone who wants information regarding LGBT issues and schools can go to the one central source at GLSEN national headquarters, which is easily accessible from its website.

GLSEN also shares its knowledge and proven strategies through conferences and training programs held annually for teachers, students, and chapter leaders. In 1998, the organization began its efforts to register GSAs in high schools throughout the country so that they could be linked together to share information and experiences. This registry of GSAs became the first way to measure the rate of expansion of the GSA movement. Although it is by no means a perfect measure, it is still one of the few available. The detailed work and strategies of GLSEN are examined more closely in Chapter 4. I included the organization in this overview of the GSA movement because of the tremendous impact it had on increasing the speed and ease with which these groups were formed. This franchisement of GSAs increased the success rate and efficiency of this movement, but it also brought with it the drawbacks associated with any social movement that becomes institutionalized. These negative side effects are explored later in the book.

THE SAFE SCHOOLS COALITION OF WASHINGTON STATE AND THE GSA NETWORK OF CALIFORNIA

It is difficult to decide where to place the Safe Schools Coalition in the history of events that influenced the development of a GSA movement. The Safe Schools Coalition has its own historical origins that predate the first GSA, the USDHHS report on youth suicide, the Massachusetts Safe Schools Program, and GLSEN. However, its origins were more localized and slower to develop into wide-ranging programs, and it never explicitly works with GSAs. The Safe Schools Coalition has, nonetheless, played an important role in gathering and disseminating information about LGBT youth, advocating for their rights and needs, and providing training aimed at making schools safer and more accepting places. The organization began as an ad hoc "Advisory Committee on Gay/Lesbian Youth," assembled by the Seattle Commission on Children and Youth in 1988 as an outcome of hearings it held on the needs of lesbian and gay youth in Seattle.[29] Its task was to help schools implement the commission's recommendations to make schools safer for lesbian and gay students. The committee focused its initial efforts on training principals and counselors in the Seattle School District to understand and be sensitive to the problems and needs of lesbian and gay students. From 1988 to 1992, the scope and reach of the committee's work expanded to larger numbers of faculty, staff, and schools. As a result of the impact of the work done by the committee, which reached far beyond the city of Seattle, it was renamed The Safe Schools Coalition [SSC] of Washington in 1993.

Over a five-year period, the SSC continued to expand its work, gathering and distributing information to schools and communities, and conducting its own study documenting the violence and harassment perpetrated against lesbian and gay students. The SSC also helped lobby the Washington State Board of Education to add sexual orientation and gender identity to its anti-harassment policies. Over the years, the SSC became a clearinghouse for information and model training programs much like GLSEN, except that its efforts were focused solely on making changes within the state of Washington. Through its visible role in legislative debates, newspaper stories on LGBT issues in schools, and its information-packed Internet homepage, the Safe School Coalition attracted attention and requests for assistance from students and educators from around the country. In response to this nationwide recognition, the group officially dropped Washington from its name and its mission.[30] Although the work of SSC is focused on educator resources and training rather than on work directly involving GSAs or student leadership, it has served to advance the GSA movement by educating the public about the needs of LGBT students and advocating for their rights in schools throughout Seattle, then Washington, and now throughout the country.

The impact of the Gay–Straight Alliance Network of California has been much more direct. The organization was founded in San Francisco by Carolyn Laub in 1998 and became a statewide organization in 2001. Several features make the GSA Network different from the other organizations that came before it. First, from its inception, it has been a group with the direct primary goal of increasing the number of GSAs in high schools throughout the state of California. Second, the organization, although it has a coordinating staff of adults, is focused on and shaped primarily by youth leadership. Third, from the beginning, the organization's stated goals included not just gay and lesbian students but also, much more explicitly than other organizations, bisexual and transgender students. Finally, from the start, the GSA Network made it an explicit goal to build coalitions, not only among LGBT and straight students, but also among students of different classes, races, and ethnicities. For all the other organizations—HMI, Project 10, GLSEN, MA Safe Schools Program, SSC—these issues were addressed only years after they began, or not at all, and for all of them, the direct promotion of youth activism and leadership was either one piece of the larger organizational activities or not directly incorporated at all.

Based on the fact that the GSA Network is the newest organization— formed fourteen years after Project 10, ten years after SSC, four years after GLSEN—it was able to start from a more solid foundation of knowledge, social awareness, and ready youth activists. When it began in 1998, the GSA Network immediately had forty previously established GSAs and all of their student members to work with. This base of energy and experience propelled the GSA Network into more rapid and direct social activism than its predecessors. At the start of the 2004–2005 school year, more than 400 GSAs in the state of California were registered with the GSA network. This represents 39% of the public high schools in the state.[31] Many factors contributed to this success rate. These factors are explored in more detail in Chapter 4, but the fact that they focus their training and resources on supporting and encouraging youth leadership in establishing GSAs is certainly a key to their success. The goals of the organization, and its programs and strategic decisions are all guided directly by a formal youth council consisting of youth involved in GSAs in their local schools.

The GSA Network and its executive director Carolyn Laub also played an active role in the passage of The California Student Safety and Violence Prevention Act of 2000 (AB 537). This statewide legislation prohibits discrimination on the basis of sexual orientation and gender identity. Since the passage of this legislation, the GSA Network has made it a goal to educate students about their rights under it and to encourage them to be watchdogs for violations of the new law, with the understanding that legislation is only useful to the extent that it is implemented and enforced. The GSA Network was plaintiff in the first lawsuit filed under AB 537, and won a settlement agreement that requires the Visalia School District to enact reforms to its school policies and procedures, including instituting mandatory teacher and student training on LGBT issues.[32] The GSA Network's work on this piece of legislation in California mirrors the legislative assistance and lobbying engaged in by many of the organizations discussed in this chapter. Throughout the history of the GSA movement, legislation and legal victories have played a crucial role in opening doors, empowering students, and establishing precedents to use and build on.

LEGAL LANDMARKS IN THE GSA MOVEMENT

By the mid-1990s, LGBT students, their heterosexual allies, and their support networks were making strides building foundations of information, resources, and experiences that all served as tools in efforts to persuade schools to provide protections and spaces for all students. The progress made was always hard fought and very incremental—one school, or one school district, occasionally one state at a time; and one issue (a support group, a GSA, adding sexual orientation to an anti-discrimination policy) at a time. This steady pace of slow incremental change was periodically accelerated by lawsuits, which, with their victories, brought powerful and standardizing mechanisms for social change. Two general types of lawsuits have been filed against public school districts by, or on behalf of, LGBT students or GSA clubs. The first type is against schools for failure to protect student(s) from ongoing harassment or discrimination directed at the student(s) because of their actual or perceived sexual orientation. The second type is filed against school districts that have refused to allow GSA clubs or have failed to treat these clubs the same as other student organizations (e.g., allowing access to school resources, publicity for meetings and events, inclusion in yearbook, etc.). Both types of lawsuits have been filed and won on the basis of existing legal statutes—The Equal Access Act [EEA], Title IX, the Equal Protection Clause of the 14th Amendment, the First Amendment, and state laws that prohibit discrimination or harassment on the basis of sexual orientation.

Between 1996 and 2002, there were fifteen major lawsuits filed against schools for failure to protect students from harassment or violence perpetrated by other students or faculty.[33] The cases have resulted in settlements for the students and their families ranging from $40,000 to $962,000.[34] The first and most publicized case, and the one resulting in the largest settlement, was Nabozny v. Podlesney. In this case, Jamie Nabozny filed suit against the principals of his former middle school and high school in Ashland, Wisconsin, accusing them of being liable for the years of abuse he suffered in their schools. The rather gruesome details of the years of abuse Jamie suffered at the hands of his fellow students, the dismissive handling of the abuse and Jamie's request for relief from school officials, and the lasting impact of the abuse on Jamie's life, were all factors in drawing attention to the case—and in winning a large settlement.

His fellow students began harassing Jamie Nabozny for being gay when he was in the seventh grade. The harassment quickly moved beyond teasing to physical violence. In junior high, several male students pretended to rape Jamie while a group of students watched. In response to this attack, the school principal told Jamie and his parents that this response from students was to be expected if Jamie wanted to be openly gay at school.[35] In high school, Jamie had objects thrown at him as he walked the halls, was beaten and urinated on in the boy's bathroom, and, in his junior year, was beaten and kicked so severely by eight students that he suffered internal bleeding and had to be hospitalized. Every incident was reported to school officials and none of the perpetrators were ever punished. During these years, Jamie tried to take his own life several times and his grades suffered considerably. Eventually Jamie, his parents, and his school counselor all agreed that for his own safety, he should drop out of school. A year later, Jamie was diagnosed with post-traumatic stress disorder stemming from his past abuse. It was at this time that he decided to sue his former schools.

The initial case was dismissed by a federal district judge, who ruled that school officials could not be held responsible for the actions of the student abusers. The appeal of this ruling was then taken on by Lambda Legal Defense Fund, an organization specializing in gay civil rights cases. The case claimed that because Jamie was gay, school officials failed to provide him with the same protections from abuse and harassment that they provided other students, a violation of the Equal Protection Clause of the 14th Amendment, which applies to public schools. The federal appellate court ruled in Jamie's favor in 1996, setting the precedent for the argument that schools are constitutionally obligated to protect all students, regardless of sexual orientation, from harassment.[36] The jury awarded Jamie $962,000, which further enforced the court ruling that schools are legally and constitutionally obligated to protect LGBT students from abuse, and that failure to do so will be financially costly. The decision in the case and the major media coverage it received resulted in its being an incredibly useful tool in persuading schools to institute protections for LGBT students and training for faculty about how to respond to homophobia and harassment. The legal precedent using the Equal Protection Clause of the 14th Amendment has held up in at least fourteen other lawsuits filed by LGBT students who were victims of harassment at their schools. This has made a powerful case to schools that it is in their interest, as well as in the interest of students, to create a safer learning environment for students and GSA clubs, which, it has been effectively argued, can play an important role in improving the climate of schools.

The landmark case involving the use of the Equal Access Act to argue for the right of GSA clubs to exist in public high schools involved East and West High schools in Salt Lake City, Utah. The story, and the issue of the Equal Access Act, actually became public and made national headlines before any lawsuit was filed. In 1996, Kelli Peterson and twenty-five other students tried to start the East High School Gay–Straight Alliance. The group initially had school support, but after pressure from religiously conservative community members, the school board voted 4 to 3 to disband all student clubs rather than allow the GSA to meet. This school board decision was based on its knowledge of the EAA, which states that if schools allow even one non-curricular student club to meet on campus, all such groups must be allowed the same accommodations.

Ironically, the EAA was established in 1984 by religious conservative leaders who were upset at decisions made on the basis of separation of church and state that had denied religious student groups from meeting on school grounds or using school resources. Interestingly, in the hearings leading up to the passage of the EAA, the point was raised that passing the act would also permit school clubs (such as a club for gay and lesbian students) that the religious leaders lobbying for the act did not approve of to meet on school property. Passage of the EAA was so important to its advocates' goal of fighting what they viewed as discrimination against religious speech in public schools that they were not dissuaded by this possibility. Ronald Reagan signed the EAA into law in 1984. The EAA is now, perhaps, the single most important tool available to students who wish to start GSA clubs, especially after the Salt Lake City case made national headlines for over two years.

The Salt Like City School Board's extreme reaction of banning all school clubs to prevent the GSA club brought publicity and protests. The students from East and West High Schools held regular protests, such as walking out of school and marching to the state capital. The students and their plight also received a good deal of sympathetic press coverage that portrayed the school as being extreme and prejudiced in its reaction to the GSA. Over time, pressured by parents and students who wanted school clubs, the district began to allow some clubs by claiming they were curricular. The school eventually even allowed the GSA to meet, but made members pay to use the school after hours. Two years later, the ACLU, supported by GLSEN, Lambda Legal, and other organizations filed a lawsuit on behalf of the GSA at East High School. In 1999, the Utah District Court ruled that the school had violated the EAA by allowing some clubs to meet and not others. The EAA is so clear and direct in its wording that all clubs must be allowed regardless of their content that it has stood up to almost all claims by any school that has tried to deny GSA clubs the right to exist. The impact of this application of the EAA has been invaluable to the advancement of the GSA movement.

This overview of the history of events illustrates the evolution and solidification of GSAs as a concept and a social movement and of LGBT and straight student allies as agents of social change. GSAs have become standard practice at schools in some areas of the country and are at least known entities to students in others. Over the past two decades, there has been considerable change in the understanding and perception of LGBT youth. They have gone from an invisible population to one known for being at risk and underserved, and now as a group of youth actively "calling their schools out" for treating them badly and demanding restitution and change. This newly emerging image of LGBT youth is a 180-degree turn from the view of gay youth that was standard through the 1980s and into the early 1990s. This difference is the subject explored in the next chapter.

TWO

IN THE TRENCHES
LGBT Students Struggle with School and Sexual Identity

The activism that ultimately led to the GSA movement was set in motion when scattered small groups of gay, lesbian and bisexual high school students started to think and speak about themselves in ways that transcended the common cultural and academic understandings of their lives. Prior to the mid-1980s, it was almost as if they did not exist. Although they were clearly walking through the hallways and sitting in the classrooms, they were invisible to school officials, academics, and most of the general public, because of the belief that the age of "realization" of a gay or lesbian identity came later in life. This "fact" erased the possibility from the minds of experts that self-aware, and certainly self-identified, LGBT students were populating the nation's schools. In pop-cultural images, too, homosexuality was presented as a personal struggle entered into in college or the early years of an attempted heterosexual marriage, not on the varsity team or at the prom. Any fragmented images of LGBT adolescents that filtered through this veil were tortured, depressed, shame filled, and confused.

Emerging from this quagmire at the end of the 1980s and through the 1990s in increasing numbers were a few self-identified, self-assured and outspoken LGBT teenagers who wanted a place in their schools. In the face of limited information, school officials were, at first, generally shocked that these students existed (and some chose to continue to deny their existence) and then tried to address their needs in the ways that this information suggested. As this chapter will show, what was advised did not meet the needs of many students. These students understood their experiences in very different terms and knew that what needed to be addressed and changed was the very structure and culture of schools, and not their sexual identity. This wisdom and the courage to articulate it became the driving force behind the efforts to establish GSAs.

HOW SERVICE PROVIDERS, THE PUBLIC, AND SCHOOL OFFICIALS VIEWED LGBT YOUTH

There is considerably more literature on LGBT youth now than there was ten years ago when I became interested, as a sociologist, in studying this population. With a few notable exceptions,[1] not much was written about LGBT youth until 1989. The1989 Department of Health and Human Services' report on gay youth suicide broadened the concern among some psychologists, counselors, teachers, and others working with teenagers. This concern resulted in a small but significant surge in research projects on this population from the fields of psychology and education.[2] The report, because it was issued by a government agency and was given a considerable amount of publicity, also prompted a surge of more news stories on the problems and struggles of gay youth.[3] Generally, these were written as tragic stories about the pain of growing up gay, or heroic stories of overcoming the odds.

What virtually all of these accounts of LGBT youth have in common is an emphasis on the developmental challenges they face. Whether the specific emphasis is placed on the risk of suicide, drug and alcohol abuse, homelessness, or harassment and abuse at home or school, the accounts portray these youth as individuals struggling to develop into happy and healthy adults. This focus on developmental problems is a result of the general ways researchers and the public understood both groups—adolescents and gays and lesbians. Adolescence is an important time for physical, emotional, and identity development, therefore, the processes and stages of this development are often the focus of research and public discourse on this population. From the late 1970s to the late 1980s, researchers sought to also understand homosexuality as a developmental process. Some of these researchers, largely from the fields of psychology and social psychology,[4] delineated developmental stages that, they argued, individuals pass through on the way to forming and coming to terms with their inherent homosexual identity. It is not surprising, then, that those who wished to investigate, understand, and assist gay adolescents focused much of their attention on the developmental problems they may face and turned to these models for assistance. By the late 1980s, the academic understandings of sexual identity in most disciplines had moved past the rather simplistic and essentialist developmental models in favor of more complex social, historical, and cultural analyses.[5] However, it is clear in reading the research and literature on LGBT youth that dominated through the mid to late 1990s that these more sophisticated academic theories of sexual identity had not filtered through to those working with these students.

HOW DEVELOPMENTAL MODELS INFORM THE LITERATURE ON LGBT YOUTH

Homosexual identity development models have heavily influenced most research and cultural understandings of LGBT youth.[6] I use the framework of these models to critique the concepts and analysis they employ and to trouble the knowledge and meanings they have produced. In my critique, I interweave the self-reports of LGBT students to illustrate the influence of these meanings on their interpretation of their experiences. The stages of personal struggle generalized in identity formation models, to the extent that they loosely exist, are significantly influenced by the socially produced stereotypes of LGBT people that have become institutionalized in public schools. The words of students themselves provide empirical evidence to the assertion that public schools are powerful forces systematically shaping these experiences.

LEARNING THE MEANING OF SEXUAL IDENTITY

The literature on developmental models suggests that individuals become consciously aware of their homosexual identities at an average age range of 19–21 for males and 21–23 for females.[7] More current research on gay and lesbian youth suggests that this average age may be considerably lower today.[8] Although no definitive age range is given, some experts hypothesize that the range is now 15–18 for males and 17–20 for females. I interviewed only self-identified lesbian, gay, and bisexual youth ages 14–20, therefore, the age at which they realized their sexual orientation was generally younger than either of these estimates.[9]

The literature states that awareness of sexual orientation is closely followed by a period of "identity confusion." This is a period in which the individual struggles to understand what same-sex attractions mean about who they really are. In other words, their otherwise "normal" identity is shaken by these emerging feelings and they must reassess their identity. I found that what at first seemed like personal confusion was highly contingent upon the messages the youth received from their social environment. For the youth I spoke with, there was a significant relationship among awareness of their sexual/affectional feelings, "identity confusion," and their interaction with the institution of public education. Sometimes such a connection was obvious and immediate in response to my initial question, "When did you first begin to realize that you might be gay?"

> "When I was younger I had a lot of really close girlfriends and I use to really like them, but never really thought about it because … In middle school I had millions of boyfriends, but everyone did. And I guess I didn't really … When it first started I was like, 'No! No!' you know. But I guess I didn't really say it out loud to myself until my sophomore year of high school; I've known though."
>
> —Becca, bisexual Jewish female, age 18.[10]

> "I guess junior high. You know? Like the whole puberty thing … When girls start talking about boys and stuff and sexual stuff. Then, I guess it just seemed like I didn't feel like all those girls did so something must be wrong with me. So, basically, I just tried to act like them, you know, talk about boys with them and stuff."
>
> —Chloe, gay biracial female, age 20.

In these responses, and many others like them, it is obvious that students mark their thinking about their sexual identity in relationship to the stage they were at in school. This indicates that, in some way, school was significant to their experience of these emerging feelings. In what way it was significant was less immediately clear. To get at a deeper understanding of this relationship, I asked more probing questions of the interviewees.

For instance, after Chloe gave the above response to my initial question about when she began to realize she was gay, I asked, "When did you know what those feelings you had meant? Did you come out at an early age?" She replied,

> "No. ... Once I realized that it was a wrong or a bad thing to feel, I tried to make myself stop. I told myself I didn't really feel that way and never talked to anyone about it. When I was a kid I knew that I really liked girls, friends and teachers, but I didn't think it was a bad thing. So I didn't try to hide it or anything, and it wasn't a secret. But once I realized it was a bad thing, it became this secret I had to keep and something that I had to fix about myself."

This statement reveals several things about the significance of the relationship between Chloe's "self-realization of sexual orientation" and school. She reports having feelings of affection for other females from an early age, and this was neither something that troubled her nor anything she felt compelled to hide. However, when she entered junior high school, with its environment of normative heterosexuality heightened by "the whole puberty thing," she learned that her feelings for other females could be labeled as homosexual. She was given the messages that this was "a bad thing to feel," that this made her different from her peers, and that she should keep this part of herself a secret and try to be like everyone else. The meaning of the messages she received from other students and the school environment was that heterosexuality was the only accepted and reinforced feeling and behavior. The force of these social norms defined her feelings as a discreditable stigma, manipulated her into believing that there was something wrong with her, and coerced her into taking on behaviors that would serve to hide or "closet" that part of herself. They also informed her that these same-sex feelings made her a specific *type* of person, which socially marked her as someone who would be the target of ostracism.

Analyzing Chloe's experience in this manner is different in several respects from the way that this situation is usually understood in the literature on homosexual identity development. If we were to apply the analysis used in that literature, we might read her actions as merely personal reactions to the self-hatred caused by her same-sex attractions that she believes are wrong. I argue, however, that the empirical evidence strongly supports an analysis of Chloe's behavior as an active or *reactive* strategy to cope with others' definitions of her feelings and the social forces around her that are hostile to that part of herself. This process, which much of the previous literature describes as an intra-psychic, personal, and staged journey of self-acceptance, is actually a social process—a process constructed by social and structural definitions and categorization of individuals' same-sex feelings and behaviors. Social and cultural definitions of sexual identity, which stigmatize and define homosexuality as unnatural and abnormal, shape and condone negative reactions to LGBT people. Importantly, these same definitions also serve as the base of information out of which LGBT people come to understand and define themselves.

Much of the psychological, counseling, and popular literature on LGBT individuals portrays them as struggling to develop a relatively positive definition of themselves *despite* their "sexual orientation." However, it is more accurate to view them as individuals battling with the social forces that *define* their feelings as an essential and problematic identity. This is further illustrated by Chloe's statement: "I mean, I'm not upset about it or anything, I'm not unhappy that I'm gay ... but ... I don't know. I guess I feel a little left out of the world."

Statements like these were made repeatedly by the youth I interviewed. Frequently, they expressed a deep understanding that it was not their feelings that were inherently wrong or deviant. It was, instead, the social world that created the difficulties associated with being LGBT. As Rick stated about realizing that he was bisexual, "It was just like the initial shock of like the first day and then I was over it. But like everybody else had a problem dealing with it. That was the problem, and that fucked me up." In relation to school, Rick stated, 'When I was at school I was always on edge. It affected me as far as how I would deal with people, you know, or I didn't deal with people at all. And because I couldn't, nobody could know the truth, otherwise I would die." Rick reported that he perceived his school as a place where harassment of LGBT students took place often and generally went unpunished by teachers or school administrators. The "truth," that he was not heterosexual, was not a threat to Rick's (and other LGBT students') self-concept. Rather, this "truth" was a threat to the normative heterosexuality of the school, and this threat put him in danger of abuse, which, in this context, was often condoned as justifiable punishment.

"Acceptance": A Setup for Failure

Overwhelmingly, journal articles and books targeted at school counselors, social workers, teachers and administrators communicate to them that the heart of the problems experienced by LGBT students is low self-esteem. That body of literature, like the homosexual identity development models that inform it, presumes that same-sex attractions are inherently unaccept-able to the individual causing self-esteem-related problems. In these asser-tions there is little distinction made between one's perception of oneself and the judgment enforced by one's environment. This de-emphasizes the reality that some individuals do not have to work to accept themselves, and yet still find it unacceptable that they are deemed intolerable by society. In fact, according to these models, an essential step in the developmental process is for the homosexual individual to "accept" the socially defined, structurally ingrained, and institutionally enforced stigma of homosexual-ity. Also, and somewhat of a contradiction in logic, these models take for granted that "self-acceptance" is fully achievable within a society in which homosexuality is so thoroughly defined as unacceptable. Such complexi-ties are not critically addressed in these developmental models or in the research on LGBT youth that has been informed by them. It is important to note that such complexities have now been addressed by a large and grow-ing body of academic theory and research, but, in the early days of LGBT activism, these understandings had not yet been used to inform the emerg-ing research on gay youth.

The concept of "acceptance" is an important one in LGBT students' lives. However, it is important in ways that are distinctly different from those outlined in the previous literature. In group meetings as well as indi-vidual interviews, the students spoke of problems with being accepted for who they are in school, at home, and in public, because they were LGBT. They also spoke of *self-acceptance*. Acceptance was something that they worried about losing and actively sought out from those they loved as well as from the social world that surrounded them.

The degree to which the LGBT youth I spoke with felt they received acceptance from others varied depending on what group of people they were referring to—the general school environment, teachers, peers, family, gay and lesbian communities, the general public, etc. The degree to which they accepted their same-sex feelings as a positive part of their own identity also seemed to vary largely in relation to their experiences with external social factors. In other words, the factors of self-acceptance and acceptance from others form a reciprocal relationship. The level of tolerance that students receive from others and from their environments influences their self-acceptance; and an individual student's level of self-acceptance influences the degree to which she/he seeks out, or worries about, the approval of others. Two major themes emerged in relation to the concept of "acceptance." The first is that, for LGBT students, school is overwhelmingly not a place of acceptance, but rather, it is a place where they feel uncomfortable, fearful or worried, and often hated. The second is that not receiving acceptance and having to worry about acceptance causes these students to have feelings of frustration and anger throughout their school experience.

I'm not good at being around kids, you know, people at school.... I am really confident outside of school, but once I'm in school I don't feel confident. It's really hard to feel confident at school, I feel uncomfortable.

—Vincent, gay white male, age 16

It's something that is more comforting to know that [my new] high school is not afraid to talk about gay and lesbian issues. It's comforting to know that I can wake up in the morning and not think, am I going to call in sick or am I just going to lie. I can just go to school and feel comfortable, you know, today is going to be a good day. I can wake up at eight o'clock in the morning and say I'm gay and feel good about it. I don't have to worry, ok who's going to say what to me today, when I get to school what's my locker going to look like. In gym class—oh god, do I skip or do I go and risk being tortured. So, it's easier for me now to walk around with my head held high, that's something that I can do now.

—Mike, gay biracial male, age 17

These statements illustrate that the way many LGBT students feel about themselves is conditionally based on their school environment. Vincent reports that his level of self-confidence drops as he enters school walls. Mike's statement illustrates the impact that both a homophobic and an accepting school environment can have on a LGBT student's life. The majority of students I spoke with reported that school made them feel uncomfortable, unaccepted, isolated, angry, or afraid.

The narrative told by traditional homosexual identity models, and much of the literature on youth that is informed by them, positions "self-acceptance" as a crucial step toward the achievement of a relatively tolerable and contented life for a homosexual individual (relative to that of heterosexuals). On the one hand, this can be read as a positive narrative in opposition to other past scientific, medical, and some contemporary religious discourses that see the future for the LGBT individual as one of misery unless they change, cure, or repress their feelings. On the other hand, it can be read as a narrative that inescapably sets the LGBT individual up for failure. It makes acceptance an accomplishment that *individuals* must work to achieve if they are to be content in a society in which non-acceptance of homosexuality is intertwined with cultural messages, institutions, and structures. This assures that acceptance is, at worst, impossible and, at best, a continuous struggle. By stressing *self-acceptance*, and submitting to the ideology that social stigmatization is justifiable, the onus is fully on the individual. It is the individuals' failure to accept themselves as LGBT that is presumed to cause the difficulties they encounter, and society is absolved.

"Coming Out": A Socially Produced Narrative of Shame and Liberation

The concept of acceptance, both from others and of self, is talked about in the literature as part of the identity-development process that builds up to the "coming-out" process. This is basically a procedure through which homosexual individuals learn self-acceptance of their stigma and the social limitations that this stigma places on them, and how to make decisions about where and to whom to reveal this discreditable feature of themselves. The terms "coming-out" and "the closet," have become a large part of the cultural discourse about gay and lesbian people. Coming-out stories and narratives of "self-discovery" are now common types of pop-cultural accounts of the lives of gay people. As a result, many people feel that, to understand a gay person, they need to know when the person "knew" he or she was gay, if the person is "in" or "out" of the "closet," and why.[11] The youth I interviewed are no exception to this. They often used the language of the "coming-out" discourse to describe their own and others' experiences. Issues of coming out—to do it or not to do it, how to do it, who to tell and who not to tell, negative and positive results of, the safety or danger of, etc.—were some of the most prevalent themes in the support group meetings I attended and the interviews I conducted.

The decision to come out or to hide in the closet is generally not based on a level of self-acceptance. It is, however, largely based on their perception of the social circumstances in which they find themselves.

> I was out to some of my close friends and I hinted about it to others and was not at all out to others. It depended on how much I thought I could trust them or how I thought they would react to it. ... I'm still afraid to be out in public and be with other gay people, to have people know that I'm gay. I don't want to get hurt or have anyone make judgments about me or anything.
>
> —**Ani, gay white female, age 18**

> It would be like suicide to come out at my high school. It is worse than the backwoods. It is such a small town and so conservative. In the eighteen years that I've lived there I've never known anyone who was gay and out there.
>
> —**Luke, gay white male, age 18.**

These LGBT students discern that it is not their acceptance of homosexuality that is most important to coming out, but rather other individuals', the institution's, or society's level of acceptance of homosexuality that will affect their experiences when and if they decide to come out.

> It was kind of scary in my school because if anybody ever found out that you were gay, everybody would know, like the whole town. There would be no place to hide from people saying stuff about you.... I thought that if anybody ever found out then, you better move out because that would be it.
>
> —**Kate, gay white female, age 18.**

Well, I came out when I was fifteen, to my family and a few close friends. But I was still in high school and didn't come out to everybody. I had people come up and ask me after rumors started flying around. I would still say no, you know, I'm straight or whatever. [laughs] I didn't want to get my butt kicked. I live in a small town.

—**Rick, bisexual biracial male, age 18.**

These students' decisions to reveal or to not reveal their same-sex attractions to others is based on an assessment of the costs and benefits, punishments and rewards, and danger and safety associated with such an action.

I'm out and nobody really bothers me. I have been out since I was fifteen and it hasn't really been a major thing. Everyone knows who I am and that I am gay and they don't really bug me much. Then again, I'm the kind of person who thinks that it's better to be who you are. I couldn't stand not being what I am. If people can't deal with it then fuck 'em—that's their deal, not mine. I mean I don't go around an-nouncing to everyone that I am gay, but if they ask me I tell them and I don't censor myself for anyone. … If they can't deal with it then that's their shit, not mine. I don't have time for it and I won't deal with it.

—**Warren, gay white male, age 16**

I tried at first to hide that I was gay, I tried really hard to act like everyone else, and to just kind of be invisible. It didn't work though, because people could just tell, like they said by the way I talked and walked and stuff, they could just tell I was gay, and they made fun of me and threw stuff at me and hit me in the halls, no matter how much I kept denying it. So, finally I just admitted it, because I was so tired of it, but the abuse just got worse.

—**Andy, gay white male, age 16.**

As the preceding statements evidence, many social factors are involved in this "coming out process" for LGBT students. For example, Ani, Luke, and Rick all perceived their school environments to be risky places to be LGBT. Based on this evaluation of their surroundings, they felt fearful of others' judgments of them and of the punishment that might accompany these judgments. For Warren, the potential risks of such judgments were outweighed by what he felt to be the cost of "censoring himself." For Andy, neither decision—to hide or to come out—could spare him from the judgment and punishment associated with being outside of the heterosexual norm of his high school. In these assessments, the students conclude that institutions of public education are dangerous places in which to come out, to be found to be, or be suspected of being gay, lesbian, or bisexual. Therefore, some choose to hide this part of themselves at school while others choose to reveal it. Regardless of the choice made, all students first assessed the relative safety or danger of their school environment.

Sexual Identity Labels: The Paradox of "Self-definition"

According to the literature on homosexual identity development models, an individual's acceptance and situational use of the label gay, lesbian, or bisexual is a sign of successful and mature homosexual identity formation. Therefore, discomfort with these labels is taken to be a sign of a personal difficulty with self-acceptance. The developmental models, and the theoretical perspective of symbolic interactionism that informs them, take the meaning of these labels for granted. They do not discuss or analyze the social construction of these labels, the "natural" binary of heterosexual and homosexual that these labels reinforce, or the compulsion to categorize people within them.

In contrast, other theoretical perspectives argue that the terms and conditions on which sexual identity labels are based, and the very concept of labeling, result from the power of scientifically and socially produced meanings of sexual identity.[12] These identity categories are used as social controls of individual behaviors and as structured enforcement of the normative dominance of heterosexuality. Many of the LGBT students spoke about sexual identity labels as categories and definitions that they felt were being forced upon them.

The use of sexual identity labels was, at times, the subject of debate at the weekly support group meetings. When I interviewed youth individually, it was revealed that many found labeling to be personally frustrating, because they felt pressured to define and categorize their "true sexual identity."

It depends on who I'm talking to … I say that I'm bisexual to people that I think are closed-minded. …. It seems like a more acceptable term. So, I guess I think that people will be more willing to accept that, or won't get as freaked out if I say that as they would if I said that I was lesbian. … I don't think that any term is really an accurate description of who I am. It makes me uncomfortable to use them and, you know, all that it means to people. Like, people make assumptions about it—like it's sexual or disgusting or whatever ….but to other people, like my closer friends, I say that I am a lesbian.

—Ani, gay white female, age 18.

I use the term gay, if I use any term at all …. I don't like the term lesbian. It's like too technical or something. It sounds like a disease or a different species or something.

—Emily, gay white female, age 16.

These statements provide examples of how many of the students make the choice of how and when to label themselves. Many do this not based on their definition, understanding, or tolerance of their attractions, but rather on their perception of the meanings that *others* have attached to these labels of sexual identity. Generally, the students had little problem with self-acceptance. However, they did have anxiety about "coming out" and about the pressure they felt to choose a label and define their sexual identity.

I don't understand why I have to label myself anything. I'm just Adam. If somebody asks me if I'm gay I'll say yes, but why do I have to go around calling myself anything? Being gay is just a small part of who I am. It happens in my bedroom, not on a big screen in the street. It doesn't affect anyone. I'm just like everybody else, I like to go to the movies and dinner and talk with my boyfriend. I don't want anything radical and I don't want to talk about it to everyone I meet. I mean, yeah I want rights like everybody else and the legal right to marry, you know, that stuff's really important. But, it's not radical.

—Adam, gay white male, age 19.

The students who respond to labels in this way demonstrate a knowledge that these terms have social meanings beyond being only a simple description of their attractions, and that these meanings are, more often than not, beyond their ability to define for themselves. They are generally uncomfortable with using these labels, which they feel do more to take away their ability to fully define and express themselves to others than to assert their identity.

> I don't use any label really. Except at group where you kind of are expected to say something. Then I guess I say gay. ... I'm not ashamed of it or anything. I just don't like... I don't go around announcing it to everyone. I don't really think that it is anyone's business.
>
> —Carol, gay white female, age 17.

> I don't really label myself that much. ... I just don't fit one and ... Well, because my sexual orientation has a bad reputation, you know.
>
> —Becca, bisexual Jewish female, age 18.

Statements like these illustrate social factors, *not* personal problems of acceptance. It is evidence of their knowledge of and anger at the ways in which others perceive the meaning of these labels and in the way such labels may be used by others to place limits on who they can be. Some of the LGBT students I interviewed took an active approach to try to define themselves outside of the definitional boundaries of these sexual identity categories.

> I use the word dyke because I don't like the word lesbian. I think when people say it, it's like lesss-bee-ann [slow and drawn out]. Like it sounds really old and ... I don't know. I'm young and. ... Ever since I've been out no one's ever used the word dyke against me in a bad way. And so ... I've been called lesbo and I've been called other things having to do with lesbian. So, I prefer not to use it because it has negative meaning to me. ... Dyke is a really powerful word, and it seems like an active word. Because when people say the word dyke, people stop and listen. And nobody stops to listen when you say lesbian. Ever. It's just like, 'O.K. Whatever. You mean you're gay, right?'
>
> —Janice, gay white female, age 19.

Not straight. Because ... I don't like heterosexuals and I don't like homosexuals, and for me each are incorporated in my thoughts .... Just things that I don't like that go along with each trait that I don't like. I don't like, extremely flamboyant people ... homosexuals especially.... And I don't like ... jock-ass heterosexuals ... hard-core heteros. Basically they piss me off. ... I consider myself bi ... I can go either way. [I: Why don't you use that label?] Because I'm not generic. (laughs) Pretty much that's it. I don't like labels.

—Rick, bisexual biracial male, age 18.

Statements like these reveal an awareness of the shaping force of sexual identity categories on these students' lives—setting the definitional terms for who they are and who they can potentially be. They also evidence the possibility of fostering a positive identity and "self-acceptance" without simultaneously passively accepting the social, structural, and institutional meanings of homosexuality. Many LGBT students are actively trying to forge an identity for themselves that rejects the stigma forced on them by society and that moves beyond the definitional limitations of sexual identity categories.

Most of the research on and writing about LGBT youth has been focused largely on the negative aspects of "growing up gay," addressing and analyzing only the negative variables and outcomes of their experiences. The motivation for such an approach was benevolent, hoping that documenting the suffering, problems, and risks involved with being a gay teenager would lead to the development of services and resources to address their needs. As I illustrate throughout the book, this focus on the sufferings of LGBT youth has brought such resources and services. However, what was missed by this focus on problems was an understanding of adolescents who have successfully avoided or transcended many of the negative experiences and outcomes associated with being LGBT, and an understanding of the factors that contributed to their success. Many LGBT teens are indeed struggling and in need of assistance. However, if effective solutions are to be found, it is crucial for researchers, school officials, social service workers, and the general public to understand the social and institutional factors that contribute to these negative experiences.

Students have been well ahead of researchers and those seeking to develop services to meet their needs. The teenagers who pioneered the

GSA movement were the first to understand the institutional forces putting LGBT students at risk and to have a vision of the direction that effective change should take. The next chapter provides an in-depth look at some first steps taken in attempts to realize this vision—one school at a time—and the succeeding chapters examine the progression from there. The assertions of positive, self-assured sexual identities and student rights served as the catalyst for a social movement and for cultural transformations in images of what it is to be a LGBT teenager.

THREE

"WE'RE NOT GOING TO TAKE IT ANYMORE"
The Beginnings of Lesbian, Gay, Bisexual (and Straight) Student Resistance

The previous chapter illustrated that many of the students I interviewed in the mid 1990s demonstrated a rather sophisticated sociological understanding and analysis of the ways in which schools affect their lives. They understood that sexual identity is socially defined and the "stigma" of homosexuality is socially enforced through cultural stereotypes, media images, ignorance, and institutionalized structures and practices such as those that take place in schools. For some, having such an analysis of the situation was frustrating because they felt powerless against the strength of these institutionalized forces; others felt empowered by the knowledge of a tangible force to resist and change. What I was observing and learning about the real-life experiences, feelings, attitudes, and wisdom of these teenagers contrasted sharply with the image of LGBT youth that was portrayed in the psychological and journalist accounts of this population.

There is no doubt that what I observed and what these other sources reported about LGBT adolescents were both real descriptions, but neither one captured the full range of their experiences. Countless LGBT high school students struggle with their sexual orientation in isolation and shame and live in fear of the potential personal and social ramifications exposure might bring. However, others see no reason to feel shame and believe they should not have to live in fear. As these unapologetic teens began to discover each other, they empowered one another to wage small battles against some of the social forces that sought to impose fear and shame on them. Their main target was their high school, because it was experiences within its walls that most united them, and its institutional force was the most pressing on their daily lives. By taking action, they hoped to improve their own lives, the lives of those who were too afraid to join in their battle, and the generations of LGBT students who would pass through their high school after they had graduated.

This chapter presents case studies of two early instances of such resistance and change. These case studies begin in 1994, before GLSEN or the ACLU had begun their attempts to organize student efforts and before much public attention had been brought to the needs of gay, lesbian and bisexual students. I provide these studies to recognize the "pioneers" of the movement and to establish the fundamental and complex issues involved in local school struggles with the controversies GSAs often spark. I highlight the reactions of students, school faculty and administration, parents, communities, and local media to the idea of GSAs, and offer an analysis of the factors influencing the opinions of these groups. I also take a look at the strategies used by members of these local school districts to try to sway public opinion to meet their own position. Finally, I offer these case studies at this point in the book as a mechanism by which to trace changes in the experiences of establishing GSAs over the past decade. These case studies give a detailed look at what it was like to try to establish a gay–straight alliance student club before teachers, parents, school officials, or community members knew there were self-identified LGBT kids in their schools or what a GSA was. Over time, some of the strategies and discourses students and teachers developed at the very grassroots level to win permission to establish a GSA at their specific high school evolved into more organized tactics of a larger social movement. These case studies provide a means to assess the social and political impact of the GSA movement by supplying a detailed look at what it was like to struggle for LGBT students' rights before the movement took off.

WESTVILLE HIGH SCHOOL:
"TRANSCENDING THE LABEL" AND "PRIDE"[1]

Westville High School[2] is a public school of approximately 1,100 students from grades 9–12. The school is located in a suburban area between two small cities. The school district is largely white (more than 90% of the students and all of the teachers at Westville are white) and middle class. It was described to me by many of those I spoke with as a conservative, "traditional," and Republican community in its general political stance. However, those I spoke with also stated that there were pockets of liberal "ex-hippies" as well as "right wing" religious conservatives who occasionally made their voice heard in the community. Westville is a quiet suburb that is geographically spread out; giving parts of the community almost a rural atmosphere.

In April of 1993, two Westville High students, Janet and Eric, decided to take a bus to the Gay and Lesbian Rights March in Washington, D.C. On the bus ride home, Janet and Eric spotted a teacher from their high school. Feeling inspired and motivated by their participation in the march, Janet and Eric approached the teacher, Ms. Smith, and asked her if she would assist them in starting a club at their high school to educate students, faculty, and staff about LGBT related issues and rights. Somewhat hesitant, but swayed by the students' enthusiasm, Ms. Smith agreed to help them negotiate the bureaucratic process and the potential resistance to forming such a group.

Janet and Eric had grown tired of the harassment they and their LGBT friends faced daily at school. They were angry at the ignorance of their classmates, and frustrated by the school's failure to provide accurate information about LGBT people, and to address the needs and concerns of its LGBT students. Both Janet and Eric had suffered harassment at school because they are gay, and both were fortunate to have found support and information outside of school from their families, friends, and books. Both had developed an informed and proud perspective about their sexual identity. They recognized that many of their LGBT classmates did not have access to such support and information, and were suffering through school in fear, isolation, and ignorance.

Discussing her decision to work to form this group, Janet said:

"Teenage suicide is becoming an important problem at many high schools; 30% of these suicides occur because of issues relating to homosexuality. If we have the chance to develop an atmosphere where gay students can receive support, even if only once a week, how can we refuse that chance? If we have the opportunity to help students be more

comfortable with their gay peers or even, perhaps, themselves, how can
we not act on it? If we have the opportunity to help the people in this
school work together more easily, how can we ignore it?"

This statement sounds like a well-crafted prepared political statement, but,
remarkably, it comes from a student who was not aligned with any larger
political faction. It was this ability to effectively articulate the need, purpose, and goals of their clubs that made student leadership such a powerful
shaping force in the emerging GSA movement.

The goal of these two students, and the several others who joined with
them, was to provide a place in school where LGBT and supportive students
could be comfortable and safe, and could talk to each other about their
experiences. What was even more important to these students was their desire
to educate and provide information to the entire school community—students,
teachers, administrators, and parents. They wanted to do more than provide a
weekly hour or two of support for the few kids who would be willing to come
to a support group meeting. They wanted to educate the entire school so that
all students would feel safe, accepted, included, and supported everywhere
within school walls. This was "Pride's" primary goal.

The two teachers who agreed to be the faculty advisors for Pride,
Ms. Smith and Ms. Patrick, also believed in the importance of the group's
mission. Both had been teachers at Westville for many years and were
cognizant of some of the difficulties the school's LGBT students faced. They
heard the name calling in the halls, they tried to stop the anti-gay teasing in
their classrooms, and they attempted to give some resources and guidance to
the students who occasionally came to them shyly seeking information and a
supportive adult. As Ms. Smith told me, "I knew that there were kids who
were gay, and there have been occasionally kids who have asked for support,
and they have become more adept at getting support and getting what they
need as the issue has become more public." However, both Ms. Smith and
Ms. Patrick felt powerless to do anything substantial to assist these students
or to advocate for changes in the school to make it safer and more inclusive
of LGBT students, because they both are lesbians. Ms. Smith spoke to me
at length about the irony of this situation. Contrary to the cultural stereotype, misconception, and fear that homosexual individuals try to "recruit"
or "corrupt" children, teachers are generally so afraid of not getting hired,
not getting tenure, being falsely accused, or losing their job that they can
not even advocate for the rights of their LGBT students.

This paradoxical situation of gay and lesbian teachers was the subject of several books in the 1990s[3]. These accounts generally discuss the frustration, fear, and danger felt as teachers struggle between their wish to create changes that they feel would improve the education of all students in their schools, and the reality of the threat such advocating may pose to their career. A typical example of this analysis from this literature:

> Lesbian, gay, and bisexual staff members are often alone in the fight against homophobia. Often we feel that we have the most to lose by confronting it. We are told that the issue is not important, or that it is solely our issue, or that there is no issue to be dealt with at all. At the same time, religious fundamentalists launch countless initiatives in attempts to deny us the right to be ourselves or to outlaw any mention of homosexuality in the curriculum. ... Our behavior is labeled inappropriate if we dare to "come out" to our students and provide role models for the 10% who will be lesbian or gay or the 90% who need to know and respect homosexuals so that they can expand their view of the world. We are accused of causing trouble, or proselytizing our lifestyle with the intent to "convert" others.[4]

Because of a lack of legal protections, teachers risk losing their jobs or tenure if they come out or if they even advocate for LGBT students, which puts them under suspicion. This threat and the possibility of sanctioned institutional discrimination serve both as a socially controlling force in the lives of these teachers and as a social control in public schools—keeping teachers silent on the subject, and therefore protecting the normative heterosexual culture. To the extent that public schools socialize students to the norms and values of society, these sanctions against teachers also serve to protect the normative heterosexuality of American society.

In the case of Westville high school, to protect their jobs and secure their futures, both Ms. Smith and Ms. Patrick had remained silent about their sexual identity (while in school and with colleagues) for the many years that they had been teachers. They both agreed to serve as advisors for Pride, because students expressed a desire to assist and educate their fellow students, and they needed faculty support in their efforts. Both women had also earned tenure and established themselves as respected and valued teachers. They felt this reduced the risk of losing their jobs for supporting these students.

In fighting for the right to establish Pride, both Ms. Smith and Ms. Patrick revealed their sexual identity at a faculty meeting. However, neither ever officially disclosed their sexual identity to the general student body or to the community. Both women felt that it was important to the establishment and endurance of the group that they not be its only advocates. Ms. Smith told me, "We tried our best to go through the proper channels. To have the head of counseling be the spokesperson rather than one of us. To have the principal be a spokesperson instead of one of us. So, it wouldn't be focused on individuals. We wanted it to be an official school organization and not just associated with a few individuals who were gay teachers, or a few kids who would eventually leave." For this reason, they attempted to frame the argument for founding Pride on meeting the needs of all students and the goals of public education—hoping to counteract the anticipated administrative, school board, and community response that Pride was an agenda of a few faculty and students.

In fact, school administrators, the school board, and the community frequently required those who supported Pride to demonstrate and explain the need for having a group that supports education about LGBT issues in a public school. Ms. Smith and Ms. Patrick reported that the superintendent and the school board regularly remind them of the stipulations placed on Pride:

> There has been lots of hassling in that regard. I guess hassling is not
> the right word, because they're always really polite. You know? But, it's
> kind of "administratese—you don't want to do anything that will offend
> anyone." And none of them have a stand on anything that anyone could
> possibly object to .... I would have had no reason to think that the su-
> perintendent would be opposed to having this student group, but all this
> effort about it made me think that institutions are even less human-like
> than I thought before. You know? Like he is completely unwilling to take
> a stand and say it is wrong for people to think that homosexuals are all
> sinners. Because there are some taxpayers who believe that homosexuals
> are all sinners, he won't say you're wrong. And, he thinks that it's his job
> to not say they're wrong."
>
> —Ms. Smith

From Ms. Smith's perspective, the principal sees it as part of his job to uphold the heteronormative order of the school because it parallels the norms of society and the community. If he allowed the inclusion of an LGBT student group into the school culture and structure, it might be perceived by community members as a threat to the morals of the broader community.

After almost every event sponsored by Pride, Ms. Smith and Ms. Patrick received a memo from the superintendent of schools reminding them of the restriction against political activity. Such a notice was sent to them after Pride, along with two other student organizations, sponsored a school dance for all students. The dance went well and was well attended; however, Ms. Patrick was notified that the activity was outside the group's "supportive" function. Ms. Patrick responded to this charge in a letter to the superintendent.

> As co-advisor of 'Pride,' I would like to respond to your March 29, 1995, memo regarding our functioning as a support group and what that means in terms of the appropriateness of the group's activities. Your reaction to the dance ... both surprised and troubled me, for I had not anticipated that we were doing anything other than saying to our members that they are, in fact, as important and accepted a part of Westville as anyone else. I, mistakenly perhaps, did not see this activity as taking us beyond the role of education and support, especially when our members benefited so by finally feeling that they, too, belonged at a school function.

It appears that the superintendent's objection to Pride's sponsorship of a school dance is that it took Pride's influence beyond the segregated confines of its weekly after-school meetings and into the general school population. Incorporating LGBT students into a dance normalizes homosexual attractions, which were at odds with the school's normative heterosexuality.

The difference in definition of, and opinion about, the "function" of Pride and its various activities centered on the concept of "political activity." There was a marked difference between what the school board and administration considered to constitute political activity and what students and faculty advisors felt was support and education. From the beginning, the LGBT students who initiated the formation of Pride at Westville wanted the group to be both educational and active. Their vision of Pride was not one of a support group in a counseling sense. They wanted to make LGBT students feel supported through the dissemination of information, through a chance to be active and meet other LGBT and supportive students, and through creating a more tolerant school culture. I asked Ms. Smith about the goals the students had for the group when they approached her with their idea to start Pride.

> They wanted it to be, well, it depends on how you use the word political, because the district, of course, didn't want it to be political. The students wanted it to be just a student organization. And the purpose of it would be education. And the education would be of the people there, who attended, and the people of the school, so that the school would be a better, kinder, more tolerant place. ... Pride is not just for gay students, it's for all students.

According to the reports of the Westville students and faculty advisors, the establishment of "Transcending the Labels" as a support group was an afterthought. This support group, which served to give more emotional assistance to students, primarily began in an effort to comply with the definition the board and administration gave of the group's purpose. The support group was established after the school's student services advisory board determined that "support" was appropriate, and Pride was allowed to continue (unofficially) as a compromise to the students' request for an active student organization. The "support group" could be kept separate, quarantined off, keeping the heterosexual students safe from the polluting influence of LGBT students and alternative understandings of sexual identity. The activities of Pride were restricted to severely limit the impact it could have on the general population and structure of the school.

The actions that the members of Pride took to educate the school community and improve the school experiences of LGBT students were often confronted with charges of "political action." Janet responded to one such charge, made by a parent, with the following statement:

> Yes, gay and lesbian teens are forced to have special interests. Hatred like that of Ms. Young creates an environment in which our physical and mental security is in jeopardy. Gay and lesbian students at Westville endure relentless harassment, threats and danger. During my senior year of high school, I was chased home and almost run over by classmates shouting anti-gay epithets. I and other gay and lesbian students developed a special interest in graduating without physical harm. Is this, as Ms. Young says, a "political gain"?

Students like Janet and the faculty advisors of Pride thought that they were being unfairly reprimanded for being too political merely because they were discussing and providing education about LGBT student issues. They thought that the restrictions placed on their activities and the constant monitoring and warnings were the result of the administration's and school board's ignorance and misconceptions of homosexuality, and their fear of parental and community reaction to having permitted the formation of such a group. From the perspective of the students and advisors, the restrictions were clear evidence of discrimination and homophobia. Janet wrote the following response to the superintendent's and the school board's request for information about what the need for this group was in a public school:

> Why is a club for gay, lesbian, and bisexual students necessary? It
> is necessary for a school to be supportive and accepting of all of its
> students. Homosexuality, like heterosexuality, is something with which
> we are born. Being an ethnic minority is also something with which we
> are born. To embrace a club such as Cultural Alliance but to simulta-
> neously condemn a club for students who are gay, lesbian or bisexual
> is sheer hypocrisy. This contradiction gives students the message that
> some students deserve to be proud of what makes them different and
> some students do not. Maybe we should begin to question if this attitude
> belongs in our schools, as opposed to questioning the validity of a club
> for gay or lesbian students.
>
> —Janet

It is clear from statements such as these that the students and faculty members who founded Pride considered homosexuality to be a natural part of human diversity. Therefore, in their view, LGBT students should be protected from harassment, included in the curriculum, embraced by the school community, and be free to express pride in themselves. As I show in Chapter five, this type of argument, articulated so well by this student in the mid 1990s, became a standard rhetorical strategy of the organizations involved in the GSA movement by the end of the decade.

The Principal: the Man in the Middle

The principal at Westville High School, Mr. Nasca, was in the position to serve as the mediator between the requests of Pride and the regulations of the superintendent and school board. As the principal of the high school, Mr. Nasca was also in the spotlight and on the front lines of school and community conflicts and controversies over Pride. Often this meant that he received severe criticisms from all sides of these debates. He tried to field all of their varying concerns, yet was unable to make decisions that could simultaneously satisfy everyone's demands. Mr. Nasca also had to negotiate his own conflicting opinions about the issue. As an educator, he was dedicated to the growth, development, and nurturance of all students. As a principal, he was required to abide by the rules and regulations of the bureaucracy of the school district. As an individual, outside of these occupational roles, he had to contend with his religious beliefs and the cultural meanings and stereotypes of homosexuality that had formed his understandings and opinions of gay and lesbian people.

One of the major forces guiding Mr. Nasca through these conflicting elements was his use of personal experiences and information as empirical basis for the development of his opinion on the place of Pride at his school. In my interview with Mr. Nasca, I asked him if he had had any previous experience with LGBT issues in his career as an educator.

> When I was at [a private school], I had a teacher's aid who was gay. Probably one of the best people I've ever met with kids. …If you talked to him, there was no overt indication to anyone that he might be effeminate, let alone whether he was gay or not. But as he got used to me and got used to the place, we accepted him as a very good teacher's aid…. I worked with him for over three years. He taught me a lot about it. He was a very special guy, terrific guy. And then when I came to high school here, there were several kids that I suspected were gay. More boys than girls, but none of them had ever spoken to me about it directly, or, as far as I knew, to any of the teachers. But there were clearly some.

Mr. Nasca negotiated what he had learned about homosexuality and gay men through cultural, mass media, and religious teachings with the empirical evidence provided by this personal experience. This professional relationship provided him with evidence that not all gay men are effeminate or otherwise obviously recognizable; that gay people could be trusted with children and be effective teachers; and that gay people could be "respectable" and "normal" individuals with whom he could develop a friendship and professional relationship. This experience provided Mr. Nasca with another frame of reference, or base of knowledge, from which to interpret LGBT individuals and issues. It did not, however, completely replace the original frame of reference, which still informed his assessment of the student body of his new high school.

I asked Mr. Nasca to tell me how the idea for forming the group Pride came to his attention. His reply began, "It was brought to me by two students and a faculty member. In fact, one of the students I knew fairly well. She was a kid I thought was probably gay, you know, but what do I know, I wasn't sure. And the teacher who was rumored to be, and I didn't have any information on that. I like her a lot, she's a great gal." Part of his attempt to understand and evaluate the students and teachers was to assess their sexual identity and, therefore, it seems, their motivation. "So, they came to me and asked if they could start this club. My first reaction was, I'll never get approval from the superintendent and the board of education to do this. I asked them what their purpose was and we talked about it, we discussed it."

Principal Nasca's initial reaction was to be skeptical of this group, not only because, as an administrator, he saw it as a potentially difficult issue to deal with in the bureaucracy and politics of a public school, but also because he personally found it to be a tricky issue. He explained the response he gave to the students and teachers, "I said 'you know, I honestly don't know what the reaction of the board will be, but I want to be honest with you, I don't know what my reaction is. Do I go publicly and say to people, we've got a club like the Key Club and some other groups, and now we've got a gay and lesbian club?' Because they clearly wanted a gay and lesbian name." This trouble in equating an LGBT student club or organization with other student organizations is a theme that runs through the history of both groups I studied, as well as through accounts of similar groups across the country. Generally, at least some administrators, school board members, faculty, students, and community members have difficulty with the idea that an LGBT group is needed, valid, or acceptable in a public school. The socially constructed and learned understandings define homosexuality as, among other things, sexual deviant, a psychological problem, immoral. Therefore, it is perceived as something that should be excluded from public education.

In Principal Nasca's case, he did not completely discount the need or appropriateness of a gay student group in his school. Instead, he sought more information about the issue. He told me, "I became interested in knowing more about it. There were not, to our knowledge, any other public high schools in New York State who had a club or organization for gays and lesbians. I called the state education department and they couldn't give me anything." This quest for more information was difficult because so little was available to educators. Mr. Nasca's search for information was coincidentally aided when, two weeks later, a local Planned Parenthood chapter sponsored a panel discussion on LGBT adolescents. He persuaded some of the members of the student services committee at Westville, the superintendent, Ms. Smith and Ms. Patrick, as well as six students, to attend this talk with him. Principal Nasca reported to me that this was a very significant learning experience for him. "I was absolutely enthralled by some of the things that these kids talked about. Not only were they bright and articulate and just wonderful kids, but they really had a tough go in high school. I decided as I drove home that night that we have really got to help these kids." As I spoke with people in communities across the country, the power of the students' own voices to change people's feelings and opinions was emphasized time and again. Every time a student speaks out, even in these seemingly small forums it propels the issue of LGBT student rights and the GSA movement forward.

Despite his personal decision to support the group, Mr. Nasca felt that more than this would be needed to convince the superintendent, school board, and community:

> I had some information, but still not enough. I ironically came by the name of a woman in Newton, Massachusetts, her name was Dr. Linda Shapiro. She was a Ph.D. psychologist who had done work in this area in the Newton public schools. I called her, asked her to come and meet with us over the summer. So, the superintendent, myself, and a couple of other people met with her. And we were really, not only taken by this woman, but also by the plight of these kids.

He thought that the information provided by an "expert" experienced scientist and academic, combined with the personal stories of LGBT students, provided the school board with more than sufficient evidence to validate the establishment of Pride. These strategies of networking and forming alliances were effective on the local level and have been expanded and strengthened by the GSA movement over time.

The next step was to formally request permission to establish Pride as an official school organization:

> We talked to the board, and said we had this club called Pride, two faculty advisors, non-paid advisors, and they hold meetings here. But they are what we consider, what the board considered, non-sanctioned clubs. See, the board wanted to cover themselves by saying, 'yeah they can exist, but [not officially] because [then] we could have a skinhead's group. So, they had this gay and lesbian group but they did not want to sanction them. They were concerned with what the public reaction would be.

Mr. Nasca's understanding of the reasoning the board used for not granting Pride official status as a school organization was that they feared the community would interpret their approval of the group as an open invitation to any group to form and force its beliefs on the school community. The school board could not, or did not, distinguish between LGBT students wanting to educate and make the school a more informed and tolerant place, and political propaganda and agendas of hate and intolerance of the hypothetical groups they claimed to be afraid of. On some level, Principal Nasca accepted this, or at least accepted that the school board was reasonable in believing that parental and community reaction might follow along these lines.

The fears about community reaction to Pride soon turned to reality. Not long after it began, the group sponsored a panel discussion of former students who were LGBT. Some parents were shocked and upset to read about this event in the local paper and learn that there was an LGBT group at their children's high school. Mr. Nasca told me that he heard from many of these community members. "Well, I caught an awful lot of flack ...I think probably ten to one hate mail I guess would be a descriptor .... Some were so vengeful and hateful I didn't even keep them, I didn't want them at home, I didn't want my wife or kids to see them. You know? Threatening kinds of things. It gets your attention, but I didn't lose any sleep over it, I didn't fear the tyranny of God or any of that crazy stuff." Not all of these hateful letters were from local community members. Many came from individuals around the country who identified themselves as "concerned Christian parents and citizens."

These letters did not cause Mr. Nasca to back down from his position on the issue, but he did seek out some support to help him cope with the criticisms and threats. The religious arguments and accusations particularly unsettled him because religion is an important part of his identity. "I am a Roman Catholic, practicing, active in my church. My parish priest talked to me one time about it. He said, 'They're all God's children, you do God's work over there.' So, that was a great endorsement from him." Mr. Nasca also found his family to be an important source of confirmation through the controversy. "My wife was very supportive. Both our boys graduated from the high school and both had known kids who they thought were gay, and they were very supportive. My oldest son just finished law school. For that period of time that that was happening he would give me information from Westlaw, they do law research, so I had some pretty good information."

This support and his conviction that he was doing the right thing for his students had to carry Mr. Nasca through years of recurring conflict over Pride. There have been periodic articles in local newspapers and a steady stream of angry letters throughout the years. Also, every year, Pride requested formal recognition and sanction from the school board. Each year, the request was accompanied by debate and has resulted in denial. Mr. Nasca's perspective on this situation was one of realistic optimism. "So, we are operating as we always have, without sanction, I guess, of the board. And we're doing fine. It's just a word. The kids were really miffed about it, and some of the adults, but I wasn't." Principal Nasca believed that the students had won a considerable victory in not being denied the permission to meet. He thought that it was a strong possibility that the school board might have decided not to allow Pride to meet at the school. However, he was prepared for this reaction, "I read the law enough to know pretty much if they brought that to the table I was ready to give them some legal citations. So, that worked out. That was the spring of the year [1996] and we finished the year in good shape."

The experience of establishing Pride at Westville high school was, perhaps, more tumultuous than Principal Nasca anticipated. However, he expressed to me a great sense of satisfaction in the work that he, the faculty members, and the students had done to change Westville high school for the better.

> I honestly believe that what we've done with Pride has improved the
> quality of this place. The milieu is very different. I think our kids are
> much more accepting. I think it's raised the level of consciousness on

the part of a lot of people, not only kids, but parents.... I think it was
an opportunity for parents to talk about responsibilities, citizenship,
character, tolerance, all those things. We are so intolerant as a group.
Our kids live in a lily white society here, not all of them, but most of
them have a good deal of money, they're mobile, they travel, there are
books in the house, most of their parents have masters or above ... so
they're a well educated group of people. But, if you don't know that
other piece, you know, you're really kind of out of touch with what the
real world is. So, I think it has really helped us .... I don't like the negative responses. I always worry about budget votes, and we've never lost
a budget since Pride has been here. But, I think it was the right thing to
do, the timing was right, and when I leave here that's one of the things,
in my own mind, I'll think back on and think we did the right thing."

From this statement it is clear that the principal of Westville learned
through his experiences that the problems experienced by LGBT students
transcend issues of sexuality, deviance, and morality or even personal identity. The debates and controversies that erupted around the issue of this
student group recalled for him the values, beliefs, and goals of public education and democracy.

The Superintendent and the School Board: Politically Concerned

I was fortunate to have access to a large quantity of documents pertaining to
the group at Westville High School. These documents included a collection
of letters and memos that had circulated among the superintendent of
Westville schools, the Westville High School principal, and the faculty
advisors for Pride. These memos date from June of 1993, when the request
for the group was first made to the board of education and continue through
January of 1996. The papers provide important data on the perspectives
and actions of all parties. They are particularly important as statements of
the superintendent's and school board's perspective, which I was unable to
attain through interviews.[5]

All of the statements quoted in this section come from memos authored
by the superintendent of Westville schools. In these memos, he often relayed
the feelings and requests of the school board. An example of this comes
from a memo sent to Ms. Smith and Ms. Patrick shortly after the request
for Pride had been presented.

We have all been spending time and effort to learn about the goals of
the request for a student group named Pride. This has been a good
educational process for the students and faculty involved …. At this
time in the process, I also want to make sure that we are all following the
guidelines the district has for the formation of extra-classroom/extra-
curriculum activities. I believe attention to these matters will provide
the solid foundation for the future decision-making regarding this
and other organizations. [list of rules] … Because these definitions are
important to the functioning of the teacher contract, the district and its
extracurricular activities, I believe it would be helpful for us to meet to
discuss them together if there are any questions or concerns.

—6/7/93

The language of this memo is clearly within a framework of bureaucratic
rationality. Clear understanding of and adherence to the district policies,
the statement argues, are essential to the "functioning" of the school system. The superintendent's statement stresses that any misunderstanding or
action outside of those prescribed by these rational and reasoned rules could
lead not only to failure of the group to get approved, but also to a disrup-
tion of the functioning of the entire school system. In this way, the superintendent passively asserts that the needs and requests of a few students
should not be placed ahead of the established and efficient workings of the
school and the district. In his view, it seems, normative heterosexuality is
an element of the rational and organized functioning of the public school
institution and, therefore, should not be radically disrupted.

The memo goes on to further list and define the rules of the district
pertaining to what constitutes extracurricular clubs, and to spell out the
rules that govern the activities of the various forms of student organizations.
At the end of this long and technical memo, the superintendent makes the
following specific statement about how he perceives Pride in relation to
these regulations [my emphasis added]:

The purpose stated on the group petition is: "Education, discussion, and
support for gay, lesbian, and bisexual students, and their friends and
supporters." In addition, during the faculty presentation, the formation
of the organization was indicated to be a response to the present lack

of such a support group within the high school guidance or other pupil service areas. Therefore, group meetings and requests for other activities should fall within a normal support group function. These generally mean discussion, education and support *for group members* and *not* advocacy or political action."

—6/7/93

This definition of the boundaries of Pride, which policy prescribes, is one that the superintendent and the school board asserted repeatedly over the years. Although the formal written request petitioning for Pride clearly places support third in their list of goals and objectives for the group, the superintendent defines it as the primary purpose. In redefining the group in this way, he places it under the category of support groups, which in the bylaws of the school are restricted to intergroup activities. Only formal school clubs are officially permitted to raise funds, have a paid advisor, and to organize schoolwide assemblies and functions. However, in defining these things that Pride, as a support group, is restricted from doing, the superintendent uses the terms "advocacy" and "political action."

The fact that the superintendent and the school board used these terms without specifically defining what actions are restricted left considerable room for confusion over the boundaries of Pride's activities. After almost every Pride activity, Ms. Patrick and Ms. Sullivan received a cautionary memo from the superintendent. The following statement comes from a memo sent almost two years after the establishment of the group. It was motivated by Pride's sponsorship of a school dance.

In past communications, on behalf of the district I have requested that the 'Pride' support group not take political action or operate as a school sponsored extracurricular activity (club). Again this year, various activities of 'Pride' or its members place the support group in positions that move beyond the agreed upon role as a support group. In particular, the participation in sponsoring a school dance.

—3/29/95

This memo is an excellent example of the superintendent and board's perspective and concerns about Pride as an appropriate group in a public high school. As the following statement [my emphasis added] illustrates, the concern is not merely about the support versus political activities of Pride, but also about the issue of sexual identity in general.

> I am writing to request your assistance in making sure that the "Pride" support group, for which you act as staff facilitator, *recognize its role* as a *support* group within the high school. This role is to provide information and assistance to students who wish to participate *voluntarily*. This support group *functions as a supplement* to what the district can offer through various programs, including guidance, student assistance, and *psychological counseling*.
>
> —3/29/95

This statement is loaded with messages about the superintendent and school board's stance on Pride and on sexual identity. The issue is thoroughly framed within the functional problems it poses for the institution and in terms of policies and procedures. However, within these few sentences, there is evidence of the effect that the social stereotypes of homosexuality had on their perspective. The statements reflect stereotypical understandings of LGBT individuals as recruiters that might potentially corrupt students. By limiting the group to a support function, it contains its influence to just those students who "sign up" for it. The suggestion that these LGBT students could find assistance through "psychological counseling" signals that he believes homosexuality to be a psychological problem to be dealt with privately behind closed doors. The superintendent went on to suggest other possible directions for the group.

> I believe this support group could *function* in other locations and the district's own staff provide the necessary support for its students to *function effectively* in their educational programs. If "Pride" finds its role as a support group in the school setting constraining, the district would assist the group in finding an outside location where it could determine its level of activity *without school connection*. I continue to be hopeful that "Pride," the district and the community can recognize its determined role and continue to work together to improve students' school lives. As staff facilitators, *your role* is to work to this end.
>
> —3/29/95

This statement does many things. First, it attempts to distance the school from the group, therefore separating the district from connection with any of the controversy the group sparks in the community. Second, it claims that the district has met all of its responsibilities to all students through established institutional programs. Finally, the superintendent's statement puts the onus on the faculty advisors and student members of Pride for the problems it is having "functioning" in the school setting— they failed to adhere to the rules and regulations.

These memos stating concern and uncertainty about the appropriateness of Pride and its place at Westville High School continued to be sent for five years after the group began. On January 24, 1996, after receiving another letter from a parent who continually objects to Pride, the superintendent sent a memo to Ms. Patrick. The memo ended by saying, "I am also considering the possibility of any interested Board members being able to meet with you and gain more information about the members of the 'Pride' group and your perspective on its *need* to exist in a *public* high school." Normative heterosexuality is an unstated and underlining rule in all of these regulations. Heterosexuality is continually assumed and reinstated as the norm and as the solely acceptable form of expression; and LGBT students are defined as outside of, or correctly separated from, the general school setting. The restrictions placed on Pride serve to provide insurance that the collective conscience of heteronormativity will be enforced and protected.

GREEN VALLEY HIGH SCHOOL:
"TRANSCENDING THE LABEL" AND "UNITY"

Green Valley High School is a public school with approximately 1,600 students in grades 9–12. It draws students from suburbs, small towns, and rural communities. These communities differ in average income level, but the majority of the school district is middle class. The district is also largely white. Green Valley, like Westville, is a quiet town and rather spread out geographically. The community, as well as the faculty and staff of the high school, were described to me as much more "liberal" than Westville.

The propulsion of Green Valley High School into the complexities and controversies of LGBT issues in public school began, as it did at Westville, with a request by students for inclusion and support. There were, however, some significant, if seemingly minor, distinctions in how the process was initiated. In this case, students approached the school social worker, Ms. Sullivan, and a guidance counselor, Mrs. Foster, for assistance.

> [Mary] came to the social worker. The social worker is a friend of mine and we had already talked about wishing we could get some sort of support group like that going here, and not really knowing how to do that, because people would then have to be out in order to be in it. And did people really want to be out in order to be in it? And how do we set it up? All of that. But, Mary got together with some of her friends and said this is really what we want to do, let's do it. So they did. And then we did.
>
> **—Mrs. Foster**

What became significant about these initiating steps is that the students asked for a support group, and not a school organization or club, as was the case at Westville. The students first wanted a safe and supportive place within their school to gather and discuss the isolation, fear, and harassment they were experiencing. The motivation originated as a desire to assist one another in coping with these experiences, not to educate or change the general school culture. This approach to starting the group, along with some other important factors, seemed to affect the reaction of administrators, the school board, and the community.

The actions, attitude, sexual orientation, and the institutional positions or roles of Ms. Sullivan and Mrs. Foster were important aspects of the establishment of the support group at Green Valley High School. As mentioned in the above statement, both women had perceived the need for a LGBT student support group long before it formally began. For Mrs. Foster, the understanding that such a support group was needed goes back to her childhood. She herself is heterosexual and married; however, she has an older sister who is a lesbian. "I was very young at the time she was out, and I think that I have always just known there was a need for it." This sister also ran a group for LGBT kids in a major city, so Mrs. Foster was very well informed on the problems, concerns, needs, and experiences of this population of teenagers. About a year prior to the inception of the group at Green Valley, a "counselee" of Mrs. Foster's told her of a friend who had committed suicide because of a long struggle with coming to terms with his homosexuality. This story moved and upset Mrs. Foster. She felt motivated to do what she could to make sure that none of the kids she worked with would suffer a similar fate.

Ms. Sullivan also had a background of experience with LGBT issues. While in graduate school getting her degree in social work, these issues were incorporated into every aspect of the curriculum. She also told me that many of the students in her social work program were gay and that, through conversations and friendships with them, she overcame some of her own personal, socially learned uneasiness with, and misconceptions of gay and lesbian individuals. This graduate school experience and knowledge did not, however, make starting an LGBT student support group a top priority for her. "It's funny, because it wasn't something that was like a driving thing that I've had in my head since I was in social work that I gotta do this." The conviction that such a group needed to be started at Green Valley came to Ms. Sullivan about four years prior to its actual establishment. She told me, "I had met a student, and he was venting about being a gay teenager and how frustrating that is, and dealing with his parents and so on. So I said to him, 'I am quite certain that there are other kids in this school who are gay. Let's do a group.'... And he freaked out." This student's response to her suggestion was one of fear that such a group would only stir up more harassment and draw negative attention to gay students. The fear that she saw in this student greatly affected Ms. Sullivan. "I think the reason why I suddenly felt that this was so important, was when I saw the panic in his eyes when I suggested it. What hit me as a person was that no one should have to live this way—in fear of getting together for support. So, that's when I first realized something's got to be done."

Despite believing that it was important for her, as a social worker and a human being, to do something to improve the experience of this group of students, Ms. Sullivan felt powerless to translate this belief into anything concrete. She did not know how to assist these students if such organized support frightened them, and she knew that the administration would not allow her to offer formalized support on the issue of sexual identity on her own. After Ms. Sullivan was frustrated by this issue for four years, the same student came back to her and said, "I'm ready, and I've talked to a few other kids and we want a group." This was an exhilarating moment for Ms. Sullivan. She had tried to give individual support to the few students brave enough, or desperate enough, to come to her on their own and ask, but felt strongly that there were many other students who needed someone to talk to. "So, it worked out nicely for us when this boy came to me with some other friends, and so we just did it." One of the students requesting the group was Mary. She had been "out" to herself, her parents, and a few friends for a while and felt relatively comfortable being on the front lines for the group. She told me, "A lot of students were being homophobicly attacked every day at school and they were too scared. Ms. Sullivan wanted to help, she was so scared for these kids, and that she might make it worse. So, she couldn't do it. And I didn't have any homophobic attacks so I said okay let's start it."

As did the teachers at Westville, Ms. Sullivan thought it was crucially important that students came to her with the idea for the group. Mrs. Foster asserted that "the big issue was that there were kids who were willing to come out. That's what you need first, the kids who are willing to be a part of it. And then you need somebody to be a facilitator." As educators, social workers, and guidance counselors within a public school, they felt a strong obligation to assist and advocate for all of their students. As Ms. Sullivan said, "I know that with difficult issues sometimes it's best not to ask too much. So, I just did it—started the group. I didn't ask permission. I am hired to be an advocate for kids, and kids were asking me for help and my job is to help them. So, I thought it's a very clear cut issue." Her conviction that this was a clear-cut issue of helping students proved to be very influential in winning support for the group within the administration, school board, and community. This perspective allowed her to remain steady in her position as an advocate and not be distracted by the efforts to complicate the issue made by opponents of the group.

The group began and ran very successfully for many months without the administration's knowledge and without any controversy. A few months later, Ms. Sullivan had a regular meeting with her supervisor, in which she mentioned the support group while updating him on the functioning of her office. She reported that he got "very concerned and very nervous" and told her, "I don't think that we should be doing this." She asked him why and he expressed concern over potential negative parental reaction and questioned the appropriateness of dealing with issues of sexual identity at school. Her response was to say, "'What do you want me to tell the kids?" Arguing that anyone who works with adolescents knows that giving teenagers something and then suddenly taking it away it will cause a great deal of upset. "So, he realized that taking it away would have created his worst fear. When, in fact, these fears were not happening." This was temporarily the extent of the resistance.

While equally supportive of the group, Mrs. Foster was a bit more cautious about how it would be perceived and received by the administration and community. She took steps to make sure they were as well informed on the issue as possible, "I did get information. I went to Westville and talked to them about their group and how they got started, while we were working on getting ours started. I also contacted the place out in Los Angeles [Project 10] and got information from them, and I had contacted this guy from Manhattan College and got information from him." One of the lessons that Mrs. Foster learned from the experiences of Pride at Westville is that it was important to administrators and school boards to separate "politics" from support around the issue of sexual identity. This lesson soon proved invaluable.

By the end of the school year, Mary and some of the other group members decided that they wanted to start a student political action group at Green Valley. The group would serve as an alliance of LGBT and "straight" students to combat all forms of inequality and discrimination, including that experienced by LGBT students. Students like Mary thought that, within the support group setting, they did not have the opportunity to do any more than discuss and comfort one another about the exclusion, fear, and harassment they faced at school. This was useful and important to the students who attended these meetings, but it did nothing to affect the forces causing the problems or to reach those students who were, for whatever reason, unable to attend these sessions. They wanted to work toward educating students, faculty, and administrators so that their school would be a more inclusive and accepting place for everyone.

Ms. Sullivan and Mrs. Foster understood the students' desire to become active and do more to work toward school change; however, they felt that it was outside of their roles as social worker and guidance counselor to be actively involved in such a group. They were also concerned that a political action group would draw more attention and controversy, which might put their efforts to offer a support group at risk. Mrs. Foster described the thought process of this decision, "We made it very clear from the beginning, the social worker and I, that we wanted to keep Unity and the support group separate. We didn't want to get into the political action stuff because that was going to be what all the controversy would be over. And we didn't want the students to lose the support group because of the controversy over the political stuff." They did, however, believe that the students had the right to organize such a group, and worked to assist them in finding the most effective approach to getting it started.

> That led us to the agreement that we would splinter off. We would have the support group and then we would have Unity, which could be more political—an after-school club. And that I, as a social worker, would stay away from that. I would be supportive of it, but I wouldn't be the driving force in that—we would find somebody else and then I would provide the support group. And that worked out beautifully …. And we strategized a bit. We involved a teacher with a very solid reputation in our district, who people think very highly of, and who also has a strong belief that all kids have the right to be accommodated.

This strategic planning was, in essence, to present these LGBT groups in a way that was as minimally threatening to the normative heterosexuality of the school as possible. Understanding that issues involving sexual identity are often controversial, particularly in a school setting, these faculty members took steps to minimize the potential negative reaction to Unity.

Once the students asked that teacher, Ms. Lewis, to advise and help them run Unity, they were required by school policy to seek the permission and approval of the school administration. Mary said that, although they were apprehensive about how their proposal would be received by the administration, the process generally went very well.

> It was a lot harder than the support group. We had to go through a lot of paper work. And just like every group has to do, but with our group it was a lot more, and it was a lot of bullshit that we shouldn't have had to go through that we did. The assistant principal said that it was fine and he thought that it was a pretty good idea, but I think that underneath he was pretty homophobic, but he was pretty cool with it. And the principal, Mr. Wilson, said that he thought that it was a wonderful idea and that it really should go into effect, and he would be there to help us. So, he was really behind us. We were all pretty shocked, I mean, we were just like wow, we didn't expect it at all.

The approval for the group did not go past this level. To avoid provoking controversy that might result in their being forced to disband the group, Mr. Wilson advised the teacher and students not to seek official school board approval.

The newly formed Unity meetings were well attended by a motivated and energetic group of, at times, up to forty students—gay, lesbian, bisexual, and heterosexual. One of the first major activities was to organize a "faculty in-service." For this, they arranged for Karen Harbeck, a lawyer, educator, author, and expert on issues of LGBT students and teachers, to provide a workshop for the Green Valley High School faculty. After she gave her presentation, a group of students spoke to their teachers about some experiences they had at Green Valley. This proved to be a very important and informative session for much of the faculty. Mary recalls the event this way:

> We told each other's stories, which was something that all the teachers were shocked about. We had everyone write down a bad experience they had at school, and of course we had more experiences than most people. We read each other's so we could keep anonymity or whatever. And I had to read one where my friend was physically attacked in the boys' locker room. And the gym teachers were appalled and shocked, and they didn't know what to do. When they left they said this to us, they said, "You don't know how ashamed I feel, that I should have known that this went on," and I said, "No. This still goes on, maybe not this bad, but all three of you, since you're here, need to know that it's not over. This still goes on every single day." It made a lot of our teachers just like, "Wow!" You know? And then we got a lot of support.

This support from administration, faculty, and students made the establishment of Unity as an official school organization at Green Valley a relatively smooth and uncomplicated process compared with the case of Pride at Westville. There were, however, two significant controversies and debates sparked by the existence of Unity.

The Principal: the Pragmatic Supporter

Before I actually sat down to interview Mr. Wilson, the principal of Green Valley High School, I had heard overwhelmingly positive things about him from the students and faculty I had spoken with there. So, despite his continued failure to respond to my letters or return my phone calls requesting an interview, I remained hopeful that he would not be resistant to speaking with me about this issue. One summer morning, it was finally time for the interview. My first impression was that Mr. Wilson was a gruff, no-nonsense kind of man's-man, which put me off a bit at first. However, once the interview began, I found him to be very honest, straightforward, and clear about where he stood on all issues concerning his school. Throughout the interview, he repeated several times that he thought the issue of the LGBT groups at his school was not solely, or even primarily, about homosexuality or LGBT rights. Instead, he felt strongly that this was a part of the larger issue of teaching students respect for all human beings. He argued that public schools have a responsibility for preparing kids not just academically, but also to relate and be successful in the world in which they will encounter complex issues. He felt strongly that the more informed students were on a wide variety of social issues the more prepared they would be to deal with life beyond the school walls.

I asked Principal Wilson if he had any previous experience with issues of homosexuality in his career as an educator. He replied that he had not had any direct experience with the issue as a professional. On a personal level, he recalled that when he was a boy he watched people harass others about being gay. He did not recall that he ever participated in harassment, but admitted that he had never, regrettably, stopped the harassment he witnessed. Previous to this experience, he said he basically thought of homosexuality as an abnormal lifestyle, but didn't care as long as it was kept away from him.[6] He told me that his attitude about gay people and homosexuality changed somewhat after the faculty in-service.

> [Karen Harbeck] turned it into some statistics and facts that kind
> of—while there may be some of that out there by choice, who knows—it
> gave me a more realistic position from a physiological stand point. I got
> my Master's in physiology. And so, that kind of triggered more with me,
> that in fact it gave some reason as to why these things occur. So, I guess
> it took me out of the ambivalent. It didn't make me a supporter. Well, it
> made me a supporter of their right to be what they were. That's what it
> made me. It didn't make me for them or against them. It just made me a
> supporter that they were just a person like I was and they deserved the
> same type of thing. It made me look at them in a little different light,
> I guess, from the support standpoint as a normal person, where it might
> not perhaps before I might not have viewed them as a normal person.

So, it was probably Karen speaking from more of a biological standpoint
that gave me insight into it.

This experience gave Mr. Wilson a way of understanding sexual identity
that was different from the meanings he had learned throughout his life.
For him, this biological argument about the nature of homosexuality was
sufficient to combat his previous belief that LGBT people were abnormal
and deviant people who were not necessarily deserving of equal rights and
fair treatment. However, his language reveals that a good amount of personal discomfort with "them" still exists.

I asked him if the experiences the students spoke about at that meeting had surprised him at all. He responded that he was not surprised that
some teasing and harassment went on, because he had been in the school
environment as a student, teacher, and administrator for all of his life
and, therefore, wasn't completely naive to these things. However, he was
surprised to hear about some of the more severe abuses that were taking
place in a school under his charge. He was surprised and regretful that these
students felt they could not report these incidents to him or other members
of the faculty.[7] This was what he wanted to focus on changing. Mr. Wilson
expressed his belief that incidents of harassment were still going to occur,
although they might be able to do something to minimize them. What he
felt he could do, and had a responsibility to do, as an administrator, was to
create an environment where students feel that they can report incidents of
harassment and that they will be listened to and taken seriously.[8]

As discussed earlier, Principal Wilson was not "asked permission" and,
therefore, not involved in developing the support group Transcending the
Labels, so he could not speak to this process. I asked him to tell me how the
idea for the political action group Unity was presented to him. He recalls
that, "They wanted to stop this whole scenario of being targets of innuendo
and comments in the hall and so forth. And they wanted to go formal right
away." This idea struck Mr. Wilson, from an administrator's point of view,
as unrealistic in its goal. He reports that he did not think the group itself
was a bad idea, but rather one that needed to be thought out with more
careful deliberation. He explained, "[I] met with Ms. Lewis and several
of the students and suggested that I wasn't really sure that that was a good
idea. I would support them meeting as a group, but to go formal might
make themselves—jumping right from nothing to everything—might make

themselves very much a target, because unfortunately that's how it works." Because he was experienced in the bureaucratic and political workings of school administration and school boards, he felt that the combination of this issue involving LGBT students and asking for immediate and full approval of the board could incite some serious controversy. Mr. Wilson wished to avoid as much contention as possible. He felt that the LGBT students would find themselves under attack at the center of this dispute, and approval for the group would be denied.

He also felt he needed to know more about the group before deciding how to respond. "I really asked them what their purpose would be? Why they would want to organize? Why they would want to go formal?" When the students informed him that they wished to advertise their meetings and to organize some educational talks on the subject of LGBT students and their rights, he said, 'Well I don't have a problem with you advertising that you're going to have a meeting without formally going through the scenario.' And so, we did that for about a year or two." In that year, the students had weekly meetings attended by between twenty and forty students, and arranged for the previously discussed faculty workshop.

The following school year, a student, described to me as an individual who liked to cause trouble and get attention, brought the group Unity to the attention of the public and the school board. This student took a sign advertising a Unity meeting to the school board and protested the group's right to exist at a public school. He also informed local newspapers of the group and his objection to it. The school board was surprised to hear of the group because they had not given it official approval. This caused some debate among board members and the community and put the future of Unity into question. The student members of Unity, Ms. Lewis, and Principal Wilson took steps to secure the existence of the club at the high school.

> The next step was we made it an official club, not with a paid advisor. And we did that kind of in agreement because we had some board members who are very much in the religious right. We've had some problems over the years with our films, with our books. And so, knowing that we were going in for a rocky road, Ms. Lewis was certainly willing to advise without getting paid, therefore, that would take the sting from the board. The board couldn't really direct me not to have a club. They have to approve a paid staff, and so if we were going to have

an organization and a club, there was jeopardy if we were going to pay
it—that we might not be able to. And rather than fight that battle and
interrupt what we already had going on, it didn't make any sense [to
fight for a paid advisor].

Some of the students I spoke with interpreted Mr. Wilson's actions as not
being fully supportive of Unity and backing down to the school board. He,
however, clearly felt that the action he took was in the best interests of the
students. As an administrator, Principal Wilson felt that he was merely being
realistic about the bureaucratic workings and political climate of public
schools. He defined his actions as the most effective strategy, under these
conditions, for the students to have the opportunity to have their group.

Principal Wilson also attempted to please the board by minimizing the
potential for controversy. This strategy may have been effective in temper-
ing public outcries of dissatisfaction with the board, but it did not completely negate them. Many parents and community members wrote and phoned
to voice their indignation over the school's permitting Unity to exist. As the
principal, and an on-the-record supporter of the group, Mr. Wilson bore
the brunt of these criticisms:

I talked to a lot of parents. My phone rang for a month. Usually negative. But I went through the whole thing and explained ... I mean ...
Obviously, the reaction of the parents being fearful themselves and not
knowing what it's all about. They thought we were teaching kids how
to become gay and lesbian. And when you finally get through and say,
"That's not the case, we have students who are gay and lesbian, they're
walking the halls, they're getting beaten up, they're getting pot-shots
thrown at them." I said, "I don't want to run a school like that. That's
not acceptable. It's not tolerable, and they're just as human as anybody
else. Whether you approve of their lifestyle or not, I'm not discussing
with you. But, I want a safe environment and everybody needs to know
that. They need to know that they're not some kind of freak."

Implicit in all of Mr. Wilson's actions is the assumption that Unity would
cause serious conflict within the school bureaucracy and the local community. This assumption is unquestioned and taken as fact, based on his
knowledge of the common cultural stereotypes of gay and lesbian people.

Principal Wilson's strong stance on the need for this group at Green Valley High and its right to exist in a public school was very effective in calming the uneasiness of parents and community members. However, when the controversy twice spilled into formal debates in the board of education, it was students' ability to effectively articulate the negative impact that the school has on their experiences that succeeded in quieting the controversy.

The Board of Education: Political Battles

I did not have access to interviews with members of the Green Valley School Board, nor the good fortune of being given documents chronicling communication among the superintendent, school board, principal, and group advisors. Therefore, my account of the school board's perspective and actions are based on newspaper articles quoting board members and reports from the students, faculty, and principal. There were only two debates in the school board over Unity. This is a sharp contrast to the repeated discussions that took place in the Westville school district over Pride. An interesting difference in the debates over the groups in these two schools was that the superintendent played a large and significant role at Westville, but there was no mention of the superintendent of Green Valley Schools in any account of the debates over Unity. The Westville superintendent was very accommodating to the objections of community members and parents to Pride, which seemed to assist in fueling the power of these antagonisms and elongating the community debates. In Green Valley, the absence of a public stance on the issue by the superintendent may have had an influence on the relatively short-lived debate over Unity.

The first time Unity became a subject of debate in the district and with the board of education, as mentioned earlier, was when a Green Valley student who opposed the group brought it to public attention. Mary provided me with the following account of the events that followed.

> This student had come to a board meeting and opposed the group—saying that it was totally immoral, saying that we had no right to be there. I had great fun arguing with him, I loved having fights with him. He got up at this meeting and he spoke. We knew it was coming up as an issue at the board so twenty-five to thirty of us sat in on the meeting, so that

they would know we were there, and that whatever they said we would hear. At the next meeting, I addressed the board members, and said, "It's about time this school actually stood up and said, 'These are our students.' This is when it was getting a lot of media attention, which was something that the board of education didn't really like that much.

Not only was the issue getting media attention from the local press, but this was also occurring at a time of school board elections. This increased the tension surrounding the issue, and, as Mary told me, served to make it more divisive. "There was a board of education race that was coming up, and a lot of the incumbents supported us and a lot of the newcomers hated us. And that was what they wanted to be elected on—whether or not they supported a gay group at school. And that's what they used as their political power, was this gay group at school." Once it was made public, the concept of a gay group was immediately understood as a politically charged issue. An individual's opinion on this issue was taken as a symbol of his or her general political stance and moral character.

All of these factors combined to force Unity to fight the community and the board for recognition and approval as an official school student organization. Despite the heightened volatility of the political climate, the group was granted official organization status. As Mary said, "We had to get approval of the board of education, and they approved us because they pretty much knew that we had all of the rights and they had none. That we are a public school, and that in a public school if you have an organization that was started by students and supported by teachers, and they want a group, you have to have it. That if you discriminate against them it's illegal." The LGBT students who stood up in defense of Unity had contacted lawyers at the American Civil Liberties Union [ACLU] and had been informed of their legal rights as a student organization in a public school. This added to the students' confidence in fighting for their right to be included at school. The strength of their conviction and reasoned argument—based on the ideals of equality and on the substance of legislation that grants students the right to extracurricular clubs—won them a favorable board vote. It is important to note that these students made this contact with the ACLU seeking support before the case in Salt Lake City made these issue of how the Equal Access Law applied to GSAs public knowledge. Again, the ingenuity of student leadership proved to be the driving force of change.

Unity came to public attention again a year later when it arranged to have Karen Harbeck provide a schoolwide assembly on the experiences and rights of LGBT students at Green Valley High School. Although students were given the option of going to study hall if they decided not to attend the assembly, many parents were upset that the assembly was being held during school hours and that they were not notified in advance. Parents heard of the assembly a few days prior to the event because it was announced to the students and reached the local press.

A few parents attended the assembly and hundreds more attended a school board meeting called to address the public outcry that followed. The succeeding passage is Mr. Wilson's account of this meeting.

> "The very next board meeting was jammed packed, just jammed. Probably 300 or 350 people and TV cameras were there. People were coming up and giving their spiel about how wrong this was. And there were about twenty, unsolicited, believe me, kids and parents who came up totally in support of what we were doing. We even had some kids who came out that night, came up and identified themselves as being gay or lesbian and what life was like and how much this was needed and how wrong it was for these people to deny us the right to have the same freedom to walk the halls that everybody else has. Boy I tell you, talk about powerful. I was a beaming person that night, but I was also equally ticked-off at some of these people and board members. But what it did ... I'm sure that when we went into that meeting and it was so packed, the board's a political animal, and I think the board was probably ... I think the board was concerned. I don't think the board disagreed with what we did, I think that they just don't like to be political. So, you know, whenever the wind blows the board kind of soft toes it. By the time the kids got through ... there was not any way that any board member could speak against it. There was just no way. What they had done was put it in such a light that any other school district in the country that wasn't doing this was wrong.

An interesting note about this school board meeting was that the local television coverage of the event only aired clips of angry and upset parents who made statements of objection to "gay sex" being talked about in their community's school. The news coverage failed to show any students or parents speaking in favor of the assembly. In spite of the lopsided news coverage and the large number of upset parents, the LGBT students prevailed at effectively arguing for the need of such education in their school.

These case studies show that, even in the early 1990s before organized efforts by GLSEN and the ACLU, LGBT students were fighting to put permanent groups in place that would work toward transforming their schools into inclusive, accepting, and safe places for all students. The capability of LGBT students to initiate these changes in their schools was affected in many ways by the opinions about homosexuality held by various participants in the formal bureaucratic power structure of the school institutions. Students were able to find support and assistance from a few teachers and faculty members who believed in their responsibility to assist the healthy growth and development of all their students strongly enough to overcome fear of the professional penalty they might pay. The principals of Westville and Green Valley high schools were caught between their roles as administrators of these heteronormative institutions and their roles as educators. In both cases, their belief in democracy and equality in education, along with the responsibility they feel to all students, outweighed the administrative pressure to maintain order and the status quo. The superintendents and the school boards most strongly represented the institutional resistance to change. The perspective and actions of these administrators illustrate the perceived threat that these LGBT student organizations posed to the school culture and structure. In their resistance to these groups, the superintendent and school boards exposed the extent of the structured and ingrained norm of heterosexuality in their public schools. In reality, much of the real conflict, controversy, and resistance to Pride and Unity did not come from within the school walls, but rather from the pressure placed on school administrators by groups of parents and community members.

In the face of all of this anxiousness, political positioning, and moral panic, the students in these two schools were able to make remarkable gains. The force that was most powerful in breaking down these various forms of resistance was the voices of LGBT students. In each of these early cases, the idea for the clubs came from the minds of students themselves as a constructive reaction to an abusive school environment. These students were brave enough to take their idea public by requesting support from their schools. In the debates among adult "officials" that resulted, it was the movingly articulated stories of their experiences and the reasoned pleas for change that were most persuasive. Through the late 1990s, cases such as these in which students struggled largely on their own to educate schools and communities about the needs of LGBT students were the norm. As the 1990s moved on, increasing numbers of students heard about GSAs in the news, on the Internet, and from students in other schools before they had the opportunity to arrive at the idea themselves. Once the prospect of such a group was made visible for them there was organized information and support already available for them. No longer do students have to discover for themselves the strategies that are most persuasive to winning the support of teachers, administrators, and community members. They had the experiences of past students and the resources of national organizations to draw upon. This has had some interesting and complex influences on local struggles to establish GSAs. The next chapter examines some of the efforts by social organizations to facilitate the networking of people involved with, and information about GSAs. The work of these organizations, their strategies, and discourse directly evolved out of the grassroots work of students and teachers at schools like Westville and Green Valley.

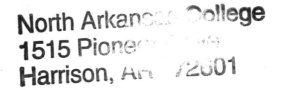

FOUR

A LITTLE HELP
FROM OUR FRIENDS
State and National Organizations
Step in to Help Out and Raise the Stakes

The battles that LGBTS [lesbian, gay, bisexual, transgender, and straight ally] students were fighting in local schools, sprinkled in sparse but accumulating numbers across the country, were having an impact on their schools and communities. Much of their success or failure, however, depended on chance. Chance that they could find supportive school faculty. Chance that their school administration would be supportive, or persuaded to be supportive, despite their personal homophobia or political fears. Chance that parents and community members would be supportive or neutral and not pressure school boards to block their efforts. Chance that school boards would not, out of fear for their elected position, try to stop or silence their efforts to avoid controversy. Every local victory by LGBTS students had the potential to increase the chances of success for the next group of students in the next school. However, that potential could be realized only to the extent that the kids, administrators, school boards, and parents in the next school knew what was being done in other schools.

In the early to mid 1990s, the sharing of stories and information had begun on a small scale, with youth from different schools meeting at gay and lesbian community centers, or other social gatherings, and sharing their experiences, or through the occasional media coverage of LGBTS student activism occurring somewhere around the country. This was true in the cases of Westville and Green Valley high schools, documented in the previous chapter. The lessons learned from one school's struggles helped to minimize the difficulties involved in starting a GSA at the next school. In 1993, the Massachusetts Safe Schools Program received a good deal of coverage, especially in the northeast, and in 1997, GSAs received national exposure though media coverage of the lawsuit in Salt Lake City. The unconscious understanding that "knowledge is power" fueled the motivation for LGBTS youth to form alliances among themselves, to educate each other about what strategies and tactics seemed to work, and what roadblocks to watch out for as they struggled with their schools. This political awareness propelled organizations like Project 10, GLSEN, the GSA Network, the Safe Schools Coalition, and others to form. The main goal of all of these organizations is to produce, gather and disseminate information, or to help formulate and coordinate strategies among LGBTS students and GSAs. Previously existing organizations, like the ACLU and Lambda Legal Defense, were also motivated to use their resources to increase the chances that the efforts of LGBTS students would succeed in making changes in their schools and beyond.

In this chapter, I explore the relationships among these various organizations and LGBTS youth activism and the GSA movement. Through this exploration I document what these various groups do to provide organization, support, information, and resources to students. All of this hard work has helped turn local grassroots efforts and the students' visions into a broader movement for social change. Throughout the chapter I present an analysis of each organization and of the GSA movement more generally, from the perspective and in the words of leading activists. It is important to let these activists speak for themselves and provide their own analysis because they think about, work on, and experience the GSA movement daily, and have done so for many years. I provide my analysis from both an outsider's and a sociologist's perspective as a means of synthesizing and comparing these various accounts with each other and with broader dynamics of social change.

PROJECT 10: PIONEERS ON A NEW EDUCATIONAL FRONTIER

As I described in Chapter One, Project 10 is the brainchild of Virginia Uribe, former teacher and counselor at a high school in Los Angeles. The foundation of Project 10 in 1984 predates the first official Gay–Straight Alliance High School club by about five years. However, the work done by Uribe and Project 10 provides important, much needed services for LGBT youth and sets essential groundwork for the GSA movement. A closer examination of the history, current work, and strategies of Project 10 offers insight about how much progress has been made in getting educational institutions to respond to the problems and needs of LGBT students, and how such progress was accomplished. It also reveals the amount of work that is still left to be done.

When I asked Virginia Uribe the question: "To what do you attribute the seemingly rapid spread of the GSA movement?" she responded:

> Actually, on a scale of 1–100, I would say we are at about a 3, to tell you
> the truth—in twenty years. If this was anything else, there would be
> a whole staff of people doing the program and it would be all over the
> United States, everywhere. But this is still an area that is under-served,
> marginalized. People don't want to talk about it, and it is an invisible
> population so they don't understand the issues gay kids have.[1]

This answer initially surprised me, because other organizational leaders, faculty, and students I spoke with, seemed to agree that they are all part of a rapidly growing movement. The difference, I soon understood, was that Virginia Uribe had been involved in advocating for the rights and needs of LGBT students for the longest period of time—over two full decades. Because her awareness of, and work on, the problems faced by LGBT students in public schools predates that of most others by as many as fifteen years, her perspective on the speed of progress is the broadest.

Uribe was hard at work battling resistant and ignorant boards of education, administrators, teachers, parents, and community members for over a decade before this "rapid increase" began. Her wider view on the history of where all this began puts the pace of the changes in a broader historical context. Uribe went on to say, "I mean I think we have made great strides. Sometimes we have not made as many strides as people think we have. There is 'Will and Grace' and all that, and we have made tremendous strides with the individual kid in school, but even though there is greater visibility, still people suffer from those same things they have always been suffering from if they are gay or lesbian."

Virginia Uribe's instruction to temper the assessment of the speed and scope of change and progress is a useful one. These things are always difficult to measure with any movement for social change, especially while it is still ongoing. This case is perhaps prone to overstated conclusions about success, because the idea of any change at all regarding LGBT issues in public school was virtually unthinkable not long ago. Even with these precautions against overstating how far change has come for LGBT students, Project 10 and others have made significant strides in changing how schools treat these students. Examining where Project 10 started and what it has developed into now, through an analysis of its structure, programs, strategies, publications, website, and the experiences and perspective of its founder and leader Virginia Uribe not only provides a picture of the historical arch of Project 10, but also reveals one important angle on understanding the complex progression of student rights and the GSA movement.

In addition to starting a support group for students in her own school, Uribe also read what little research there was on the developmental risks and needs of LGBT youth and prepared and distributed documents that advised counselors about how to work with these students. This initial action would seem to indicate that Uribe believed the problems of LGBT students were personal and inherent—borrowing from the logic of the stage models of homosexual identity development. It would not be surprising if Virginia Uribe did take this position, because that was overwhelmingly the conclusion of the limited research available on LGBT youth at the time. However, this was not Uribe's view. From the very beginning, she understood that, although the problems and struggles LGBT students faced did result in personal pain and suffering, they were caused, in part, by the climate and policies of public schools. The support groups began in LAUSD schools as a way to address the damage done to these youth, and Project 10 continues to develop other programs to ameliorate the conditions in public schools that cause harm to LGBT students.

It is significant that this historic first LGBT in-school student support group, and the district-wide program that followed from it, like nearly every major development in the GSA movement, was student initiated. As we discussed the beginnings of Project 10, Uribe told me that she learned of the incident of severe anti-gay harassment from a group of LGBT students who came to her concerned for their own safety:

Some students who kind of sensed, I don't think they knew I was a lesbian, but they kind of sensed that I would be sympathetic, came and told me about it. They were so upset that we decided to sit down and just talk about it a little bit at lunchtime. The more we talked about it, the more I realized that this harassment they were speaking of was not confined to this one student, but was really pervasive in the educational system. It just infuriated me so much, that I decided that we would start a little informal group and that's really how project 10 started. It was as a grassroots, informal lunchtime group in Fairfax High School in Los Angeles and it was a group of gay kids and it was generated by this incident, that was really the catalyst.[2]

This first Project 10 support group looked very little like a typical GSA today, in terms of its purpose and goals. The students who prompted the group were looking for support, empathy, and a safe place to talk truthfully about their lives and experiences. Although they were unhappy with the hostile school environment that made their experiences as LGBT students frightening and painful, they were not looking to be agents of social change. However, when they took the risk of divulging their sexual orientation to a teacher and then revealed to her the truth of what it was like to be a LGBT high school student, that is exactly what they became. The names of these students are not public. Their actions were limited to a specific time and place, and the motivations for their actions were largely based on self-interest; nonetheless, they were the catalyst for changes that extended well beyond their own lives.

In her own words, Uribe's assessment of the significance of this initial group of students is: "I think what Project 10 did was give voice to a group of marginalized students whose voices had never been heard in the educational system, and when they were heard they were treated with hostility. That's what I think the great contribution of Project 10 was, that we started to talk about something that had never been talked about before."[3] Fortunately, these voices found an ally in a teacher who was willing to advocate for their interests. Virginia Uribe had no plans to become a leader in a new social movement or a controversial public figure, but the trust her students put in her, and her sense of responsibility as an educator, resulted in exactly that.

Anyone who works on LGBT issues or with GSAs in public schools to-day has to be amazed at the success Project 10 was able to have in 1984. More than twenty years later, although there have been many successes, the issues are still, more often than not, fraught with conflict, controversy, fear, and resistance. Project 10 would eventually become controversial, but the reaction Uribe initially received from her school administration and board of education was supportive. After weeks of meeting with her group of students, listening to their stories of an isolating and often hostile school environment, and doing her own research, it became clear to Uribe that the problem went far beyond Fairfax High School. Here is her account of what followed:

> I went to talk to the principal of Fairfax High School and to my great
> surprise he was extremely supportive. He was supportive in a way that
> was very interesting. He was not gay himself, he did not even know
> anything about gay people, but he said, "You know, we are public educa-
> tors and we have a responsibility to serve the needs of all of our students
> and this is part of our population and we need to serve their needs too."
> I suggested that he make contact with the people at the board of educa-
> tion and see if we can expand this further than Fairfax High School ....
> Most people have never even heard of him in connection with Project
> 10, but had it not been for this principal we would have not been able to
> get started. His name was Dr. Warren Steinberg, and he really gave the
> green light in a totally educational way. He was simply not threatened by
> the issue.[3]

The need to offer support and services to LGBT students was pre-sented to the board of education within the context of the LAUSD's stated dedication to diversity. The expansive district serves nearly one million students from as many diverse backgrounds as you will find in any school district in the United States. According to Uribe, supporting diversity had been a kind of "mantra" of the board of education years before she pre-sented them with the idea of Project 10. Although this mantra of diversity previously omitted any consideration of LGBT students, Uribe was able to successfully use it to relatively easily win the board's support for develop-ing and implementing programs that assisted LGBT students and educated school personnel about their needs. Project 10's support groups and train-ing workshops began to slowly spread through the district, as faculty and staff in various schools heard about the programs and contacted Uribe for information about and assistance with integrating the programs into their local schools. The more the requests increased, the more formally organized Project 10 became. It spread organically, and without conflict or controversy, for over two years before their efforts were contested.

This honeymoon period ended when, in Uribe's words, "The right wing became aware of it and they started with their phone calls and everything and their attacks on Project 10." The voices of opposition gained volume and persuasive strength over some political officials. Eventually, Reverend Sheldon of the Traditional Values Coalition, a conservative Christian organization, spearheaded efforts to pressure state education officials to stop Project 10. Under this pressure, the State Assembly's education committee in Sacramento passed a resolution stating that all state funds to the LAUSD would be cut unless the district disbanded Project 10.[6] This action drew the attention of the media and a swell of public reaction. Uribe told me that all this came as a surprise, especially after almost three years of relative calm progress, "I didn't realize the power of the right wing at that time. This was twenty years ago and I was basically naïve about the political implications of all of this at that time." [7]

The media coverage was overwhelmingly positive in its assessment and support of Project 10. However, phone calls poured in to the Fairfax High School principal, berating him for allowing Project 10. According to Uribe, his commitment to the program never wavered, "He would always say the same thing, 'We are public educators, we serve the needs of all students.'"[8] The board of education's support for Project 10, won years earlier, held as they defended the program to state officials, eventually winning the ability to keep both the group and its state funding for the district. Although there is still periodic organized opposition to Project 10, and a rather consistent stream of relatively small numbers of objecting letters and phone calls, the programs continued to grow and expand at a slow but steady pace without any really serious threat.

Being thrust into this political struggle by the religious right made Virginia Uribe more politically savvy (or at least less naïve) and solidified her conviction about the need for programs like Project 10 to provide services for LGBT students and work to counter some of the pervasive homophobia perpetuated by those groups who sought to stop her efforts. As a result of her pioneering work with LGBT students—both through her work with Project 10 and her academic work (during this period she completed a doctorate degree in psychology)—Uribe began traveling the country at the request of groups of educators and LGBT groups who wanted to utilize her knowledge in their own local areas. During our interview, Uribe told me that it was during one of these trips in the late 1980s that she briefly met a man named Kevin Jennings. She recounts the event this way, "One of the places where I went to speak was at Harvard, at their gay and lesbian group, and there was a fellow in there named Kevin Jennings. And after that talk he said, 'this is a great thing that's happening in Los Angeles, but I want to take this nationwide and enroll the teachers.' And I believe that he started the organization called GLSEN." Jennings remembers that this meeting took place at Phillips Academy.

While news of Project 10 spread throughout the country, undoubtedly inspiring and informing other scattered efforts to services provided to this population, Project 10 continued its work in the LAUSD. Even though Project 10 had survived threats of dissolution and won the support of the district's board of education, it did not gain much in terms of a budget or financial support for the programs. This limited the Project's reach. However, after word spread about the work of Project 10, unsolicited donations from private individuals and corporations started finding their way to Uribe. To use these funds fully for the service of students, Uribe established a nonprofit organization and named it Friends of Project 10. The donations that come into this nonprofit organization allows Friends of Project 10 to do many things they simply would not be able to afford to do if left at the mercy of their small school district budget. These donations are used to fund everyday activities, such as producing and distributing resources and information on LGBT issues to school personnel, sponsoring diversity training workshops, and maintaining a telephone information line and the Project 10 website. In addition to these routine activities, the foundation is able to hold a conference, called "Models of Pride," for LGBT students from across the state every year; sponsor an annual LGBT prom; and support a college scholarship fund.[9] These privately funded activities allow Project 10 to reach out to more youth than would be possible on the school district budget alone.

The only real expense that the district funds is the pay for one Project 10 adviser for the entire district. This adviser is responsible for responding to all requests for LGBT training and information, and responding to any incident of LGBT-related harassment or conflict that occurs throughout the enormous district. The advisor must do this without a budget other than his or her salary.

I interviewed Project 10's current paid staff member, Gail Rolf, and asked her how she was able to manage the program with such limited resources. Her response revealed the need for networking skills,

> The way this program has been able to survive and do what it does, because I am just a one-person operation for a district that has close to 800,000 students—and you can imagine all the administration and layers of administration and teachers and support staff that goes with it, including the school police—[is] that I have formed a lot of community and district collaborations or coalitions. So I have brought lots of key people including the LA City and LA Human Relations Commission on board, the Antidefamation League, PFLAG, the gay and lesbian center here in LA, GLSEN, you know, anybody who is anybody, and I have brought them into the mix and so we have a very strong power base here in the city of Los Angeles and the district is well aware of it. I've helped them to become aware of it …. This position has been threatened a number of times because of budget cuts and because we are so small and when it comes time to cut budgets and programs sometimes they forget about Project 10, so I have also forged very healthy relationships with board members in that respect. So, anytime there is a threat to the program, we have board members and we have our community people and the district people saying "no no no no you can't cut Project 10."[10]

As with all of the organizations that provide services for LGBT students, survival, expansion, and success comes primarily through the tireless work of alliances of diverse individuals dedicated to the cause.

Participation in any or all of the training and counseling programs offered by Project 10 is strictly voluntary. Although the programs have the approval of the board of education it is not mandatory that individual schools implement them. Therefore, there is a continual need to educate local schools about the experiences of LGBT student and why they should be interested in addressing them. I asked Virginia Uribe what her twenty years of experience has taught her about the sources of resistance to Project 10. Her response was surprisingly basic:

I think one of the psychological factors is that they feel that if they are too interested in it that people will think they are gay. And I think another is just a lack of real understanding of the issue ... like at an elementary school if some kids are calling a kid a "fag" a lot of times teachers will be afraid to step into that. Why are they afraid? They are afraid that they will either be thought of as gay themselves or that they are promoting homosexuality. Those I think are the biggest psychological factors.[11]

After more than twenty years of work exposing the educational community to LGBT issues, it is intriguing that the main force of resistance she cites are the most primal homophobic ones.

At first glance, this might seem to indicate that nothing much has changed, despite all the efforts. However, I think it speaks to more complex dynamics of change. Project 10, GLSEN, Lambda Legal Defense Fund, the ACLU and other groups have been able to use the rationality of both existing and new laws and policies to get schools to provide equal accommodations to LGBT students, because, by reason and procedure of law, they understand that they must. This has resulted in institutional changes, but does not necessarily reflect cultural changes in stereotyped understandings of LGBT people or culturally perpetuated fear of the stigma of being homosexual. This is a common, if complex, pattern of social change. Civil rights and women's rights movements, for example, after long hard-fought struggles, made considerable strides getting legislation passed to provide groups access to, and equal treatment in, a variety of social institutions. However, volumes of social science research show us that a great deal of racist and sexist cultural attitudes and stereotyping, as well as institutional discrimination, still exist despite the legal victories. The relationship between cultural stereotyping and institutional practices is dialectic. It is impossible to fully eradicate institutional forms of discrimination when cultural stereotypes abound, and vice versa. It is also often the case that progress in one area outpaces change in the other. These dynamics are all present in the GSA movement, making a clear assessment of progress difficult.

In light of fact that some of the roadblocks to progress for LGBT students are basic struggles to break down stereotypes and fear, I asked Uribe for her assessment of what has been achieved in the past twenty years. "I think we opened the door. I think if Project 10 hadn't been there, who knows if GLSEN would have ever started, and if GLSEN hadn't been there, who knows if the GSAs would have started. So, I think that is our function. Historically, our contribution was to open the door, and I mean, when we opened the door, nobody said the word 'gay' and nobody said the word 'lesbian,' I'll tell you that." Project 10 did not universally or widely convince educational officials and the public that LGBT students' issues need to be addressed; however, it did set an example for LGBTS students, concerned teachers, and lesbian and gay rights activists, showing them that one could speak of gay and lesbian issues in school and not only survive but be taken seriously.

I asked what impact Uribe thought this had on LGBT students themselves, and she responded, "I think that there is a greater comfort level for a certain number of kids. I am hesitant because I don't think there is a comfort level in Kansas. There might be in Los Angeles on the west side or in the Valley or there might be in the east if you are near Boston or if you're near a big city. I do think the comfort level has been increased a little bit." I then asked if she felt that youth acceptance of their LGBT peers has increased over the years. "I think that has everything to do with religion, to be honest with you. If you're in a school like Fairfax High School, that's got kids that speak 50 different languages and you have all different kinds of ethnic groups and the gay kids are around, you know, then I think there is a lot of acceptance. But you go into a strictly religious environment and you're going to find a lot of intolerance." Uribe's perception of drastic local and regional differences in the level of tolerance for LGBT student concerns is supported by various sources of preliminary empirical evidence—such as concentrations and absence of the number of GSAs by state and by urban, suburban, or rural location.

One of the most significant features of the GSA movement is that it produced a group of skilled, dedicated, and experienced young LGBT-rights political activists. I asked Uribe for her assessment of the impact Project 10 has had on activism among LGBTS youth:

> I think that Project 10 groups are very affirming and empowering to
> kids …. How powerful is the voice of youth? I'm not sure. The gay and
> lesbian voice is not very powerful … As a group, when they talk about
> voting blocks, you notice nobody is mentioning the gay voting block …
> so I don't know how much power as a group we have. And then most of
> the gay power is in the adults, not in the youth … So, do I think that the

youth movement has much influence? It's got to have influence because just in the evolution of our culture you see more gay figures, you hear more discussion, so it has got to have some influence. Every time there is visibility it has got to be visible to someone else and so I do think that it has influence. So, what the overall influence would be, I don't know. We'll see. If, maybe in your lifetime, you'll see civil unions or gay marriage validated in the federal sense, then that will show how much influence we ultimately have had.

I asked Uribe what she thought the future of the GSA movement and Project 10 would be:

> I think what has to be done is to continue to do what we are doing and get more aggressive about it. In other words, I would like to see the influence of Project 10 spread to further and further school districts, and I would like to see more and more young people become active, and I would like to see the educational system be much more understanding on this issue. I think that the education system has failed miserably with regard to its gay and lesbian population and I believe they need to address it. And if they have to address it by being afraid of lawsuits, so be it, but they have to address it. I think that every kid has a right to a safe and equal education and that is what I will dedicate myself to for the rest of my life.

I then asked her what, other than lawsuits, she thought would instigate change.

> I just think that more and more of these kids will become active and they will go back and they will do their thing with their school districts and I think the evolution of it all is what will happen. I don't think there will be a single event that is going to make this happen; it's just going to be a process and it is going to be a process of education really. And through education will come the empowerment … The more you know about yourself and the more you understand the issue and its relationship to society the more powerful you become, and, the more powerful you become, the less likely you are to capitulate to whatever the forces are that are working against you.

Despite all the work that she and her organization have done, it is youth resistance, empowerment, and leadership that Uribe still sees as the key to social change.

THE SAFE SCHOOLS COALITION:
EMPHASIZING THE RESPONSIBILITY OF ADULT LEADERSHIP

The founders of the Safe Schools Coalition [SSC] differed from those of other organizations in that they believed adults, rather than youth, should be the focus and leaders of the movement for change. The SSC began in 1988 as a local organization in Seattle, Washington. In 1993, the group expanded to a statewide organization, and in 2001, marked the expanse of its reach by declaring itself an international organization. It has expanded in this way as a response to requests for information and assistance from groups from farther and farther afield. The group's beginnings are much like Massachusetts' Safe Schools Program, although the SSC emerged out of a city commission on the needs of gay and lesbian youth rather than a statewide one. As was discussed in more detail in Chapter One, the goal of the commission was to develop recommendations for making schools safer for gay and lesbian students. The group evolved from there to developing programs out of the recommendations, organizing and coordinating efforts in schools across the city, developing and running staff-training programs, to building a clearinghouse of information and contacts on their webpage. The focus of the organization from the beginning was to get the adults who work with students to take responsibility for serving and protecting them equally.

I interviewed Beth Reis, current co-chair and one of the founding members of SSC. In her view, the SSC's evolution as an organization focusing on policy and training educators distinguishes it in some ways from other groups that have been formed since.

> One of the ways in which safe schools coalition has differed from some
> of the other organizations in the country – too much of the change
> that there has been has been entirely a function of youth activism
> and not grownups taking the responsibility they are supposed to have
> for kids. I mean, it's great that youth are doing this work, but they
> shouldn't have to. Students should not have the responsibility for
> making schools safe. Students should not have the responsibility for

making the curriculum inclusive; that's just wrong. And adults in too
many places have advocated because it's easier to have students do the
work... It's wonderful that they are doing it and they are finding ways
to do it, I don't mean to minimize that at all. It's just that I think, and
because other people are supporting their work in that is part of why
Safe Schools Coalition has been putting over the years so much more
of our energy into working with policy makers and teachers and nurses
and counselors and all the grown up groups, because other people are
supporting youth in that activism.[12]

This focus away from youth activism was based on a sense of responsibility, but also on efforts to find the most effective strategies for changing
schools. As Reis argued:

Most of the work of the coalition has been grownups trying to work
with other grownups to do what they should have been doing in
the first place so the youth wouldn't have to .... and my feeling is
that youth are very effective educators with other youth, but they are
less effective with adults ... So, it's wonderful to get youth trained as
speakers and at the same time if you want to do a lot of professional
training, you need professionals.

SSC's decision to focus its resources and energies on adult educational
training is not just based on the belief that professionals are more adept, but
also that this type of training can have a broader impact on changing schools
than youth activism. Although the SSC supports GSA work by LGBTS
students, they do not actively work with youth to help start them. Reis explained this decision based on the organizational leaders' assessment of the
impact of GSAs on improving the educational conditions and outcomes of
LGBT students. "Such a small percentage of LGBT kids are using these
groups when they exist. I think the combination of a school having inclusive
policies in place and well disseminated so that everyone knows what they are;
along with gay straight alliance and ideally both and LGBTQ youth support
group; along with the inclusive curriculum K–12, along with universal staff
training both in harassment prevention, but also in LGBT cultural com-
petence is necessary. You know, I think research has shown that when you
have got all of those pieces in place, you absolutely have a much safer school

and kids are much more likely to succeed academically."[13] Although there is, unfortunately, not a large body of research to decisively prove Reis's assertion, the logical rationality of it cannot be denied. Research of the type that Reis speaks is not possible because nowhere in the country is there a state, or a district, or a school that employs all of these tactics together. The potential impact of such a coalescence of factors remains a goal rather than a reality.

I asked Reis how effective she thinks the SSC has been at meeting these very wide ranging goals:

> I think we have helped people become much more aware of the higher risk and greater likelihood of self harm and risk-taking behaviors of LGBT youth. And we have wanted them to move beyond that into resilience. I think that's still a big struggle, and into moving with schools beyond just trying to make themselves safe—although they are not so great at that yet, they are working on that at least. But trying to get them to think beyond that to trying to meet the needs of LGBT youth beyond safety and trying to educate all youth about LGBT people in culture, to help schools to be more LGBT culturally competent, and I think that is sort of what we are beginning to work on now, and schools are just in their infancy around that. It is much easier to get schools in terms of safety than it is in terms of actually doing anything to provide LGBT role models or anything else like that.

The focus on safety over larger cultural changes has been a trend in the strategies of the organizations that compose the GSA movement. This strategy appears to have developed both in response to the pressing need to protect LGBT students and out of a desire to find the most pragmatic inroad to creating change in America's schools.

THE GAY LESBIAN AND STRAIGHT EDUCATION NETWORK: NATIONAL ORGANIZATION AND LEADERSHIP

Ask anyone involved in efforts to address LGBT issues in schools where to go for information and resources and they will immediately respond, "GLSEN." The Gay Lesbian and Straight Education Network, is the main "go-to" organization for anyone seeking information on LGBT issues in education. The organization's national leadership position is a long way from its humble beginnings as a network of gay and lesbian independent schoolteachers in Massachusetts. Social and political circumstances, combined with the vision and ambition of dedicated leadership, thrust GLSEN onto the national educational landscape. GLSEN's founder, Kevin Jennings, began his journey with the GSA movement as a young history teacher at the elite boarding school Concord Academy. In 1988, he and one of his students, the heterosexual daughter of lesbian parents, began what is believed to have been the first official gay–straight alliance student club in the country.[14] Jennings also began an informal coalition of gay and lesbian private school teachers (and named it the gay and lesbian independent school teachers network—GLISTN) to share experiences and information and provide support to one another. When the Massachusetts Governor's Commission on Gay and Lesbian Youth was formed in 1992 with the task of assessing the school climate for LGBT students and developing programs to improve it, Jennings volunteered his resources, experiences and energy to the cause. His participation in the political, legislative, educational, research, and public relations processes involved with establishing the Safe Schools Program in Massachusetts' public schools taught Jennings many important lessons about what it takes to bring about change around LGBT issues in schools. These lessons provided him with a valuable set of skills and resources of knowledge and also a clear example that change is possible. Inspired and knowledgeable, Jennings sought to share the lessons with others across the country in the hope that they could bring about change in their own communities.

In Kevin Jennings' accounting, the decisions to make GLSEN a national activist organization, to make the work his full time job as the organization's executive director (and initially its only paid employee), and to move and set up physical headquarters with an office in New York City, were primarily made in response to a growing need. The exposure that Jennings, and the then-named GLISTN, got through its work on the Safe Schools Program prompted teachers from around the country to call and write looking for information and advice. Jennings told me that, after months of fielding these calls, "it became very apparent to us that nobody was doing this work other than us ... It really wasn't something that we had envisioned or planned on doing but there was a need and the need really came down to the fact that there's no one in the education world that focused on LGBT issues and there was nobody in the LGBT world that focused on education. So, we had two fronts that we were working on at that point."[15] This speaks to some essential and distinctive features of the GSA movement. Each of the main groups that took an interest in LGBT issues in schools was deficient in its ability to bring about change. Students had plenty of first-hand experience with, and knowledge of, the problems they faced in schools, but lacked institutional power and understanding of the politics and bureaucracy of education. Concerned and sympathetic educators had experience and skills in the workings of educational institutions, but lacked an understanding of the workings of homophobia and the politics of sexuality. Lesbian and gay activists and community members had acquired skills in sexual politics and confronting homophobia, but were not familiar with educational politics. GLSEN, which at the time was largely made up of lesbian and gay teachers, filled in many of the gaps that existed in the skills and knowledge of these three groups.

Fear was an element that joined all of these groups, but it also served as a formidable barrier to any of them successfully fighting for change on their own. Although there were many courageous individuals in all of these groups, many more were afraid of the all-too-real, potentially negative consequences of lending their voices to this cause. Students feared further harassment from their peers and potential rejection of their family and friends. Teachers feared losing their jobs and potential accusations about their sexual orientation and their motivation for being involved in this cause. Lesbian and gay rights activists and community members feared the stereotypes that would be called up if they aligned themselves with youth. As Kevin Jennings viewed it at the time, "A lot of folks didn't want to touch the issue, quite frankly. The LGBT community didn't necessarily want to touch it because they were afraid of the accusation of recruitment or promotion. Education groups didn't want to touch it because they didn't believe that the students were there—simple as that—so, the motivation [to make GLSEN a national organization] was partly because we saw the need and partly because people were asking us for assistance in their community and we said we couldn't do it anymore as volunteers."[16] The grouping together of gay and lesbian educators into a formal independent organization that was removed from any specific school district or state and was not an offspring or division of any lesbian and gay rights organization gave them an insider/outsider position from which to operate.

GLSEN began working as a national organization headquartered in New York City in 1995 and, for several years after this, much of its work involved establishing local chapters throughout the country, and training and assisting those chapters to work in their own local communities. Jennings explains the reason for this type of structure in this way, "Basically, what we were choosing to do was to replicate what we had done in Massachusetts. In Mass, we kind of pulled people together and helped them to organize in their schools, in the community, etc. And then we thought, 'well let's export this model to other communities. You know, we'll get people in Albany to get together. And the idea at the beginning was very much, it was very organic that people in Albany were the experts in Albany and would know best what needs to be done in Albany." This process involved Jennings, and later a few other paid staff members, traveling throughout the country to provide guidance and inspiration for fledgling local chapters.

GLSEN today still operates local chapters, with more than ninety nationwide. These chapters are all joined by the bylaws set by the national headquarters, and the leaders of most chapters attend an annual leadership training conference run by the national office. Chapters have access to and make use of the enormous information and strategic resources compiled by the national organization. This allows even the newest chapter to begin working to effect change in their local schools almost immediately. Being associated with a well organized and highly publicized national organization also gives even the smallest local chapters a considerable amount of legitimacy and influence with school officials. While each chapter works with the schools in their own local areas, the feeling and spirit of being involved in a larger movement for change is fostered through GLSEN's Internet site (through which local chapters can communicate and share information), various print publications, and annual conferences.

For the first four or five years of GLSEN's existence as a national organization, the focus was on establishing these local chapters, training local activists and leaders, and educating as many local teachers about the struggles, needs, and rights of LGBT students. The membership of these chapters was largely educators and former educators. Jennings told me that this restricted membership was, in part, an unintended consequence of the organization's name. "Because in the beginning years, there was the name 'teachers' in it, there was a perception that GLSTN was for teachers only. And I think that was a barrier to involving community members and students who were put off by the name."[17] Although there might be some truth to this, it was also true that the majority of GLSTN's activities and strategies during the first four or five years were geared toward educators. The organization moved to expand its membership and field of influence in 1997 by changing the acronym of its name (while retaining the pronunciation) from GLSTN to GLSEN. This officially marked the progressive shift in focus from its origins as a small networking group for gay and lesbian teachers to a national organization focused on the broader goals of educating schools and the public about LGBT issues as they relate to students and educational outcomes.

At this same time, GLSEN began to make fostering and supporting student leadership one of its main goals. Although the organization had always been an advocate of the impact GSAs could have on schools and provided support to students who requested it from them, for the first four years it did not have a formal mechanism in place to work directly with students. In 1998, GLSEN took its first steps toward networking student leaders by instituting the project "Student Pride USA," which sought to account for as many of the GSA student clubs in schools across the country as it could and to establish channels of communication among them and with GLSEN national and its local chapters. By the year 2000, the Student Pride project, through community outreach, the community connections of local chapter leaders, and the Internet, had registered over 700 GSA clubs.[18] In the year 2004, the number of GSAs registered was more than 2,000 nationwide.[19]

It is always more difficult to organize groups that are geographically scattered rather than concentrated in areas where they are immersed together in their shared oppression. For example, women vs. African Americans in the segregated South; and workers across industries vs. unionizing workers within one company or one industry. Feminist philosopher Simone deBeauvoir referred to this problem, in relationship to the women's rights movement, with the phrase "women dispersed among men."[20] She argued that one of the fundamental barriers to a successful large-scale women's rights movement was that women's interests were more likely to be aligned with the men in their lives (fathers, husbands, sons) than with other women. In addition, the likelihood that women would recognize that they shared similar experiences of oppression was minimized by the fact that they lived with men (the source of the oppression with a different experience of life) rather than with other women who shared their social position and experience. DeBeauvoir contrasted this situation of women with that of racial and ethnic minority groups, who, in general, lived segregated from the dominant group and, therefore, could clearly see and discuss the similarity in their experiences of oppression. This was a tool used to maintain inequality, but it also created a strong base and motivation for collective organized resistance.

Karl Marx theorized the difficulties of organizing a mass workers' rights movement in terms of the lack of a unified class consciousness. Workers in different industries might come to understand that some of the conditions of their workplace are unfair or unjust, but not see the connection to the experiences of workers in other industries. Without making this connection, according to Marx, workers cannot come to understand that the system of capitalism, not individual heads of industry, is the source of oppression for all workers in every occupation. Only getting workers to talk across industries and educating them on the workings of capitalism could bring them to a realization of their common social position. The terms "class consciousness," in Marx's writings, and "consciousness raising," in feminist writing, both speak to the importance of facilitating communication among scattered members of oppressed groups. Although kids are coming out younger and in larger numbers than at any other point in history, the reality still is that there are relatively few students who are out in any one specific local community. GLSEN's efforts to network and facilitate communication and the sharing of experiences among LGBTS students from across the country is an effective strategy to unify a scattered oppressed group, raise consciousness, and build the power of numbers. Many other groups have since followed this example.

GLSEN's efforts to network GSAs so that they could learn from and support one another, of course also gave GLSEN considerable access to, and influence on, student leadership. I asked Kevin Jennings about the relationship between GLSEN and individual high school GSAs. His response revealed that he had been asked this question, under more accusatory circumstances, many times before.

> "What's very important to understand is that gay–straight alliances have a legal right to exist only if they are formed and led by students. So, you know, if they are organized by an outside group they lose the legal protections granted to them under the Equal Access Act of 1984.

So, the deal is that we provide support, resources, assistance, training, but the students have to start it and run it. And that's not something we are uncomfortable with because we honor student leadership; we think it's great when young people are taking the lead. But there is also the legal reality that if it is organized or led by an outside group it has no legal protections in the school. So, therefore, we are very careful to make it very clear that we provide support, assistance, and resources to the students if the students start and run them."[21]

The fact that GSAs must be student initiated and run means that, regardless of the resources provided and influences of organizations like GLSEN, it continues to be students who take the lead in making local change. GLSEN's student organizing efforts try to make this less risky and challenging for students by providing them resources and guidelines for how to successfully get a GSA approved and to provide them with advice and/or legal assistance when and if they run into resistance. This is done, in large part, through the Internet. On GLSEN's website, dozens of documents provide students with guidelines for how to find a good faculty advisor for their group, how to run interesting meetings, how to deal with resistance from school administration, what their legal rights are, etc. These easily accessible resources, combined with the networking efforts of the student organizing department, leave very little of students' efforts to begin and lead a GSA in their school to chance. In Kevin Jennings' assessment, this support and guidance provided by GLSEN is needed because LGBTS students can rarely find it within their school faculty or administration.

I asked Jennings if GLSEN's efforts to provide students with all of these guidelines largely explained the sharp increase in the number of GSAs over the past several years. Did it speed up the process because now students do not have to reinvent the wheel every time?

Exactly. It's funny, because I now do a lecture at Harvard Business School every year and the main value of a national organization like GLSEN is what's called "leveraging learnings across the network," in business-school-speak, which is, in common-people-speak, "not reinventing the wheel." The individuals starting a gay–straight alliance in Albany doesn't anymore have to figure everything out on their own, they can go to the GLSEN website and get activities, get guides, they can connect with other students who are doing the same work, they can maybe come to a training. That's a really important support in a time when a lot of this, first of all, is still being invented from the ground up. This is not the French club, which has been around forever and everybody knows what to do. It doesn't receive the same level of support as the French club either.

In addition to the concerted efforts of GLSEN, Jennings believes that media coverage of events like the battle over the GSA in Salt Lake City and the killing of Matthew Shepard helped to inform and motivate students throughout the country to work to create change in their own communities. These news events, along with increasing media images of LGBT people, have also brought greater visibility and awareness of gay and lesbian issues to a more general audience, which helps to improve people's receptiveness to the issue.

Those who study social movements know that the transition from a grassroots movement to something more formally structured and organized usually yields both gains and losses to the movement's ability to effectively reach its goals—increasing efficiency and access to institutional powers and decreasing its creativity. With this in mind, I asked Jennings if he thought that the alliance of GLSEN with local LGBTS students ever had any negative consequences on the students' ability to create change in their schools:

> Well, I think that the extreme right sees it as 'See, see, see, it's a gay plot!' And I think that has been used against some GSAs in some places. People trying to portray other people like they are puppets, which I think is just so profoundly disrespectful and for that reason … it's not only not true, it pisses me off, because you know it's saying they can't think for themselves, which makes me very upset. But, I think that the extreme right has tried to denigrate the leadership of the students by brandishing the connection to GLSEN as if GLSEN is some kind of marionette.

As I will discuss in more detail in following chapters, this accusation of a gay plot or "the gay agenda" infiltrating schools by way of confused students being used as the pawns of the gay rights movement, is one that is regularly voiced by religious conservatives in opposition to GSAs. I asked Kevin Jennings if it was his experience that such accusations were a major roadblock to LGBTS students' early efforts to win support of school officials and community members, or if there were other larger points of resistance:

> I think that [in the beginning] people were in total denial that there were these students. The students themselves were terrified to actually come out and almost, virtually all the gay–straight alliances ... we use to joke that they were "straight–straight alliances."... I think the general denial of the existence of these students, the fear the students themselves lived in, the fact that they were so rare at that point gave the charge that they were adult plots being foisted on kids more credence. Now it's hard to pull that off. It's like there's eighteen hundred of them, "oh yeah, all of these kids are just dummies" you know. But, when there were ten gay–straight alliances it was like "oh it's those gay teachers behind them that are making it happen." So, I think that those were big barriers.

I asked Jennings if these same barriers existed now or if there were new ones. He responded:

> I think it continues to be a lack of support from school systems, you know, the fact that young people are still left on their own to make them happen. I think the intense opposition of the religious right to these groups, and I think, also, the fact that schools in general are besieged right now—they have less and less money, more and more competition for attention—I think that gay–straight alliances are just getting pushed to the side."

In response to this, I asked him how much of its resources GLSEN spent trying to educate school administrations about the needs and rights of LGBT students:

> You know we do the best we can. We've provided a guide for administrators about the legal rights of GSAs. We've got an article in the *National Association of Secondary School Principal's Magazine* about them. We try as best we can to educate them about what their responsibilities are, legally, and also why they should support them—not just because they might get sued. But it's hard, what is there, something like 23,000 high schools in America? And we are a very small organization, and finding a way to reach all those principals is a real challenge.

In addition to the enormous task of trying to educate all of these schools, the challenge is further complicated by the political nature of school administration. As Jennings instructed me:

> You've got to remember that 54% of all school board members in America are religious conservatives,[22] so they [school principals] report to people who are not into this. And they, how do you put it, the primal instinct of all administrators is to avoid controversy, controversy is *bad*. So, anything that starts potential controversy, because they are appointed officials, superintendents in particular, they are very nervous. I talked to a very supportive superintendent in Ohio recently and he gave me a funny metaphor. He said, "School superintendents are the highest paid immigrant workers in America." And what he meant was, basically, you're in a system for three or four years and you kind of get pushed out and you go to another system, and so there is a lot of pressure on these folks.

This observation is an interesting statement on American politics and institutional practices: elected officials and institutional leaders are pressured by the public to choose between upholding/enforcing the law and catering to the religious beliefs and personal prejudices of their constituency.

The bulk of Jennings' answers to my questions about the successes and progress of GLSEN and the GSA movement focused, understandably, on the work of GLSEN national rather than on the students themselves. So, eventually I asked Jennings how important he thought students' voices were to winning support for themselves. His response was concise but strong, "Critical. Students put a human face on the issue. It ceases to be about some, you know, network television agenda, it starts being some young person in your community and that is, that changes the whole terms of the debate." After this brief answer, I asked him if he thought that LGBT student activism and GSAs fit in with larger struggles for gay rights and what, if any, impact it had on these struggles. His response was very intriguing:

> Well, one of the things I'm very fascinated by is that this really seems to be a movement that is free and clear of the "gay movement." GLSEN itself arose out of teachers and students. This is a movement arising out of teachers and students—we are the entry point into organized politics

for most of our members. Most of them are not ...... either because they are too young or because they are teachers or whatever... they're not kind of "hardcore" political activists. They get into this because they are experiencing a need themselves in their community. So, I think that one thing that we are doing actually, is providing an entry point into these issues. For a lot of people who weren't involved before—young people, straight people, teachers. And I think that will pay off enormous benefits in the long run. I think that the young people running the GSAs today are going to be the congress people of tomorrow. And I think, secondly, as a historian, there's never been a successful social justice movement in America that didn't have a heavy involvement of young people, the GLBT movement is the first one to even try, and so, I think that the fact that we are helping all these young people into the movement, I think has got to have payoff benefits.

This response struck me as intriguing in three ways. First, I was taken aback that Jennings was giving GLSEN the credit for the entry of youth into politics when, in fact, students were involved in struggles for GSAs and building alliances with teachers, administrators, and among students many years before GLSEN stepped in, in an organized way, to help coordinate their efforts. I think it is more accurate to say that LGBTS students provided activists like Jennings entry into educational politics; at least initially—and now the opposite is also true. Second, I was surprised that he recognized the significance of youth activism to successful social movements. Finally, I was intellectually intrigued by his analysis that GLSEN and the GSA movement were not part of the gay rights movement. This statement struck me as both true and false. It is true that students clearly were acting independently of any formal organization and focused only on changing their own schools. It is also true that organizations like GLSEN, and Project 10, and the Hetrick Martin Institute before them, were indeed founded by individuals and not as an offshoot of any existing activist organization, gay rights or otherwise. However, the statement also rang false in the sense that the goals of GLSEN clearly mesh with, and serve to advance, some of the goals of the lesbian and gay rights movement even without this formal institutional connection.

I explored this further by asking Jennings what connections, if any, GLSEN now has to gay rights organizations:

We don't get any funds. It is important to recognize how GLSEN defines themselves, by the way, GLSEN defines themselves as an education organization that works on LGBT issues. We do not define ourselves as a gay rights organization. And what I mean by that is, not that we don't have strong relationships with folks in the gay rights movement, but what we're really about is making sure every young person gets an education. So, we're working very hard to strengthen our already existing ties with the NEA [National Education Organization], the AFT [American Federation of Teachers], folks like that. We're really calling the shots in education, so we do have strong ties ... we established a group several years ago called The Schools Network, which meets monthly by teleconference to—it's largely LGBT groups—to talk about work people are doing related to schools so that everybody knows what everybody else is doing. And I think that one of the things that has changed since GLSEN was started ten years ago is that virtually every LGBT organization—Lambda, PFLAG, HRC—is somehow involved in schools now, which is, like, a great credit to GLSEN. So, we definitely have relations with them, but we don't really think of ourselves as a gay rights organization. We think of ourselves as an education organization, and that may sound like a small distinction to say "instead of being a gay rights organization and focusing on education, we're an education organization that focuses on gay rights," but to us that's a big difference.

The difference is one of focus and legitimacy. All of GLSEN's resources and efforts are focused on making changes that will improve the educational experiences and outcomes for LGBT students, rather than divided among a variety of issues. This uniform focus and self-declared status as an educational organization helps to legitimize GLSEN with school officials and parents, particularly amidst charges from religious conservatives that there is a gay agenda to take over America's schools. By articulating its mission and goals clearly in terms of safety and educational outcomes, GLSEN makes its agenda a student rights agenda rather than a gay rights one, thus attempting to avoid the negative stereotypes of a "homosexual agenda."

I have often been asked, in conversations about my research, how the experience of LGBT students is any different from the experience of other students who are teased and harassed for a multitude of other reasons on a daily basis at school by their peers. Why focus all this attention and resources only on helping LGBT kids? I asked Kevin Jennings how he responds to comments like this, particularly in light of GLSEN's stated position as an educational, and not a gay rights organization, dedicated to "teaching respect for all":

> Well, the first thing that I say to anybody who says that to me is "you're absolutely right," and we think the schools need to take action to stop all forms of harassment, and GLSEN supports that kind of activity, we are totally in favor of it. So, we don't disagree. The issue with LGBT kids is then, you bring back what the statistics say, while there's a lot of name calling in schools, we're talking about a group of kids who are dispro-portionately singled out. You know, and you just go back to the statis-tics and the harm and stuff like that and say, "we think we need to deal with all forms of harassment and bullying, but our particular focus is on this group because they are so, they are systematically being harassed and driven out of schools and that's wrong."... That is the difference. I mean, yeah, there's lots of name calling, but when you are systematically, repeatedly, targeted because you belong to a particular group, that's a different ball game.

To be fair, while GLSEN's research does document that LGBT students endure a great deal of verbal and physical harassment on a con-tinual basis, it does not investigate any other type of harassment—on the basis of gender, race, weight, etc. So, Jennings' empirical claim about the relative nature of the harassment LGBT students face is not firmly grounded in actual comparative research. The focus of GLSEN's research on harassment certainly matches its focus on educating school officials and the public about the needs of LGBT students, but expanding the research to multiple forms of harassment might more powerfully accentu-ate the organization's assertion that educational institutions grossly fail at "teaching respect for all."

It is interesting to note that students seem to understand both the similarity and distinction between the harassment of LGBT students and the ostracism faced by all students who stray from the norms of popular and youth culture. A major theme that emerged through interviewing and surveying faculty advisors and former student leaders of GSAs, was that a large number of GSA members were non-LGBT-identified kids who were drawn to the group by a sense of empathy and in search of a place to fit in. I asked Jennings to comment on this phenomenon:

> I think they've become the kind of place where if you're young and you're different, you go. It's kind of a way of solidarity. I think the majority of young people involved in GSAs are straight-identified. And I think they are doing it, certainly because they are sympathetic to the cause, partly because they have gay friends or gay family or neighbors, partly because it's a way of kind of saying "screw you" to the establishment, all kinds of reasons.

I then asked Jennings if he saw this phenomenon of GSAs being heavily populated by straight students, as also signifying that LGBT students still do not feel safe enough in schools to risk being involved in these clubs. "Yeah, I do. I think that, for a lot of LGBT students, they're still afraid to walk through that door because they're afraid they're going to get targeted if they do. But, what I've also heard from these students, often after they graduate, was 'yeah there was no way I was going to go to that group, but, boy, it made a big difference to me to know it was there." This impact is nearly impossible to measure in any systematic way, this is also true of trying to accurately determine how many LGBT students are not participating in GSAs and why. However, it does seem to be a sign to activists like Jennings that, despite the increase in numbers of GSAs, more work needs to be done to make schools comfortable and safe places for LGBT students to learn and socialize.

One of the alliances that GLSEN formed to help make this possible was with the American Civil Liberties Union, which has been instrumental in many high-profile cases fighting for the rights of LGBT students and GSAs. I asked Jennings about the ties between GLSEN and the ACLU:

> They are great. The ACLU Lesbian and Gay Rights Project has been probably the most important litigators on students' rights, particularly around gay and straight alliances in the country. We did a joint pamphlet about three years ago on the rights of gay straight alliances, so they are a part of The Schools Network. I can't say enough about their work, they are great .... I think that we would like to think that everybody does the right thing because it's the right thing, but the reality is that some people do it because they don't want to get sued.

The ACLU, along with the Lambda Legal Defense Fund, and the National Center for Lesbian Rights, aligned themselves with each other and with LGBTS students to very effectively make the case that schools can and will be sued if they fail to protect LGBT students or if they fail to allow a GSA in their school.

THE ACLU:
HELPING STUDENTS UTILIZE THE POWER OF THE LAW

The Lesbian and Gay Rights Project of the American Civil Liberties Union[23] has made defending the legal rights of LGBT high school students one of its top priorities since the mid 1990s. The Project has used a basic two-pronged approach of first litigating impact lawsuits that establish strong legal precedence for the rights of LGBT students and then engaging in extensive educational campaigns to make students aware of their own rights and school officials aware of the legal ramifications of failing to support LGBT students. This strategy is nicely illustrated by this statement from a page on their website that summarizes their major legal victories, "If your school hesitates to do something about anti-LGBT harassment, you should let them know about the following successful—and expensive—student harassment lawsuits. This summary reinforces the importance of adopting and enforcing LGBT-inclusive safe schools policies and training faculty on how to prevent harassment."[24] The Lesbian and Gay Rights and AIDS Projects began as a specialized division of the ACLU in 1986, and issues of youth and schools became one of its priority areas in the late 1990s. Currently, youth and schools are one of the Project's four focus areas—along with, family (concentrating on parenting rights), relationships (focusing on civil unions and marriage rights), and discrimination (focusing on employment, housing, and criminal justice inequalities).

Making youth and schools a priority area has brought to the efforts and struggles of LGBTS students the expertise, strategies, and resources that have proven successful for the ACLU on so many civil rights issues for decades. According to their mission statement, "The Project's legal strategies are built on the idea that fighting for civil rights means not just persuading judges but ultimately changing the way people think. As we litigate for change, we implement targeted media, online and outreach campaigns to change public attitudes through education and to give people on the frontlines the tools they need to act."[25] Attorneys from the ACLU's Lesbian and Gay Rights Project have litigated dozens of cases on behalf of LGBT high school students since the mid 1990s, and in countless other instances the Project has stepped in and advocated for these students' rights through letters and phone calls to school officials. According to the ACLU's literature, the Project's program on schools has a broad, yet directed, focus, "Our "Every Student, Every School" program is a special initiative on LGBT youth and schools. Through this program we're working to make schools safe and bias-free for LGBT kids and teachers. For students, this includes the right to free expression, to establish gay/straight alliance clubs, to bring a same-sex date to the prom, and to be taught in an environment respectful of their sexual orientation or gender identity."[26] As I discussed in Chapter One, since the mid 1990s the ACLU and Lambda Legal have won major legal victories in all of these areas. As a result of these victories, which have set powerful legal precedents as to the First Amendment rights of LGBT students, the Equal Access rights of GSAs, and schools' legal responsibility to protect LGBT students from harassment, the program is now able to concentrate its resources largely on educating students about their rights.

The "Every Student, Every School" program's website is filled with information about these rights and very detailed instructions about how to start a GSA, get a safe schools policy passed in their district, and how to get safe school training for the faculty, staff, and students at their school. These instructions are all written in very accessible language, while at the same time framing everything in its legal context. For example, this statement about starting a GSA:

> While school administrators sometimes balk at allowing students to start GSAs, federal law guarantees that students have the right to do so. There are two types of clubs in public high schools: curricular clubs (those that relate directly to things that are taught in the school, like Math Club), and non-curricular clubs (those that don't relate directly to things that are taught in the school, such as Key Club). The federal Equal Access Act says that if a public high school allows students to form non-curricular clubs at all, then it must allow students to form any non-curricular club they want, and the school must treat all non-curricular clubs equally. If you're trying to start a GSA at your school and you

encounter resistance, or if your school places limitations on what the
GSA can do that it doesn't place on other clubs, keep reading for tips on
what to do and how to contact us for assistance.[27]

All of the information on the website is fashioned in a "do-it-yourself"
way, providing students all the tools and supplies they need to confidently
make changes in their schools. Every instruction ends in a similar manner
to the one above, by reassuring readers that the rights are on the students'
side so everything should go smoothly, but if it does not, the ACLU will be
there to support them.

Students are instructed not only about what to do and in what order,
but also about what to say to those who might oppose or question their
rights. These instructions are written by attorneys and staff members at
the ACLU who have had a considerable amount of practice defending the
rights of LGBT students against every argument possible from the opposition. Providing students with clear and rational responses to all of the major
charges generally used to try to dismantle their efforts can make a tremendous impact on the divisiveness and speed of change. In the years before
groups like the ACLU and GLSEN were widely distributing this information, students and teachers, like those in the case studies in Chapter Three,
were left to formulate responses to these accusations on their own. This
allowed for a degree of creativity and conversation, but it also often resulted
in prolonged debates over issues that, while provocative, completely distracted the issues away from LGBT student rights and the right of GSAs
under the equal access law. By providing standardized responses to these
accusations that have proven to be most effective, the ACLU, GLSEN,
Lambda, and others were able to stem many potential controversies before
they began. This has undoubtedly sped up the process of change. There
is no way to accurately measure the impact of these strategies; however, in
Chapter Seven, student leaders and faculty advisors for GSAs from across
the country speak to their usefulness in their own efforts.

The ACLU's history of representing the rights of all groups, even those
that others do not want to defend, made it a logical defender of LGBT high
school students. Years before working on equal access cases, like the Salt
Lake City GSA case, the Lesbian and Gay Rights Project at the ACLU
worked on several cases representing LGBT college students and student
groups. Many of these were free speech cases involving sodomy laws. Even

as recently as 1997 the ACLU defended a college LGBT group at a public university in Alabama that was disbanded by the university on the rationale that the state's sodomy laws precluded the students' first amendment rights—in other words, that the LGBT group was inciting people to commit sodomy, which was an illegal activity and, therefore, not protected by the first amendment. Lawyers from the ACLU's Lesbian and Gay rights project won this case by successfully arguing that there was no rationale by which to argue that the group was about sex or inciting people to engage in sodomy.[28] This ruling was an important precedent-setting one for high school GSAs. Since the court had already ruled on this matter, accusations that high school GSAs are "sex clubs" had no legal footing (even if these accusations continue to be made and stir up emotional reactions in parents and community members).

As mentioned earlier, LGBT high school students are now one of the four priority areas for the Lesbian and Gay Rights Project at the ACLU. During a phone interview, I asked staff attorney Ken Choe what went into the Project's decision to make youth and schools a priority:

> Well, the criteria we use in setting our priority was to look at vulnerable populations within the LGBT community. Those who probably need the most assistance, and youth certainly struck us as a population that did, where there really was a tremendous need ... where there was tremendous vulnerability, obviously. The experience that one has with the youth can shape one's experience with a gay, lesbian, bisexual, transgender person in all areas of one's life in going forward. It just seemed like something we really wanted to focus on.

LGBT youth are a perfect fit for the ACLU's focus on impact litigation. This focus is a strategy to devote its limited resources to fighting cases that have the potential to create new laws and protections for LGBT people, and that can also assist in the larger struggle for winning equal civil rights. In this way, youth cases establish new law, because they were a previously invisible population and they impact the larger struggle for civil rights by bringing in heterosexual allies who may not have been previously sympathetic to LGBT rights, but are sympathetic to youth and student rights.

The ACLU's focus on impact litigation also means that it does not defend the free speech rights of everyone who needs or requests their services, but rather just those cases that will have large legal impact on or the potential to impact public perception toward a group or an issue. This strategy is used to maximize the use of the organization's limited resources. These guiding principles, however, have been bent somewhat in the case of LGBT youth. According to Ken Choes:

> The one exception we made is in the schools area. We have a "making schools safe project" where we have set up a separate email account on our website, and we try to get the word out there in literature where people can email us or call us—students, parents, school personnel, anyone in the school community—if they have problems or questions. And we actually try to answer every single one of those questions, even if it is providing them with a referral, but we try to respond to every single one. So, we really have made this … it's sort of a very special priority area for us.

A substantial amount of effort and resources are put into informing students and school staff about the rights of LGBT students and the services that ACLU can provide. Mailings are sent to schools, with packets of information and flyers that can be posted to inform students of their rights, and links to the project's webpage are posted on a wide variety of Internet sites that are visited by LGBT youth. The special effort to get the word out is motivated by the priority of the issues to the project and the understanding that most teenagers would not automatically know that their rights had been violated, or, if they did recognize this, think to call the ACLU for assistance.

One of the tools that is provided for LGBT students to use in their struggle is what they call "demand letters." These are letters sent from an attorney at the ACLU alerting the school administration that it is violating the law by not protecting LGBT students from harassment or by blocking the formation of a GSA, and informing it that the ACLU will file a lawsuit against it unless the matter is resolved. According to Choe, these letters have proven to be very effective:

> Usually schools and school districts are good, once you send them a letter they actually get it most of the time. And so usually it does just take a letter to resolve these issues. … I think they are very litigation

averse. Also because usually there is someone in the school district who has a good head on his or her shoulders who not only gets the law but gets the policy as to why this is bad for the school community for there to be discrimination or censorship. These are obviously educators and they theoretically understand.[29]

The biggest reason for the success of these letters, however, is the strength of the law that backs them up. The lawsuits and settlements won by the ACLU and other groups provide a very strong foundation on which to make these demands. The law has become so clear, according to Choe, that the project has made form demand-letters available on their webpage to empower students to use them without ever having to contact the ACLU in person. He believes that services like these are the most important contributions the Lesbian and Gay Rights Project has made to the GSA movement:

> I think that providing resources to these students to be able to stand up for themselves is probably the most significant thing we have done. We have really tried to find ways of empowering students to stand up for themselves in their own communities, and then to be willing to back them up if they aren't successful. I think all these outreach efforts we have had and all the materials that we have prepared have had an enormous impact beyond probably what we could ever know. In some ways, the whole point was to put it out there and for students to take advantage of it on their own and we may never know about it.[30]

Educating LGBTS students about the laws that protect their rights empowers them to be confident and strong in efforts to start a GSA or get an antidiscrimination policy passed. Their confidence is bolstered by the knowledge that the law is on their side and that a powerful organization like the ACLU is there to back them up if they need it.

As effective as the ACLU has been over the years at defending the free speech rights of all sorts of groups, and as well known as it is, not everyone has a positive reaction to its name. Conservative groups like those from the Christian right that are often the source of opposition to GSAs are inclined to have an aversion to groups like the ACLU, which they see as bastions of liberalism. Given that this is the case, I asked ACLU attorney Ken Choe whether he thought that LGBTS students' alliance with the ACLU had ever hurt their cause more than it had helped:

> There are two reactions that we get. One is, as you say, it sort of gets people's backs up when an outside group comes in .... Because the ACLU has a unique ability to talk about the First Amendment, I think people recognize that, whether they agree or disagree, there is an institutional expertise there when talking about free expression issues. I think people take us seriously at least. I mean, they know that they have to take us seriously even if they disagree with us on the outcome. So, I think, actually, that ends up outweighing whatever natural sort of defense comes up when some outside, seemingly wacky, liberal group comes in. I think that at least these students have an institution that will take them seriously on their side.

I asked Choe how large an impact he thought the law and the ACLU's support of LGBTS students has had on the rise in the number of GSAs in recent years:

> I think it is obviously a confluence of factors. I certainly think that the social climate is different these days. There are more students who both have a need for these kinds of organizations, and who are willing to put in the effort and put themselves out there in attempting to form these organizations. But then I think, also, they are just encouraged by the fact that they should know that the law is on their side now.

Those associated with the ACLU Lesbian and Gay Rights Project feel very strongly that the law is on the side of LGBT students and that this has been proved time and again in the courts. Their main strategy now is to get the word out about the rights of LGBT students and to use their influence to help students use these rights. I asked attorney Choe if he thought there was any way that those who sought to stop a GSA from forming could win a case if it were to go to court:

> I think that what we are seeing now is people who are determined not to allow GSAs are getting more clever. I think that they get that they can't just say, "Well, you're a gay group so we are not going to let you form."

I think there was a time when they thought they could get away with that. I think they are getting more sophisticated. They understand that's probably not going to be a winning argument so they are actually looking for pretext. They are looking for, "Well, you forgot to file this form, you didn't get this signature, you didn't fulfill this technicality." … The discrimination is becoming a little more submerged, which is a little distracting."

The Project has already begun to address these new tactics from the opposition. Instructions on the Project's webpage on how to start a GSA include explicit warnings about being sure to follow every rule and procedure, and to file all the paperwork required. I asked attorney Choe if he saw this change in tactics by those who oppose GSAs as a sign of the success of students and the ACLU. "Yeah, exactly. And I think that is true in general. I think the more success you have in any movement, your opponents just get more clever and it becomes more difficult to deal with." He added that other major factors slowing down the pace of change and the effectiveness of the legal arguments are the cultural differences in different regions of the country and the power of local courts to make their own rulings. The largest areas of concentration for GSAs have been on the West Coast, in the New England States, and in the upper Midwest, and more heavily in suburban and urban areas of these regions.[31] One sign of the success of the movement is that students in southern and more rural areas are increasingly learning about GSAs and becoming empowered by this knowledge to try to start a group in their school. When this happens, it is often the case that the allegations against GSAs that have long since been discounted and overturned through litigation elsewhere, have to be fought all over again in these new locations. Because of these factors, the Lesbian and Gay Rights Project at the ACLU anticipates that they will continue to have to litigate on behalf of LGBTS students on these issues for many more years to come.

THE GAY–STRAIGHT ALLIANCE NETWORK: A FRESH NEW TAKE ON LGBT YOUTH ACTIVISM

Carolyn Laub was only twenty-four years old when she founded The Gay–Straight Alliance Network in 1998. Since that time she has used her creative energy, vision, dedication, and networking skills to assist students in expanding GSAs into approximately forty percent of California's public schools. Unlike Virginia Uribe from Project 10 or Kevin Jennings from GLSEN, who both circumstantially stumbled into their involvement in and then dedication to fighting for the rights of LGBT students, Carolyn Laub's entrance into this movement was much more deliberate. Much of this can be attributed to social and historical circumstances. Carolyn Laub was a high school freshman the year Jennings started his GSA in Concord, Massachusetts and a junior high school student while Uribe was establishing Project 10 in Los Angeles. In other words, her adolescent years were ones in which LGBT youth were acknowledged, and some groups were trying to provide services for them. After graduating from Stanford University with a BA in cultural anthropology, Laub began working with youth as the director of an AIDS prevention program in the San Francisco area and later started a community support group for LGBTQQ (lesbian, gay, bisexual, transgender, queer, and questioning) youth. By this time the GSA movement was already underway. During this time, Laub also participated in lobbying efforts to get state legislation passed that would protect LGBT youth from discrimination and harassment (California Student Safety Violence Prevention Act, otherwise known as AB537 finally enacted in the year 2000).

While doing this service-oriented work, Laub became "interested in working with young people in ways that were really about empowerment and community activism as opposed to social services. "I was interested in a different set of strategies for change and making change in people's lives,"[32] she said. Then, one day late in 1997 a girl from a local high school came to Laub's support group and told the story of how she started a GSA in her school in an act of solidarity with the students at East High in Salt Lake City. At the time, the case in Salt Lake City was making headlines across the country. The student, who was so motivated and committed to changing her school and making a statement, revealed to Laub that now that the GSA was established she did not know what to do with the group. It struck Laub that, "The student had all the right instincts as a student organizer, but she had no support. She was totally isolated and she didn't have any mechanism for connecting with other student organizers and student activists like herself." Laub recalls that, as she listened to this student tell her story and saw the mixture of excitement and frustration in the reaction from the other group members, a light bulb went off in her mind and she knew what she should do:

I should create an organization that supports student activists like this girl and helps network students with other young people so that they can learn how to create a gay–straight alliance club at their school. And then to channel the gay–straight alliance clubs toward student activism on campus. To really change—not just to create a safer environment within the club meetings, a safe haven for students to go to, because that's obviously an important function of the GSA clubs and that's been since the history of the clubs in the late 80s and early 90s that's really how they started. But in the mid 90s I became very interested in how to use GSA clubs as a vehicle for doing the kinds of things that this one girl had her instincts to do, which was to really change the school climate. And it seemed like GSAs were an incredible mechanism for student empowerment for teaching skills around activism and social justice work and changing school policies and school climate, and that's really still to this day, still the focus of our organization. It's about empowering young activists, and it's also about changing school climate and changing school policy.

This overt focus on helping to create young social activists is the first thing that makes The GSA Network different from its predecessors. Although other organizations eventually made this part of what they do, it was neither their initial nor primary focus. Again, this is, in part, a reflection of the success of these groups. They had created a safer and more secure environment, which now created the potential for greater activism. However, it is also partly the result of the standardizing efforts of GLSEN and the ACLU that Laub perceived such a large need to support and develop youth leadership in the GSA movement. Although these organizations made the work of LGBTS students simpler and less fraught with frustrations, they also unintentionally stifled some of the creativity and energy of youth activism, because many students who want to start a GSA now simply turn to the website of one of these organizations for a step-by-step how-to guide. Because they no longer need to figure it out on their own, the potential innovation of students is often no longer tapped by the movement.

GLSEN had existed as a national organization for two years before this "light bulb went off" in Laub's head, so I asked her what knowledge she had of GLSEN and Project 10 at this time. She reported that she did know about them and was excited about the work they were doing on youth and school issues, but she was also dissatisfied and disappointed, in some ways, with the direction of these organizations. The main sources of Laub's dissatisfaction were the lack of representation of people of color and analysis of issues of race and class; the complete exclusion of, or lack of real attention paid to, issues of gender and gender identity; and the lack of active youth leadership in these organizations. Laub wanted her organization to be diverse and inclusive, to really address the issue of gender (and the transgender in LGBT as more than just a politically correct letter add-on), and to focus on developing student leadership—starting with the organization itself.

Over the years, Laub has seen changes in other organizations as they have responded to pressures to be more inclusive. She said, "I definitely have seen real change and growth. For example, GLSEN didn't have gender identity and expression even in its mission statement six years ago and they do today. There is definitely more of a commitment from the organization to look at those issues."[33] I discussed with Laub the 2003 national GLSEN conference I attended in which youth of color protested GLSEN's lack of diversity and attention paid to racism. These protests created a fair amount of tension at the conference as people celebrated all of the good that GLSEN does and its successes, while also trying to acknowledge what it could do better. Laub was well aware of the student protests at these conferences and the tension. Her analysis was that it is much harder for an organization to change and try to add diversity later, so it is better to be as inclusive as possible from the start:

> Those changes [at GLSEN] have come because there's been outside
> pressures on them and then, internally, there have been advocates
> to better address race and class issues or gender identity issues.
> I haven't seen it come from the core within the organization from
> the outset because obviously that wasn't initially in their mission.
> So, I do see changes in terms of who is working there, what kind
> of materials they are putting out, all that kind of stuff, it seems like
> some of that has been in reaction that these youths protest every year.
> What we've tried to do at GSA Network is actually have, those issues
> central to how we've plotted out and envisioned our work and created
> our mission.

Laub's academic training and collegiate experience with social activism informed her decision to make inclusion important from the start. I asked her how effective she thinks this strategy has been and is she satisfied with the results?

> There has been a real intentional effort on our part and the part of our staff to focus on helping GSAs get established in schools that serve youth in a lot of different kinds of schools: in urban predominantly youth-of-color schools, in low-income schools, in schools where the climate is extremely conservative. Sometimes that crosses all kinds of race or class levels. And then also, we focused on some of the urban spaces. Right now, for example, this year we've been really trying to support GSAs getting established in south LA, which is mostly Latino and African American. We've worked to establish some GSAs in Oakland, serving mostly African American students. And that's been really intentionally. It's not been whoever just comes to us, we've actually been really seeking out partnerships with people in the local community to be able to enable those GSAs to get established. And then the other thing that we do is focus on developing the leadership capacity and the skills of students of color, so now … when we first started, just because of the population of California, about 40% of the youth we worked with were youth of color, and about 60% were white and now that's almost reversed."

From the start, the conscious effort Laub made to build a network across class, race, ethnicity, and gender as a main goal of the organization motivated her not only to build coalitions, but also to work to understand the social, cultural, and psychological barriers to youth of color becoming involved in the GSA movement. The Gay–Straight Alliance's efforts to reach out to youth of color and work to effectively get them involved in GSAs has played a large role in the success they have had in rapidly increasing the number of GSAs throughout the state of California.

This central focus on addressing race, ethnicity, class and gender identity directly is one thing that makes The Gay–Straight Alliance Network different from other organizations that service LGBT students. Another feature that makes it different is its focus on youth leadership. The GSA Network not only focuses on developing youth leadership through GSAs in high schools, but also makes youth leadership the core of the Network itself. In Laub's words:

> Our organization is a youth led organization, so we actually have something called the youth council. There are three youth councils in California that we run—one in the northern California region, one in the central California region and one in the southern California region—and there's usually anywhere from 15 to 20 youth at each youth council and they are the ones that actually do the trainings. They run the camp, they do the leadership trainings, they make decisions about programs, they provide input on organizational decision making that happens, they are sort of the leaders of the leaders. And then each year several of those youths from the various youth councils across the state serve on our statewide governing board. So, youth in decision making positions and leadership positions within the organization is one of the other ways in which we do our youth leadership work.[34]

Students are central to the leadership and decision making process of the GSA Network because Laub recognizes that ultimately the organization exists only because of these students, and every action taken by the organization directly impacts their experiences and future. The stake that students have in the outcome of school board's and administrator's decisions about GSAs and antiharassment policies also makes their voices and leadership powerfully effective. Laub asserts that it is important to recognize this:

> All the evidence is that when students go and they present to their faculty or they present to the administration or school board members and they tell their stories about why they want a club or if they have a club what they are gaining from that club, the sense of safety, that they are developing their leadership skills, developing their voice ... it's very persuasive.[35]

Given this emphasis on youth leadership I asked Laub what role the Network plays in the local struggles of LGBTS students to establish GSAs. Is it left to the student leadership that they have fostered or is there more active involvement?

We try to help students figure out who the allies are and then try to build
alliances that are going to strengthen their position and sort of build
their power base. And then if it seems like their rights have already been
broken or there's a potential that the law is being broken or their rights
are being broken or violated, either as individual students experiencing
harassment or as a GSA club and their right to exist and meet and advertise their events and all that, then we will refer them out to an attorney
with the ACLU and the national center for lesbian rights or one of our
legal partners. For transgender students, we also work really closely with
the transgender law center. And then we will get an attorney to either
make a phone call or write a letter explaining the law, and sometimes
that's all it takes, because schools don't want to be sued.

This relationship between adult organizations and student activity
relates directly to Laub's foundational philosophy for the Network—that
LGBT students had all the right activist and leadership instincts, but,
because of their age and marginalized position, often lacked the resources to
use these instincts to create real change.

Since the mid 1990s, the numbers of resources made available to
student leaders by GLSEN, the ACLU, The GSA Network, Project 10,
and numerous other groups, grew by leaps and bounds. All of this resource
mobilization was aimed at breaking down the barriers that stand between
the LGBT students' desires to make their schools safer and more accepting places and the reality of starting a GSA and getting an antiharassment
policy passed. Laub's assessment of the changes in the barriers to these
goals brought about by all of this resource mobilization was quite similar to
the analysis of all the activists I spoke with:

Now what we're seeing is we're not seeing as many cases where administrators say, "No, you can't have the club," but they are saying things like,
"Well, you can have the club but it's really not a—you really shouldn't
call it a gay–straight alliance, let's call it something else that doesn't have
the word 'gay' in it." So there's censorship that's still a barrier and then
there is still the factor of some students who want to have a club, they
are scared to start one, they are scared for their own safety, there's issues
about their own personal safety, the reaction from peers, the reaction
from teachers and administrators.

Laub, like the others I interviewed, stated that as the strategies of the students and the organizations that support them are proved more effective, and as the law has been repeatedly proved to be on the side of LGBT students rights, those who oppose GSAs have gotten more creative in putting up new hurdles for students to have to clear:

> I think one of the new frontiers of resistance for a GSA club or barriers for GSA clubs, is around parental permission, parental permission to be in the club. ... I actually talked to one of the school board members who was behind this [in a Texas school]. They allowed the club to meet but they changed the bylaws to the club that you have to have parental permission for all clubs. And, of course, it doesn't affect all clubs in the same way. This particular school board member was at the national school board association conference at my workshop at GSAs. He was spouting about, "I support the GSA but what I'm going to tell all you school board members out there is [to] pass policy now that says for any club membership you have to have parental permission, and that way, basically, this is the way to deal with your GSA." You can't ban these clubs but you can require parental permission and you can, in effect, disable these clubs from being able to really do anything .... I think this issue about parents' rights, I think that has a lot of sway with other parents and it is also ... And vice versa, when there's a parent who says, "I have a kid at this school and I want my child to be safe" that's also again a really influential statement, and both kinds of parental voices can influence an administrator's decision."

As students rights are repeatedly proven under the First Amendment, the Equal Access Act, and equal protections laws under Title IX, those who oppose LGBT students' goals of changing schools have countered by asserting rights and protections of their own. The newer strategy of an assertion of parental rights (and sometimes taxpayers' rights) combined with the continuing ignorance, fear, and homophobia that surround the issue, still have an impact on local school debates. However, they have not manifested enough resistance to stop the spread of GSAs through the country.

Of all of the organizational activists I interviewed for this book, Carolyn Laub was the most enthusiastic about the speed and rate of progress that has been made by the GSA movement:

Seemingly so quickly, yeah. Believe me, I'm aware of how fast this is growing. It's really exciting. My take on it is that it's amazing and that it's incredibly powerful and it's huge. GSAs represent just an incredible base of students, tens of thousands of students in the country, and even in California, that are mobilized and engaged in LGBT civil rights issues and LGBT student safety. So it's very powerful. We just increased tenfold; we just hit the tenfold mark, because we started out as a network in '98 with about 40 GSAs that already existed and now we're at four hundred and…well, we're over 425.[36]

This assessment contrasts sharply with Virginia Uribe's view that progress has been slow. This is, at least partially, because Laub has a more compressed view of the history and timeline of the GSA movement—involved with working to change schools for six years rather than twenty. Both views are correct. The longitudinal view is that it took considerable time, work, and small incremental steps to get to the point where now rapid change is occurring. As with the others I interviewed, I asked Laub for her analysis of the factors that have contributed to the recent growth of GSAs. She argues that this was largely a combination of grassroots word-of-mouth diffusion of an idea from one group of students to another, as well as the mass media and Internet, which accelerated this word-of-mouth process:

There has been a couple spikes in the growth in GSAs, the biggest spikes being after the Salt Lake City case. And that makes a lot of sense, because GSAs were sort of, really [a] very organically spread concept until the mid 90s; you didn't have many of them around the country. And people all of a sudden heard about GSAs in the national media and that certainly resonates with how I heard about them and how this girl that I was working with heard about it. … Then the murder of Matthew Shepard also is one of the other spikes in terms of the growth of GSAs following all of the, again, national media attention about his murder. … There have been other kinds of high-profile GSA cases where the GSA itself is being contested and that definitely, I think, contributes to the spike in GSAs.

Stories of real-life struggle and conflict served as inspiration for others to take a stand and be counted, providing the sense that something larger was going on beyond their school, and by taking action they could become a part of it. There is little doubt that there were also others who were further frightened into silence by these stories of conflict and struggle. Over time, other stories also began to surface, as Laub noted:

> What I would say now is that there's been other kinds of media coverage
> about GSAs, more success stories about what students are doing,
> stories about events like the Day of Silence and the Transgender Day of
> Remembrance where there's participation by GSA clubs in these national
> days and there's lots of local stories on what students are doing … Some
> mainstream shows … "Boston Public" has a GSA, "Once and Again" had
> a GSA story, the "Queer as Folk" had a GSA story, so both mainstream
> and queer media have covered this issue and not just the legal cases but
> also the stories about what students are doing and why they get involved,
> what they work on as a GSA, how they are changing the school, how they
> are changing attitudes and all that kind of stuff. So, I do think that helps.
> And then, I still think that GSAs basically spread like the same way they
> did in the early 90s in a very kind of, organic, word of mouth kind of way.
> Students will meet somebody and, like, "Oh you have a GSA, how did you
> do it? I want to do it at my school." Really basic stuff that is just still very
> powerful for spreading the movement.

Organizations like The Gay–Straight Alliance, Project 10, GLSEN, and the ACLU are able to take this idea that is spread by word of mouth and give it structure and substance. When students or school teachers anywhere in the country hear a story of a GSA and are intrigued by it and interested in finding out more, it now takes them only a few seconds to do an Internet search and find multiple sources that provide all the information, step-by-step instructions, and personal and legal assistance they need to turn the idea into reality in their own school. There is no doubt that this has also been a major factor in accelerating the spread of GSAs by providing narratives of victory and empowered role models for LGBTS youth, rather than only models of victims of suicide and abuse.

Carolyn Laub speaks very passionately about the power of youth activism that she has dedicated herself to help to foster. It is clear that she feels this youth activism is having a large impact on schools, but I asked her if she thought it had caused any changes in the larger gay rights movement:

I would say it just may be a little bit harder for me to comment on because of my own age. I just turned 30, so I can comment on the last ten
years. Even ten years ago there was still this very really entrenched belief
stereotype about gay adults' recruiting—if they work with children, they
are going to recruit them to be gay. And that actually stopped a lot of
adults. My understanding of what's happened because of that is that it's
actually prevented a lot of adults and adult LGBT organizations from
working with young people or feeling like they could work with young
people. There's a lot of misunderstanding between adults and youth in
the LGBT community, so I think that particular entrenched fear about
recruitment has shifted, I don't feel that anymore from adult LGBT
organizations. In fact, I see the opposite, sort of like, everybody sees this
really cool stuff happening with GSAs and everybody wants a piece of
it …. Even five years ago there were a handful of LGBT community
centers that included youth programming in their services, and five years
ago almost none of them had anything that related to schools or GSAs
and now they all do.

As the GSA movement evolved, won legal victories, and received a
good deal of sympathetic media attention, youth became a potential source
of power for the adult lesbian and gay community rather than an Achilles
heel (by virtue of calling up negative stereotypes). LGBT youth have been
validated as a group that deserves increased legal rights and protections, in
many ways more so than the adult LGBT community. As a result, supporting and advocating for the rights of LGBT youth can be viewed as an asset
to achieving these goals for the adult lesbian and gay community.

In the next chapter, I examine how the GSA movement tried to make
the most of this asset. I offer an analysis of the general strategies and
discourses developed by all of the organizations discussed in this as is the
case with every movement for social change, the GSA movement has faced
organized resistance. This most systematic form of opposition has come
from organizations associated with the religious right. The efforts of these
groups to counter the goals of the GSA movement have had an impact on
public perception and opinion of the issues and, to some extent, the movement's progress.

FIVE

CAUGHT IN THE CROSSHAIRS
Becoming the Latest Target of the Religious Right

"Revolutions don't happen overnight. Homosexuality is being widely accepted in schools now by administrators, school boards and some parents and students because of diligent, aggressive people who believe its okay. Some work for large, well-financed national "gay" activist groups; others are local volunteers. Some are practicing homosexuals who are educators; others are their relatives or sympathizers. Regardless, this process has happened because traditional-minded parents and communities weren't watching closely enough, and many thought supporting homosexuality was part of being kind, compassionate and tolerant. Most people never thought it would get this far. But it has gotten very far"—Mission America[1].

The statement above could read as an affirming declaration of the success of LGBT and straight ally students and all the organizations that support and assist them. However, it is decidedly not a positive claim of victory. Rather, it is the opening statement of a call to arms. Mission America is a "Christian ministry started in 1995 as a publication and a website,"[2] with the primary organizational goal of mobilizing Christians and other concerned "moral" citizens to combat organizations like GLSEN, Project 10 and the ACLU, the existence of GSAs, and all efforts to make schools safer for, and more inclusive of LGBT, students. It is one of a multitude of conservative Christian or religious right organizations that have devoted significant amounts of their resources and time trying to counter and derail the efforts of the GSA movement at the local and national level since the mid 1990s. The "revolution" referred to in the statement is viewed not as a rebellion for liberation and justice, but rather as an overthrow of morality and order. The statement gives credit to the success the GSA movement has had in making schools more tolerant of LGBT students and issues, but this victory is understood as truly a failure of parents, community members, and schools to guard against the forces of the "gay agenda." Objectively, however, the statement does speak at least to the success that GSA movement participants have had in effectively defining the negative experiences of LGBT students as a social problem that deserves public attention and official action.

Completing the process of collectively defining a social problem and constructing a strategy for dealing with it are just the initial steps in the process of making an issue one of public concern. Once these definitions are made and the strategies are put into action, the social movement is put to the test as it becomes the subject of discussion, conflict, and controversy. Individuals in the social movement who are advocating for change inevitably collide with groups that strive to protect their interests by resisting change.[3] When a movement's assertion of a social problem is contested, it is a sign that others take it as a strong enough claim to pose a credible threat to their interests. It is also an early marker of a movement's success, because the debates and conflicts over meaning bring more media and public attention to the issue.

The most organized form of opposition to the definitions and claims made by the GSA movement come from already established organizations of the religious right—The Family Research Council, The Christian Coalition, American Family Association, Citizens for Excellence in Education, Concerned Women For America, just to name a few. These groups have objected to Project 10, GLSEN, and student activists' claims that the negative experiences of LGBT students in public schools is a serious social problem that needs to be rectified. More specifically, these religious right organizations have defined a social problem of their own. From their perspective, the emergence of GSAs and policies to protect LGBT students' safety is a social problem. In a diverse society such as that of the United States, in which citizens have a wide range of values and interest, it is not uncommon that debates over social issues involve political conflict at even the basic level of definition.[4]

The opposition and resistance to any social movement always influence what it does and says and its successes and failures. Although this is only one of many factors that play a role in determining the direction and the fate of a social movement, it is a significant one worthy of attention. Therefore, to develop a fuller understanding of the GSA movement, I believe it is essential to examine the most organized form of opposition it faces. In this chapter, I analyze the discourse and strategies used by the opposition and consider how they match up against, and influence, those of the GSA movement. In the next chapter, I examine how well each side is doing at influencing media representation of, and public opinion and support for, their position. Throughout both chapters, I argue that this comparative discourse analysis, combined with a comparative assessment of empirical evidence, reveals that the GSA movement's discourse more strongly relates to the civic discussion of public policy and is rooted more closely to empirical reality than is that of its conservative Christian opposition. In spite of this, conservative Christian groups are often able to use their claims to moral authority, combined with baseless accusations, to cause significant fear about, and conflict over, the efforts of LGBTS students and the GSA movement. They are able to have this disruptive impact largely because their presence in the discussion draws the conversation, and the GSA movement, into a debate about the larger, long established "culture war" waged between the religious right and gay rights groups.

THE RELIGIOUS RIGHT AS A COUNTER MOVEMENT

Although the state, or some governmental institution, is the ultimate target of most social movements, it is often not the main source of opposition. Research on social movements recognizes that their actions and demands often stimulate the mobilization of a counter movement that becomes their main source of opposition.[5] This is clearly what has happened in the case of the GSA movement. Counter movements are groups of individuals who make rival claims on matters of policy and politics, and contend for exposure from the mass media and the public's attention to their perspective.[6] It is only logical that movements spark the creation of their own competition. Their claims inherently stand in opposition to some elements of the social structure or cultural value system, otherwise they would not have a reason to mobilize. Therefore, it is inevitable that some group will organize in an effort to protect against the change from the status quo, or to argue for an alternative change.[7] In the case of the GSA movement, not only was opposition inevitable, it was predictable. Regardless of the fact that the movement was started by students and teachers to make schools safer and more respectful places for all students to learn and thrive, driven by concern for students' safety and well being and not gay rights more generally, they drew the attention and wrath of the religious right. Conservative Christians have long opposed any attempts to decrease the social stigmatization and institutionalized discrimination of gay and lesbian people. In their view, such changes serve to establish a judgment about homosexuality in America's institutions and culture that run counter to their own moral judgment. Rather than argue that the problem with this is that it deflates their moral authority over these institutions, the religious right argues that such changes threaten to destablize the foundations of the nation.

The ability of conservative Christians to use religious morality as a political tool in American democracy is interesting and complex. Our founding fathers strongly believed in the necessity of secular governing to eliminate the influence of particular religious beliefs and values in the construction of federal and state laws and policies. However, religion clearly influences the political climate, political debates, and, at times, public policy.[8] An important question is how this has happened. Even though the United States constitution established the government explicitly to be secular, there have always been religious undertones in American politics. Once understated, Christian religious themes have gradually become more explicit and influential since the 1960s. This blurring of the boundaries between religion, politics, and morality was "caused by historically contingent events (Vietnam, Watergate, Roe v. Wade) and by structural changes in the political economy, including the educational revolution, the rise of the 'new class,' and new forms of state penetration into areas of daily life formally defined as private" (Wuthnow 1988: 113). All of these factors prompted some members of religious communities to feel that their cultural values and morals were not being represented in, and were in some ways threatened by, governmental institutions, policies, and laws. This belief mobilized them into political action. The history, tactics, and political impact of this conservative Christian mobilization has been documented and assessed by many political scholars.[9] I encourage anyone interested in the GSA movement, and in gaining a general understanding of the current state of American political power, to explore some of this research.

Catherine Lugg's (2000) research on the Christian right reveals that, in addition to cultural shifts, another important factor in the politicalization of religious groups was a shift in dominant Christian ideology from fundamentalism to reconstructionism. "Reconstructionists differ from traditional fundamentalists in that they believe Christ will not return until his kingdom is established on earth. Consequently, they are dedicated to reconstructing a national government based explicitly on Christian tenets" (Lugg 2000: 625). The use of the term *reconstruction* rather than construction in Lugg's statement is significant. Reconstructionists believe that America was once a Christian nation, but the increasing separation of church and state has caused its moral decline, and the nation's social ills will be relieved only when the two are unified. This belief has made political activism a moral imperative for members of these religious communities—creating a religious "political ethic."

Didi Herman's extensive research on the religious right and its influence in American politics is in agreement with Lugg's analysis. She argues further that an anti-homosexual agenda is central to this religious political ethic that conservative Christians feel morally mandated to uphold. They believe that any institutional policy that signals a tolerance for homosexuals is tantamount to the institutionalization of sin, and this takes them further away from the goal of the unification of church and state, which is required (among other things) to bring forth the millennium.[10] The religious right's conviction that the policies and ruling principles of the government and institutions of the United States must sustain a narrow and specific fundamentalist Christian doctrine explains the ardency with which they have led a pubic antigay agenda for over three decades.[11]

The duration of the struggle between gay- and lesbian-rights groups and conservative Christians has solidified the conflicts between them. Given this prolonged battle, they must be analyzed as opposing movements. Opposing movements not only directly battle with one another over issues, they also impact each other less directly by altering the social, cultural, and political environment in which they both operate. An opposing movement plays a critical role in shaping the structure of political opportunity the other side faces.[12] In very basic terms, opposing movements are like monkeys on each other's backs, following them where ever they go and getting in the way of their attempts to clearly articulate their perspectives and goals. At every turn, each is reminded that the other is lurking, ready to counter everything they say and do. As a result of the consistency of this, both sides eventually develop strategies and discourses that seek to anticipate the inevitable move of the opponent. Since the 1970s, social and political scholars have analyzed the effect of these dynamics in the struggles between gay rights and the religious right over many specific issues—from American Psychiatric Association's classification of homosexuality as a mental illness to the continued struggle for same-sex marriage rights.[13]

I was interested in how large a role these dynamics played in shaping the strategies and discourse of the GSA movement even though its leaders attempted to establish a movement that was separate from the gay rights movement. In my interviews with the executive directors and active members of the major organizations supporting the GSA movement, I asked them about their experience with opposition from conservative Christian groups and how much time they spent trying to anticipate and counter their position. Although all of those I asked agreed that these groups play an instrumental role in the resistance to the goals and advancement of the GSA movement, they had different assessments of the effectiveness and power of this opposition. Beth Reis of the Safe Schools Coalition argued that they "have been strategic and have more power than their numbers would imply," but that power is more influential on some specific issues than on others. For example, they have wielded a significant influence over the content of textbooks, regarding sexuality in general and homosexuality specifically, through strong lobbying efforts in Texas and California, which, by virtue of their size, are the markets that set the standard for textbook publishers. In contrast, Reis argues that, although they have been vocal in their opposition to GSAs, they have been less effective in stopping them largely because of the proven protection of the Equal Access Act.[14]

When I asked Kevin Jennings what he thought were the biggest roadblocks to efforts to start GSAs, he named the religious right among his top three (along with lack of support from school administration and lack of school resources in general). In response to my question about how much power and influence he thought the religious right's moral arguments against homosexuality had in determining outcomes of debates over GSA, Jennings stated, "I think it only has weight with their core audience. I think outside their core audience, it actually engenders a lot of opposition. Because people don't like the idea of having religious values shoved down their throat. So, I think that it works for their people and it doesn't work for anyone else." Given that assessment, I asked him why he listed the religious right as the second major roadblock to his organization's goals. "You have to remember one thing here, which is that only about 15% of people vote in a school board election. Nobody votes in the school board election. So to continue to control our schools, they don't have to get everybody to agree with them; they just have to get their side to vote, which they are very good at doing. So, I think that, with the general public, their religious argument is not very effective. I really don't. But I think that with their core audience it is very effective, and that's enough people to control the school boards, unfortunately."

I asked what, if anything, GLSEN was doing to address this phenomenon of conservative control of school boards. "We are definitely trying to get more people more engaged with school board elections, attending school board meetings. We have our safe schools action network where you can directly email superintendents, and stuff like that. So we definitely are trying to get people, and young people especially, more engaged in the political process, because right now it's a forfeit." I asked Jennings if, in addition to trying to mobilize more GSA movement supporters into political action, GLSEN also spent time trying to formulate rhetorical arguments to counter those made by conservative Christians in their opposition to LGBT issues in schools. He strongly asserted that he does not waste his time or the resources of his organization trying to debate their position on the issue. Jennings' strategy for dealing with the religious right is based on advice given to him by a friend who is a very successful business owner. As Jennings explained to me:

> The first month after I launched GLSEN and started talking about
> the religious right, he said to me, "Why are you talking about these
> people?" and I said, "Well, they are our opponents." He said, "When I
> started my business I never worried about my competition. I made my
> product better and better and better, and now I don't have any competi-
> tion anymore." And that has really been how we deal with the religious
> right's arguments. We have the strongest argument on our side, because,
> in my opinion, the best defense is a good offense. I would rather have
> them explain why schools should not take action to keep people safe, why
> it's okay these young people get beaten up, than answer their ridiculous
> 19th-century arguments about promoting homosexuality.

In reality, of course, public debates are not just easily won by those who objectively have the best argument. All arguments are faced with the subjective judgment of their audience. Therefore, a social movement may be able to avoid directly defending itself against attacks from its opposition, but it must also know their strategies well enough to construct an offensive that will score more points with the public audience. They do this by trying to "frame" the issue in ways that clearly articulate their interpretation of the problem in a way that resonates with cultural values and understandings already held by some portion of the general public.

Constructing the Best Offense:
A Brief Summary of the General Framing Strategies of the GSA Movement

The term "framing" refers to the purposeful strategies used by social movements to help the public understand their movement, the issues that they address, and why action should be taken.[15] Social movements try to win advantage with authorities and the public by framing their demands in ways that are most persuasive as to the validity of their cause.[16] The most effective way of doing this is to discursively link their frames with larger cultural themes and values. Doing this makes the frame accessible to larger audiences, because it will "resonate,"[17] with their preestablished cultural understandings.[18] Social movements draw on existing cultural definitions of rights of responsibilities to underscore what is wrong with the current social order, and to suggest directions for change.[19] Framing strategies of social movements generally do not redefine cultural norms or social understandings, but rather work within preexisting ones.[20] What is creative about effective framing strategies is their ability to transform these common understandings into calls for new social action.

Opposing movements have both a positive and negative effect on the success of each group's framing strategies. Leading social-movement analysts Benford and Snow argue that a social movement's framing activity typically challenges the logic and effectiveness of solutions advocated by opponents as well as offering the rationale for its own remedies. It is important to realize that opposing framing activity can affect a movement both by putting movement activists on the defensive, at least temporarily, and by frequently forcing them to develop and elaborate on predictions more clearly than they might otherwise have done.[21]

This can be both an asset and a hindrance to effective political mobilizations. Well-established positions or "master frames" of a movement may provide a degree of effectiveness, because their ability to resonate with a particular audience becomes reliable; however, they also, at times, serve to constrain the movement.[22] Organizations occasionally get so locked into their own established position, or master framing strategy, that they become unable to adapt to changing social circumstances or to move beyond their initial political gains. I argue that when this potentially constraining effect of master frames is combined with the dynamics that exist between opposing social movements, the result can be conflict between groups that no longer actively engage one another in political dialogue. Instead, they speak only of each other to the general public for the purpose of discounting or dismissing the other's claims. This is the case in the conflict between those in the gay rights movement and the religious right. The give and take of opposing movements' framing strategies has evolved into two completely polarized political framing tactics. The GSA movement has become entangled in this pattern.

In a prolonged battle between opposing movements, framing strategies become intensely fought battles for control over the social, cultural and political meaning of the issue in question. Sometimes the very conflict between the groups is framed as having larger cultural meaning.[23] This is exemplified in the history of battles between gay-rights and religious-right organizations. In fact, the definition of "larger value cleavages" has been so strong that gay-rights and religious-right groups have come to represent completely opposite cultural-value orientations. To align with one of them over any issue is to symbolically choose sides in a political war that does not define a middle ground. These frames, in a sense, paint the opposing groups into their respective corners, from which they cannot dialogue with each other or with any audience that has not already chosen, or is not willing to choose a side. The framing strategies of the gay rights movement firmly anchor it in identity- and civil-rights claims, and framing strategies of the religious right firmly anchor it in morality claims.

This dynamic spilled over into the GSA movement. When LGBT and straight ally students first began this movement, they simply stated what they wanted and why they wanted it, without thinking about frame alignment strategies or anticipating oppositional frames. This lack of a plan freed students from these constraints for a while. However, as a result of organizational efforts to increase students' chances of success, the GSA movement eventually developed a set of framing strategies that closely mirror those used by the gay rights movement in its culture war with the religious right. In a sense, the movement's leaders were forced to do this, as a practical matter, as a means of anticipating and countering this most vocal form of resistance to their goals. Nevertheless, in doing so, they curtailed the potential students had to develop frames that broke free of the predictable circular no-way-out discourse to establish a new and innovative framing strategy unique to a new GSA movement. The result is that the same argument was applied to the new battleground of schools and is drawing much the same opposition that has proven effective elsewhere. On this battlefield, however, students' concerns and voices are often able to provide some advantage to the GSA movement.

Many of the groups that make up the GSA movement have defined the need for LGBT inclusions in public education, not only in terms of the personal sufferings of students, but also in terms that connect the system of public education to the perpetuation of discrimination and oppression of gay and lesbian people. They have also implicated the responsibility of society to change the practices and policies in public education in ways that strive to alleviate this as a matter of democratic civil rights. In other words, they have defined it as a social issue rather than an individual problem caused by immoral behavior.

An early version of GLSEN's mission statement defines the general social meanings of this issue as one that is separate from issues of religious morality.

> The Gay, Lesbian, and Straight Education Network strives to assure that each member of every school community is valued and respected, regardless of sexual orientation. We believe that such an atmosphere engenders a positive sense of self, which is the basis of educational achievement and personal growth. Since homophobia and heterosexism undermine a healthy school climate, we work to educate teachers, students, and the public at large about the damaging effects these forces have on youth and adults alike.[24]

In statements like this one, the problems of this population are blamed on the lack of information and the environment of intolerance in public schools, therefore implying that public education, a major institution in American society, is responsible for these sufferings of LGBT students.

To ground these definitions of the problem in reality, empirical evidence is used to support the argument. Suicide rates among LGBT adolescents are the research and statistical estimates used most frequently as grounds for statements about the problem of gay students. The statements "30% of all completed teen suicides are gay teens" and "LGBT teenagers are three times more likely to commit suicide than their heterosexual peers," are used repeatedly and almost always in any statement made by these groups to define the social problems of LGBT students. The fact that these estimated suicide rates are taken from a study conducted by a governmental agency is used to substantiate the credibility of the frame and the seriousness of the issue. These suicide statistics are generally coupled with citations from their own or another organization's research, and statistical estimates of verbal and physical harassment, school dropout rates, substance abuse, etc.

To increase the success of this frame alignment and the credibility of the numbers, social movements generally combine these statistics with personal accounts, or "real-life stories," with the goal of giving a human face to the problem. The personal face of the social problem is commonly provided through the use of "horror stories,"[25] "atrocity tales,"[26] or "worst cases."[27] They are effective because they attract media and public attention to the issue, shape the general public's perception of the social problem, and serve as "real-life" reference points for the issue in general. This strategy of using horror stories in the process of defining an issue as a social problem provides evidence to the claims made by social movements that this issue is one of injustice and, therefore, should be considered a social problem[28]

The GSA Movement uses this strategy often and very effectively. Personal statements and detailed stories of LGBT students' experiences with harassment at school are often intertwined in the literature produced by these organizations and in statements made to schools or to the press. In public hearings or debates around this issue, LGBT students are usually present to provide the personal face to the issue and give real-life evidence to the negative experiences of LGBT students in school.

It is necessary for these organizations to define the problems of LGBT students away from these common cultural understandings of homosexuality and toward other shared meanings. In these frames, the conclusion the general public should come to is that this is a serious social problem that needs local and national attention. The public should recognize that the problem is caused, in large part, by the failure of public schools to fulfill their purpose of educating students to be productive and active citizens in a pluralistic democracy. In failing to include and protect LGBT students, schools are denying all students the total fulfillment of this goal, and, consequently, they are damaging children's identity development, and their ability to be productive and critically thinking adults.

HOW THE RELIGIOUS RIGHT ATTEMPTS TO DISCOUNT, DISCREDIT, AND MOBILIZE AGAINST THE GSA MOVEMENT

Conservative Christian organizations provide a very different definition of gay and lesbian inclusions in education as a social problem. The broadest theme of their framing strategies is that of a "homosexual agenda," which seeks to infiltrate social institutions and destroy American values and culture. In an article from its online journal entitled, "Homosexuals push for control of schools: Pro-family groups prepare national strategy to counter threat," the American Family Federation (AFA) summarizes the problem from its perspective:

> U.S. public schools, already a hotbed of liberal agitation, are quickly
> becoming a battleground for the soul of a culture that has been jolted
> off its Judeo-Christian foundations. As homosexual activists rush into
> the vacuum created by insulating schools from the influence of religion,
> AFA and other pro-family groups are formulating strategies to protect
> America's school children from homosexual propaganda ...The irony is
> that activists are getting into schools by pleading for tolerance, but once
> inside, they are fiercely intolerant of those who oppose them.[29]

These common themes of agendas, cultural values, and danger to children are used in all arenas of conflict between gay rights and religious right organizations—marriage being the most visible recently.

The following passage from a report by Focus on the Family about the 2003 GLSEN national conference illustrates the framing of the threat to public schools.

> GLSEN is a cultural hurricane that's hitting our schools with the kind
> of force and devastation that may take years to fully assess. Let me try

to paint the picture. GLSEN is a self-styled pro-gay education network targeting our kids in public schools. The danger is how they seek to accomplish this mission. In effect, GLSEN's objective is to cut out parents and adult leaders in the child's life who don't agree with the LGBT agenda. Every speaker at the national conference made this very clear:[30]

In this arena, the "homosexual agenda" threatens not only schools, but also families, parental authority and, most seriously, the minds of children. According to conservative Christians, this undermining of core and foundational social institutions and, therefore, the future of the nation, is the social problem that must be addressed:

> If all forms of harassment are wrong, then all forms of harassment—without distinction—should be banned. In fact, singling out "sexual orientation," and including it with traditional categories like race and sex, serves not a "safety" function but a political one. When harassment based on sexual orientation is explicitly banned, school staff are inevitably trained that the *reason* that such harassment is wrong is not because all harassment is wrong or that all people should be treated with respect, but because *'there is nothing wrong with being gay or lesbian.'* Such an assertion is not only offensive to the moral standards of most Americans and to the historical teachings of most major religions, but it flies in the face of hard scientific data showing the high rates of promiscuity, physical disease, mental illness, substance abuse, child sexual abuse, and domestic violence that result from homosexual behavior.[31]

Members of the religious right strongly align their frames with religious definitions of the immorality of homosexuality to provide the discursive power and legitimacy to their claim that LGBT inclusions in public education must be opposed. This knowledge is used to legitimize the claim that such inclusions are a threat to the morality of children and society. The "hard scientific data" about the high rates of promiscuity etc. does not actually exist, but this fact is, most likely, irrelevant to the audience who is predisposed to the particular religious underpinnings of the statement. The success of these types of assertions are contingent on the fact that they will resonate with such prejudiced beliefs.

The following statement was made at a July 2, 1996 Capital Hill briefing regarding the Defense of Marriage Act that was sponsored by the Family Research Council [FRC]. The statement illustrates the threat that the religious right perceives LGBT inclusions in public education poses to children and to what it views as the essential values and morals of American society.

> At one time in the history of our country, education was virtually synonymous with moral training. The traditional virtues and cultural mores were passed down from generation to generation because they work. Our students have been guinea pigs in Russian roulette with their futures long enough. Same-sex "marriage" is a result of a destructive, narcissistic way of thinking and of "value-neutral" curriculums. One can only shudder to consider the horrific possibilities which may occur on the sexuality continuum with the perpetuation of such policies.[32]

In this statement, the teaching of "tolerance" or "value-neutrality" on the topic of homosexuality in public schools is argued to be against the traditional moral training of students in "American" values that public schools were meant to uphold. Teaching tolerance for, or acceptance of, homosexuality is situated in this frame alignment as counter to the proper functional role of public education. A shift toward acceptance of homosexuality in one institutional realm (schools, marriage, media, etc.), they argue, will disrupt the accepted and necessary moral order of American society, which is considered linked to normative heterosexuality.

These organizations provide research studies and critiques of research studies to discount gay rights organizations' empirical claims. These research studies are almost always authored by a medical doctor or Ph.D. associated with a Christian hospital or university. The research is not taken from publications in credible medical or academic journals, but rather in publications produced by various conservative Christian groups. The primary objectives of these research articles are to prove that homosexuality is not natural, but is an unhealthy and destructive lifestyle; or to disprove the LGBT youth suicide statistics. The horror stories that are used to put a personal face on their claims are generally stories of "recovered homosexuals" who are now leading a "moral" heterosexual life, and stories of explicit sexual acts that were supposedly discussed in a public school classroom somewhere. William Martin (1996) found that the latter category of horror story has been consistently used by the religious right since the 1960s. He argues that the fact that these stories were always false did not take away from the power of the myth they substantiated.

Conservative Christian groups argue that the general public, and particularly Christian citizens, should recognize that homosexuality is immoral and any provisions granted to LGBT individuals will, therefore, serve to decay the moral values of America. From their perspective, permitting GSAs in a public school is not only condoning an immoral lifestyle, but is also failing to help children suffering with the "disorder" of homosexuality. Including LGBT topics in the public school curriculum not only promotes an immorality but also makes a mockery of "true" knowledge and education. According to the conservative Christian groups, such changes in public education, as a main institution for ensuring the perpetuation of "American values," will lead to the corruption of children and society as a whole. They believe this is a social problem that needs to be rectified for the sake of America's moral future.

The GSA movement defines the function of public education and American values very differently, their definition is as essential to their framing of the social problem as the religious rights' definition of it is to their own:

> Is it not precisely the role of education, and schools, to prevent igno-
> rance? Yet, schools continue, through their own ignorance and fears, to
> censor all fair and accurate information about LGBT people. And what
> is the result? Obviously, LGBT young people grow up isolated, afraid,
> lacking self-esteem or role models, disliking themselves. ... LGBT young
> people, denied their right to the truth about themselves through ap-
> propriate schooling, experience a host of societally imposed problems:
> harassment, hate violence, parental abuse, job discrimination, medical
> mistreatment, etc. Schools are failing in their responsibilities to these
> young people.[33]

This statement asserts that the difficulties faced by LGBT youth are socially imposed. It also speaks to the rights of LGBT students within the public schools. The rights of these students, in the eyes of many, are contingent on whether they meet the criteria of a valid minority group.

OPPOSING FRAMES OF THE MINORITY GROUP STATUS
OF LGBT PEOPLE

The main framing processes used in debates over GSAs are strongly tied to those used by gay-rights and religious-right groups in the past. Historically, much has been debated about the "meaning" or truth or morality of sexuality, particularly homosexuality, and this debate over meaning shaped the gay rights movement's attempts at identity politics. The definition of a common homosexual identity was used in the American mainstream to designate and regulate individuals in this category to an inferior and subordinate status in American culture, society, and politics. The definition of common lesbian and gay identities was used by the gay and lesbian mainstream to designate this group of individuals as a minority group—not by choice, but by birth—that deserves the same rights and protections granted to other minority groups in America. This "minoritizing" strategy established the gay- and lesbian-rights movement firmly in line with civil rights politics, and the movement could, and did, draw from the framing strategies used by the black civil-rights and women's-rights movements. A common framing strategy in all of these movements has historically been to identify the group as one that is, but should not be, discriminated against in a democracy. This always requires redefining the qualities commonly used to socially and culturally understand and oppress the group.[34] Although the gay rights movement has evolved over time into a multitude of organizations that have developed a variety of strategies to politicize gay identity that are more complex, this minority strategy is the one employed most often by the GSA movement.

The most frequently used ideological strategy in the GSA movement is to frame LGBT students as a legitimate minority group whose needs are not being served and whose civil rights are being violated by the current state of the system of public education in America. To succeed in having gay students collectively defined as a legitimate minority group, the GSA movement has had to combat the commonly accepted socially constructed meanings and understandings of sexual identity as a natural human deformity or a deviant and immoral lifestyle choice. To overcome this roadblock, the groups that make up the GSA movement make strong statements about "the truth" of sexual orientation. For example, Project 10 asserts:

> It is the basic assumption of this program that homosexuality is a normal variation in both orientation and sexual behavior. Negative attitudes

toward homosexuals are primarily the result of homophobia, a prejudice similar in nature and dynamic to all other prejudices including anti-Semitism, racism, and sexism. Continued exposure to societal prejudice results in a stigmatization of the homosexually oriented through which their social and personal identities are, to use Goffman's (1963)[35] term, "spoiled." As a result, gay people become members of a minority group, a term defined as any segment of the population that suffers unjustified negative acts by the rest of society.[36]

This statement very clearly illustrates that Project 10 understands the importance of defining homosexuality as a "natural" or "normal" biological human variation in order to legitimately claim that LGBT students are part of a minority group. Once defined as such, it can be argued that they suffer unjustifiable social discrimination. This frame clearly attempts to remove any discussion of morality from the issue. Literature published by Project 10 frequently includes strong statements backed by research or quotes from a medical doctor or Ph.D., asserting the fact that "sexual identity is not a matter of choice."[37] The importance of this assertion is, of course, that if sexual identity is considered by the public to be a "choice," then the resulting problems are individual and the solution is to fix the LGBT person, and not the social institutions.

The literature produced by GLSEN also devotes attention to separating the issue of sexual identity from the notion that it is a moral issue or choice. GLSEN's approach to articulating this is, however, less forceful than that of Project 10:

> Our sexual behavior and how we define ourselves (our identity) is usually
> a choice. Though some people claim their sexual orientation is a choice,
> for the vast majority, this doesn't seem to be the case. ... Possibly in
> an ideal world devoid of homophobia, few people would construct a
> personal identity based on sexual orientation. Since we do not live in this
> ideal world, however, people define themselves to assure their visibility in
> a society that wishes to shove them into a closet of denial and fear....[38]

This statement conveys an understanding of identity that is more complex than the statement of Project 10. It articulates a separation between the terms sexual orientation, which is biologically defined, and sexual identity, which is socially defined. It also asserts that social forces create and make declarations of sexual identity politically necessary. However, the statement still asserts the basic minority group status of LGBT people as the criterion on which they deserve civil rights guarantees.

The religious right strongly opposes the efforts of the gay rights movement to establish LGBT people as a legitimate minority group. They have repeatedly attempted to undermine efforts to gain basic civil rights by discounting the claims to a common identity that are politically necessary to gain access to such rights. They have taken two main approaches to dismantling these claims. The first is to assert that homosexuality is not a natural sexual orientation with which an individual is born, but rather it is a deviant behavioral choice, or psychological or moral sickness that can, and should, be redirected or cured. The success of this framing strategy often rests only on social stereotypes and selective biblical passages. Occasionally, attempts are made to provide "evidence of these claims" by providing testimonies from "reformed" homosexuals as examples of the ability to "correct" homosexual behavior through religion or counseling. There are countless examples of this claim from every conservative Christian group that opposes the GSA movement. The following from the Family Research Council is just one example:

> Singling out "sexual orientation" for special protection cannot be
> justified on logical grounds, and it could have consequences not clear
> at first glance. Lumping "sexual orientation" together with "race,
> color, national origin, sex, and disability" for special protection
> is illogical because the latter qualities are inborn (except for some
> disabilities), involuntary, immutable, and innocuous—none of which is
> true of homosexuality, despite the claims of its advocates. Evidence that
> homosexuality is inborn (that is, unalterably determined by genetics
> or biology) is ephemeral at best; while same-sex attractions may come
> unbidden, homosexual behavior and adoption of a "gay" identity are
> clearly voluntary; the existence of numerous "former homosexuals"
> proves that homosexuality is changeable; and the numerous pathologies
> associated with homosexuality demonstrate how harmful it is.[39]

It is clear from reading any piece of literature published by any conservative Christian group that they view the argument that homosexuality is a choice, not biological, as the linchpin in dismantling the GSA movement. It is interesting to consider how much the GSA movement's successes have actually hinged on an argument of "in-born" identity. Evidence that their success is not solely conditioned on this argument can be found in the religious right's other strategy for discounting LGBT people's claims of being a legitimate minority group.

The second attack on gay-rights claims for minority status and civil rights has been to dismantle the validity of any minority group's claim to civil rights. Patton (1995) argues that, since the early 1980s, the religious right has been working to discursively change the meaning of civil rights in such a way as to make identity- and minority-group claims invalid grounds upon which to be granted civil rights. The religious right argues that "true" civil rights are meant for groups who, regardless of their race or ethnicity, prove their loyalty and good citizenship through assimilating into "American culture" and upholding "American values." Patton argues that, for the religious right:

> The 1960s was rewritten not as a high point for the civil rights movement but as a drift away from the "original" (post-American Revolution) civil rights ... the new right quietly sought to destroy the grounds for making remedies to those who faced systematic oppression. "Civil rights" ceased to mean the inclusion of groups excluded by an evolving hegemony and became instead the erasure of the marks of difference through which those exclusions had been publicized."[40]

From this perspective, if groups are facing discrimination or oppression it is a result of their lack of effort or ability to prove themselves good citizens, and not an effect of their race, ethnicity, or sexual orientation. There is room in this perspective of the religious right to accept that sexual orientation is a condition with which individuals are born; however, it is not a basis for claims of discrimination or civil rights. From this vantage point on the meaning of civil rights, LGBT people are not deserving of "the extension of 'special privileges'" because they are "viewed as having disavowed the Christian, family lifestyle, which was the condition for those deserving the benefits of the social contract."[41]

While most LGBT social movement organizations seek to portray their objectives as civil rights issues, their opponents frame them as moral issues

and frequently cite biblical literature and its prohibitions against homosexuality.[42] This is in sharp contrast to identity- and civil-rights politics,
where groups must first prove they are a valid minority group. To do this
they must provide evidence or arguments to counter the heavily ingrained
social, cultural, and religious beliefs that homosexuality is abnormal, deviant, or immoral. The Christian right's strategy of morality politics uses the
power of these beliefs, not empirical evidence, to win support for its perspective on LGBT issues.

OPPOSING FRAMES ABOUT THE RESOLUTION OF THE ISSUE

After making framed arguments, in an effort to collectively define LGBT
students as a true minority group with a collective identity and a common
set of experiences, the GSA movement is able to more effectively use the
symbolism and ideology of equality in America's pluralistic democracy. The
language of democracy and the symbolism of America as a rich and diverse
mix of cultures are conjured up in their most idealistic terms for the purpose of legitimizing the rights of these students within the system of public
education. The general articulation of this frame is to state that, if public
education is meant to uphold and ensure the democratic values of American
society, then public schools have a responsibility to provide and guaran-
tee the equal treatment of all students, including LGBT students. Kevin
Jennings offers an excellent example of this type of frame alignment:

> Our program calls upon people to overcome their stereotypes, to leave
> behind old ways of thinking, and to embrace a new way of relating—one
> that is, in the end, healthier, happier, and more in line with American val-
> ues of justice, equality, and fairness. ... Why am I so confident? Because
> I went to public school in this country, schools where each day I pledged
> allegiance to a flag which, I was taught, stood for "liberty and justice for
> all." Homophobia is un-American; it violates the pledge we've all said
> since we were little kids in elementary school. ... I can't imagine a better
> lesson for any educator—gay, lesbian, or straight—to teach.[43]

This statement makes the concepts and imagery of the ideals of American
democratic foundations vivid for the reader, connects these values to the
goals and purpose of public education, and personalizes the issue to the

common experiences of every American citizen who attended public school. Framing the issue in terms of a violation of American values and associating the solution to the problem with the fulfillment of these ideals is used in groups' tag lines: GLSEN, "teaching respect for all"; and Project 10, "with liberty and justice for all."

In his study of the history of the religious right, William Martin found that, "One of the aspects of culture that deeply troubles most pro-family activists is an increasingly widespread view of homosexuality as normal, and even more galling, of homosexuals as people entitled to special protection against discrimination."[44] In interviews with leaders of religious right groups, Martin draws out the connection between the religious right's stand on homosexuality, civil rights, and inclusions of LGBT topics in public education. The following statement from an interview with Gary Bauer, the former president of the Family Research Council, is an example of the discursive linkage of these issues:

> We have devoted a great deal of time and energy to the gay-rights issue because we see this issue as saying a great deal about the country and how we think about liberty and virtue. Most Americans believe in "Live and let live. What your neighbor does behind closed doors is his business." But when the gay-rights agenda goes into the public square and says "We want the right to teach children in school that homosexuality is no better or worse than heterosexuality," or "We want to be included in civil-rights laws," so that we will have to consider sexual orientation as much as we do now race and gender, then we think it's imperative to counter that agenda.[45]

To more fully assert the need for Americans to oppose the inclusions of LGBT topics in public education, conservative Christians have developed a frame alignment strategy that removes the issue from the realm of civil right identity politics and places it firmly in the context of morality politics.

The religious rights' use of the symbolism of American traditions and ideology to legitimate its claims is, arguably, more difficult to support than that used by the GSA movement. These groups are in the precarious position of arguing that including and tolerating this group of students is un-American. Although they make repeated claims to the immorality of homosexuality—according to religious morality, which is equated with

American morality—conservative Christians generally avoid references to democracy and equality in their frame alignments on this topic. When these issues are raised, it is only to summarily dismiss homosexuality as a topic that warrants considerations for such rights. (The GSA movement, of course, does the same thing when people bring up the issue of morality in debates over this issue.) This is illustrated in the Family Research Council's position statement on "the homosexual agenda in public education":

> FRC believes that homosexuality is unhealthy, immoral and destructive to individuals, families and societies. FRC opposes any attempts to equate homosexuality with civil rights or to compare it to benign characteristics such as skin color or place of origin. The Family Research Council opposes sex education programs that treat homosexuality and heterosexuality as equally desirable, that teach any sexual behavior between consenting people is a human right, and that idealize homosexuality and the homosexual lifestyle.[45]

Groups like the Family Research Council believe that homosexuality is clearly outside of consideration in discussions of civil rights and equality in America. Their frame loses its power outside the realm of morality politics, and it is, therefore, in their interest to avoid a discussion of the issue in terms of civil rights. In much the same way, it is in the interest of the GSA movement to frame the issue away from one of morality politics in which their position has little resonance.

The time, energy, and thought put into these framing strategies is wasted if they are unable to influence the outcome of battles over GSAs and the rights of LGBT students. To have such an impact, the frames need to be heard and, once heard, they must resonate with the public. The next chapter examines newspaper coverage of GSA and LGBT student rights to see how effective each side has been at getting its discourse out into the public and how well its message is received.

SIX

MAKING HEADLINES
Media Coverage of the Debates over GSAs

The main objective of all of the frame alignment strategies developed by social movements and oppositional movements is to use them to sway the opinions of those who make decisions about institutional policies and practices. To do this, movements must get their frames heard and deemed legitimate by "experts" and the general public, who have the power to influence these decision makers. Although some of the tactics implemented by movements are direct (i.e., direct mailings, workshops, lobbying), one of the most expedient tools that movements can use is the mass media. A movement getting the media to cover the issues surrounding its group in the ways that it wants them framed can accelerate its efforts. Both the GSA movement and religious conservative groups who oppose them have worked to get their interpretations of the problems faced by LGBT students and the purpose of gay–straight alliance clubs covered by newspapers across the country. How well they succeed at influencing this news coverage impacts their ability to reach their goals—to make it easier or more difficult for students to establish GSAs or change school policy—by influencing expert and public opinion.

Overall, the newspaper coverage of LGBT school-related issues from 1984 through 2004 was fairly balanced. The majority of articles included a discussion of the positions of those advocating for LGBT students and those opposed to schools addressing their needs. Most articles also included quotes from interviews with people on both sides expressing their opinion in their own words. When I broke the news coverage down into categories—

feature stories, news items, editorials, and letters to the editor—I found that
the coverage was less balanced within categories. Reports of a current news
item—local controversy, lawsuit, school board meeting, etc.—and letters
to the editor about a current event tend to be very balanced in covering
both sides of the argument. However, the featured stories and editorials
by newspaper staff were largely sympathetic to the struggles of LGBT
students or supportive of their rights. This trend became stronger over
the years. As lawsuits decided in favor of LGBT student rights established
rather strong precedents, and as more research was done documenting rates
of harassment and suicide, editors seemed to take this as a solid base of
evidence from which to assert support for GSAs. For example, the following excerpts were taken from an op-ed piece in the Washington Post. The
piece was written in response to right-wing talk-radio personality Laura
Schlessinger's homophobic commentary directed at LGBT students and
schools with GSAs, and in support of the protest against her:

> Led by the San Francisco-based Horizons Foundation, more than
> 180 organizations and individuals, including some of the country's most
> prominent scholars, psychiatrists, pediatricians, rabbis and ministers,
> have written Schlessinger a letter expressing concern that her statements
> are contributing to fear and hatred of gay people. "We are especially
> concerned that your commentaries are teaching otherwise happy and
> healthy young people to hate themselves," they write. … But the harsh
> reality of the situation is that she spews venom about homosexuals that
> would have knocked a radio personality off the air in five minutes if he
> had applied it to African Americans. Imagine what would happen if one
> of the shock jocks declared that being black was a "biological error."
> He wouldn't even get the Greaseman's shot at resurrecting his career
> on a 6,000-watt station in the Virgin Islands. Sadly, homophobia has
> not risen to the level of racism and sexism in our cultural taboos. And
> as it is with any group that is "different," it is the children who suffer
> the most."

The article goes on to cite research studies done by the Massachusetts
Department of Education and the Harvard School of Public Health, which
document the high rates of harassment, abuse, and suicide for LGBT youth.
The editorial then states:

While gay bashing is flourishing, it is a tribute to the tolerance and good sense of many youngsters that some 600 [in the year 2000] gay–straight alliance clubs have sprung up in high schools and middle schools throughout the country, according to the Gay, Lesbian, and Straight Education Network. Some schools have encouraged them, understanding the value of support groups for gay students and the children of gay parents, and the value of those clubs in teaching tolerance. But predictably, in Orange County, Calif., the school district is trying to ban such a club.[1]

The strength of support offered in this op-ed piece is clearly bolstered by the fact that its author feels confident that the experts and the weight of the evidence back her position. The important significance of the research on LGBT youth and support for GSAs by educational and health experts and the law is discussed in more detail throughout the chapter.

Another pattern that emerged from my analysis of newspaper articles is that, over the years, as conflicts over GSAs became fewer and generally less heated and drawn out, featured stories became less about local conflict or moral controversy and more often about the activities and accomplishments of LGBTS students. Since the late 1990s, there have been more frequent featured stories about the political activism of these students—their work on getting anti-harassment policies passed, their efforts to educate their schools about homophobia and discrimination through a school activity such as the "Day of Silence"[2]—and more stories about their courage in facing harassment, overcoming depression, or coming out to their family and peers. The following example comes from a featured article that appeared in the *Los Angeles Times* on August 3, 2004:

The clubs are formed and run by students (though they have an adult advisor) and are endorsed by the American Civil Liberties Union and can be found in more than 2,000 middle and high schools across the country. In 1998, California had 40 of them. Today, the state has 422, with a membership of more than 6,000 students. ... At a retreat center in Pacific Palisades, about 25 kids from more than 20 Southland high schools recently plotted, networked and drank punch at the fourth annual Southern California Gay–Straight Alliance Activist Camp. Adult representatives from the network attended but stayed out of the way; it was clearly the teenagers' show.[3]

In these accounts, LGBT youth are generally still presented as going through developmental issues, being a group "at risk," and being victims of ill treatment. This same article began with several students talking about the problems they suffered and included these quotes from students: "I hated myself; I was trying to find something to live for." "It was pretty bad. I'd walk down the hall and people would shout 'faggot' or 'dyke' every day, everywhere I went. ... I felt like a prisoner." Unlike earlier accounts, this is not the end of the story. It is, instead, the premise from which to understand the magnitude of their bravery and accomplishments.

The more objectively balanced coverage of news items and the editorial efforts to provide a forum for both those who favor and those who oppose LGBT school groups have increasingly tended to reflect a more positive supportive view of LGBT students and GSAs. Some would argue that this is a result of the "liberal bias" of the news media. My own analysis is that it is largely a result of both the imbalance between the strength of each side's argument (framing of their position) and the strength of the evidence supporting each side. Even the most balanced news coverage indirectly exposes the weaknesses and the bigotry of oppositional arguments, and the rationality, fairness, and evidenced reasoning of those supporting the rights of LGBT students. This is revealed, not through biased media coverage, but through the very words used by those on each side of the debate. Media representation of social issues is an important marker of social movement success—for both movements and counter movements—and also an important avenue for influencing public opinion and, hopefully, winning support.

SOCIAL MOVEMENTS, THE MEDIA, AND PUBLIC OPINION

The relationship among social movements, the media, and public opinion is complex. Social movements are always interested in influencing public opinion about issues concerning their groups—to win support for their cause, recruit new movement participants, solicit donations, etc. However, they are never in full, or even primary, control over how the issues that concern them are delivered to and received by the public. Two other major factors in determining public sentiment are experts (or elites) and the mass media. Of course, the wild card in all of this is always the individual psychology of members of the public. Predicting how the public will interpret and react to a social movement, messages from experts, and the media is far from an exact science, but there are patterns.

The "politics of knowledge" has always been central to the lesbian and gay rights movement.[4] Lesbian and gay social movement organizations have continually battled medical experts, religious leaders, politicians, and the media over accurate information about, and descriptions of, LGBT individuals. As a disenfranchised minority group, they have had, like women and racial and ethnic minority groups, relatively little control over public knowledge, stereotypes, and opinions of their group. The authors of knowledge about them have been experts in the medical field, who, until 1973, defined homosexuals as diseased and mentally ill, and continue to be relied on for the truth about the natural or unnatural origins of homosexuality; religious leaders who claim authority over morality; and powerful media conglomerates, who disseminate the "expert" knowledge of these elites along with a host of cultural stereotypes that deliver insidious meanings of their own. According to elitist or "top down" models of public opinion, "experts" are used by the public as sources of reliable and factual information or "truth claims." Citizens look to social, political, and scientific experts to provide them with interpretations of events and direction for what stance they should take on social issues. This, in turn, influences public opinion.[5]

Sociologist C. Wright Mills[6] argued that public opinion in contemporary American democracy does not arise from actual lived experiences and debated perspectives of the citizenry—although he felt strongly that, in a true democracy, it should. Instead, public opinion derives from that of the politicians, institutional leaders, scientists, and academics who have claimed positions as elites. He contended that, over time, the general public has been made "psychologically illiterate" by their dependency on these groups to tell them what is true, how to understand the word, and what they should think and feel about it. He used this term "psychologically illiterate" to assert that the general public did not have the capacity to understand events or even know how to feel about them on their own. This illiteracy, according to Mills, resulted from a culture that teaches its members to rely on experts to tell them the truth and what the right opinion is, rather than emphasizing the critical thinking skills that would make them active citizens. Mills asserted that the influence experts and elites had over public opinion was assisted and amplified by the proliferation of mass media, which allows them to uniformly and repeatedly dictate their views on issues to the masses. In Mills' analysis, this is an entirely top down imposition of opinion—the elite/experts form their understandings, which serve their own interests, and then work to manipulate the public into agreeing with their perspective.

Although this top-down model does capture important dynamics in the shaping of public opinion, it omits the fact that "experts themselves may be susceptible to influence by the social actors about whom they are supposed to be experts."[7] This is where social movements come in. They target experts and the media in attempts to influence the knowledge claims and cultural images that shape public opinion, and the policies, laws, and cultural practices that fashion their lives. The impact of social movements' efforts to change public opinion is difficult to determine succinctly, because such change is also conditioned by demographic, cultural, and ideological changes. However, there is general agreement among contemporary sociologists and political scientists who study public opinion that social movements can have a significant impact. Prominent social movement researcher William Gamson examined the research done on the media's influence on public understanding and opinion, and came to two broad conclusions. First, that "the media generally operate in ways that promote apathy, cynicism, and quiescence, rather than active citizenship and participation."[8] Second, that "the undetermined nature of media discourse allows plenty of room for challengers such as social movements to offer competing constructions of reality and to find support for them from readers whose daily lives may lead them to construct meaning in ways that go beyond media imagery."[9] This first finding supports Mills' top-down theory, but the second is more hopeful. Although there is big corporate ownership and control over most of the major media outlets, and these are often used as Mills' suggested, there is still some room for expressions of diversity. There is also room left for reconstructing, at least partially, the "expert view" of social issues that is carried by the media.

It is within this contested space that social movements hope to win influence. All social movements target experts in an effort to persuade and educate them to formulate opinions favorable to the interests of their group. In the case of the GSA movement, teachers and school administrators have been major targets of groups like GLSEN, Safe Schools Coalition, the ACLU, and others, because they are looked to as the authorities on what is best for students and educational outcomes. Educating these groups, in turn, changes the "media information environment"[10] because the media goes to them for information, facts and expert opinion. By working on educating elites about the issues and concerns that affect their group, social movements influence public opinion and political debate through a process of "conceptual revision."[11] This process refers to one in which social movements work to redefine deeply entrenched and longstanding understandings of their group.[12] This influence is important because opinion changes often, but not always, translate into shifts in behavior and alterations in political decision making.[13] Social and political theorists and researchers have offered analyses of the complex dynamics of the multifactored effects on public opinion.[14]

PATTERNS AND SHIFTS IN PUBLIC OPINION ABOUT HOMOSEXUALITY: A PREDICTOR OF PUBLIC REACTION TO GSAs

Research specifically aimed at surveying the general public's opinions about homosexuality and the rights of gay and lesbian people[15] consistently shows that there has been change in public opinion, but the change is split on two issues—morality and civil liberties.[16] Multiple studies have found that Americans distinguish between the morality of the sexual behavior of homosexuality and the civil liberties of gay and lesbian individuals.[17] Americans' opinions became increasingly negative regarding the morality of homosexuality from 1973 through 1990, but since then, their attitudes have become increasingly favorable. However, slightly more than fifty percent still feel that homosexual behavior is morally wrong.[18] Interestingly, over the same time period, there was a steady decline in Americans' willingness to restrict the civil liberties of gay and lesbian people.[19]

Public opinion research indicates that, over time, Americans have generally become increasingly liberal about civil rights, particularly with regards to women and African Americans, and there is evidence that this opinion is slowly expanding to gay and lesbian people.[20] Social scientists have presented various theories to analyze and explain these changes in the public's attitudes, including changes in American demographics, particularly increasing educational levels; changing cultural ideologies (primarily becoming more liberal or conservative regarding sexuality in general); and the efforts of the gay rights movement to legitimize LGBT people as an unjustly treated minority group.

Research on public opinion about homosexuality generally concludes that older, less educated people, African Americans, people living in the South or Midwest, males, people residing in small communities, and religious fundamentalists are more negative towards homosexuality than are younger, more educated people, whites, those living on the Pacific Coast, females, residents of big cities or big suburbs, and religious liberals.[21] If we look only at demographic indicators, population shifts since the 1970s do indicate that there would be both positive and negative attitude changes. An increase in college graduates, a rise in the number of people living in cities and suburbs, a decline in the numbers of people living in the Midwest, an increase in the population on the West Coast, and a decrease in the number of fundamentalist Protestants from the mid 1980s through the late 1990s would influence opinion changes in a more favorable direction. On the other hand, the aging of the population, slight decreases in white and female populations, and an increase in the population of the South are all indicators of negative shifts in opinion. Social researchers generally conclude that demographic changes counteract each other in terms of their effect on opinions held by the entire population.[22] Since these demographic shifts cannot account for the national trends in public opinion, what other factors might account for both the change in attitudes and the division in opinion over homosexual behavior and civil rights?

A 2001 research study of this pattern of public opinion offers this analysis:

> Two possibilities help explain this distinction. First, the morality question of the GSS [General Social Survey][23] concerns homosexuality as a practice, while the "civil liberties" questions concern gays and lesbians as a group. Thus, the morality question focuses directly on homosexual behavior, particularly sexual behavior, while the civil liberties questions focus on issues on minority group status. The morality group question may be picking up Americans' puritanical attitudes concerning sexuality in particular, while the civil liberties questions do not call up these puritanical attitudes.[24]

This analysis indicates that the framing strategies of both lesbian and gay rights and religious right organizations, discussed in Chapter five, have been somewhat successful.

The efforts of gay rights groups to frame issues of homosexuality as matters of civil rights for a minority group appear to have been partially, if not largely, responsible for the increase in public support for the civil liberties of gay and lesbian people. However, the framing strategy of the religious right to perpetuate a religious view of homosexuality as an issue of deviant and sinful sexuality has also been rather successful at maintaining the public's opinion that homosexuality is "always wrong." Although each side feels that these are contradictory opinions for one individual to hold, apparently a significant portion of the population does believe that homosexual behavior is immoral and yet gay individuals deserve civil rights. It illustrates that, even though each group focused energies where they are in fact most effective, both will have to work to improve their frames if the goal is to win full support for their positions. In other words, if the goals of the GSA movement include not only legal rights and protections for students but also social cultural acceptance, which would decrease the stigma and homophobia that fuels the harassment in the first place, they will have to confront the issue of morality more directly. If the goals of conservative Christian groups include not only maintaining and strengthening the ideology that homosexuality is immoral but also persuading school officials, judges, and the public that LGBT students should be denied civil liberties, they will have to address the issue of civil rights more concretely.

Another frequently offered theory to explain the public opinion divide over morality and civil rights emphasizes the impact that people's belief about the cause of homosexuality has on their attitude about behavior and civil rights. Discussions of morality tend to involve a debate about the choice of homosexual behavior and identity. Opinion research has found that those who believe homosexual behavior is a personal choice are more likely to view it as immoral and not a group basis for civil rights protections than do those who believe that homosexuality has a genetic cause.[25] This analysis helps to explain why each side spends so much time and energy framing the issues, as described in Chapter 5. Both sides understand these opinion polls and try to work them to their advantage—using the media to carry their message, and trying to persuade experts and elites of the truth as they see it. The GSA movement can claim some measure of success when newspapers carry stories that discuss the injuries done to students through institutional denials of rights and protections. The opposition can claim a similar measure of success every time newspapers run stories that include discussion of the potential dangers or moral objections to GSAs.

THE INFLUENCE OF OPPOSING MOVEMENTS ON MEDIA FRAMING OF STORIES

Social scientists generally agree that the media frames the news in ways that significantly shape the public's knowledge about and opinion of issues, events, and groups of people. However, this is not simply a one-way imposition of opinion.[26]

Social movement organizations work to exploit this vulnerability by trying to get their understandings of issues and events into the media and out to the public. In doing this, they hope to influence the public to "decode" the news in ways that are informative about their group's expert perspective and favorable to the interests of their group. Making an impact on how the media frames stories related to their interests is one way in which social movements measure their progress.[27] In this sense, once a social movement has developed a framing strategy it feels is most effective and gathered supporting evidence for it, the focus becomes getting it out to the public as often as they can. Social movements, at that point, must have faith in the strength of their argument—knowing that, once they put it out there, they cannot ensure that every individual will react to it the way they would like, but having confidence that the majority will react positively. However, public opinion polls can indicate to social movement organizations how the public will respond to their arguments if they frame them in relation to larger cultural values and beliefs.

A critical factor in getting the media to pay attention to a group's perspective is to establish the organization as an "expert" on the issues. Yang (2001) has argued that "the expansion of exactly who is an expert on a particular area of social and political life is reflected in the battles of lesbian and gay activists to become their own experts on questions of homosexuality."[28] My analysis of the newspaper coverage of issues related to LGBT students shows that GLSEN and the ACLU have successfully positioned themselves as experts. National and local news coverage often identify them as leaders in the field, citing their position, their research, and the legal cases they have won. The fact that GLSEN initially consisted primarily of teachers and other educational professionals helped convince the media that they could speak as experts on this topic, and their early work helping to start the successful Massachusetts Safe Schools Program enhanced their credibility. The ACLU's long-established expertise on First Amendment rights gave them almost instant status as experts on the rights of GSAs, and their early victory in the Salt Lake City case solidified this position. Other groups, such as Project 10, Safe Schools Coalition, and the GSA Network, have also been rather successful at establishing themselves as expert resources of information, at least in their home states and regional.

Despite these successes, organizations that make up the GSA movement have continued to have to compete with others who have also been positioned as legitimate pundits on the subject matter. The nature of LGBT issues makes it more difficult for gay and lesbian groups to establish themselves as the main source of knowledge:

> When one considers the whole range of issues of concern to lesbians and
> gays, questions of expertise become more complicated, in part because
> issues that can be intelligibly framed as matters of rightness or wrong-
> ness, health and sickness, equality, respect for difference, and civil
> rights, for example, invite a plurality of possible "credible experts."[29]

As the research on public opinion indicates, the fact that the issue of homosexuality has long been framed as an issue of both morality and civil rights gives both gay rights groups and religious groups a position of expertise on homosexuality. When issues of adolescent development, education, free speech, student rights, etc. are added to the mix, a whole host of groups assert that they have a legitimate position from which to claim expertise. Parents, community members, psychologists, lawyers, students, and educators can all voice their opinion, claiming that they have some degree of expertise on GSAs in schools. They can frame their opinion as experts about their own children, about the academic needs of students, about developmental concerns, about religious morals and the values of their community, etc. An analysis of the newspaper coverage on this subject from 1984 to 2004 makes it clear that, although those involved in the GSA movement have had some success in establishing themselves as experts, many other groups and individuals who oppose them are also often given expert status by the press.

WHAT MAKES THE NEWS: SIGNS OF WHO IS WINNING
THE BATTLE FOR EXPERT AND PUBLIC OPINION

The argument against GSAs that is most frequently cited in news articles about a local controversy is that they are part of a larger "gay agenda" to change American cultural values and social institutions. Newspapers give a good amount of coverage to this frame and usually give some of those who hold this view an opportunity to explain it in their own words. The use of the gay agenda frame has been consistent over time, but it has increased in its intensity and detail. As the following excerpt from a 1988 news report illustrates, this argument has been used since the start of Project 10:

> Nearly one hundred friends and foes of Project 10 aired their views Thursday on the Los Angeles Unified School District's controversial counseling program for gay and lesbian students at the district's downtown headquarters. Speakers at the public forum, which erupted from time to time with boos and cheers, included Project founder and director Virginia Uribe, a teacher at Fairfax High School, and a representative of the Roman Catholic Archdiocese of Los Angeles, who read a statement from Archbishop Roger Mahoney condemning the program as "a camouflaged method to legitimize homosexuality" and an example of "blatant social engineering" on the part of the school board."[30]

Although the phrase "gay agenda" is not directly used in the Archbishop's statement, the warning about it is clear. As time goes by, the assertion that there are larger forces at work and larger issues at stake orchestrated by homosexuals becomes increasingly direct.

For example, a 1998 news story from St. Petersburg, Florida about a heated local battle over a GSA reported:

> The school board has had to respond to outcries of opposition to the group that have been perpetuated by David Caton, a Hillsborough County resident who is president of the Florida Family Association. Caton and his group launched a letter-writing campaign last month to oppose GSA. School board members were deluged with postcards and letters that protested against the district using federal and local money to "fund a pro-homosexual organization" the letters and postcards said.[31]

Reports such as this state that GSAs are more than just another student group, rather they are part of a larger movement to promote the idea that homosexuality is normal and/or positive. Based on an analysis of this gay agenda argument in newspaper stories over the years, it is clear the long-range strategy is to make the charge more detailed and more frightening so that it will capture the attention of readers. The successes of GSAs throughout the country have made the issue more of a pressing concern over time. For example, in a 2000 *USA Today* story about a court ruling in favor of a California GSA, the opposition was presented in this way:

> Protesters shouting anti-gay slogans and carrying placards blasted the
> ruling. A woman who refused to give her name taunted lawyers and the
> gay students' parents, calling them 'puppets of propaganda.' This judge
> is allowing high-powered homosexual attorneys to come into a school
> district and trample the rights of parents and school board members.[32]

Part of the articulation of this frame often is to exclaim the power of homosexual leaders and activists and the influence they have over the decisions of political and cultural elites. Claiming the success of your opponent to win support for your cause is an unusual strategy, but it is an effective way to mobilize those who agree with you to take action to stave off an imminent threat.

A *USA Today* story about the same case, which appeared earlier that year, offered an even more detailed description of the threat of the gay agenda:

> Opponents carried "Grades not AIDS" signs and quoted scripture to
> argue that homosexuality was morally wrong. Parents said they feared
> that their children would be "converted" to homosexuality. They
> attacked the club's organizer, sophomore Anthony Colin, 15, and said
> he was nothing more than a puppet of national gay organizations that
> were trying to force their political agenda on schools across America.
> School board member Bill Lewis was quoted as saying, "The bible says
> we're all sinners, but this in my opinion is asking us to legitimize sin."...
> Campaign for California Families, a parents' rights group, lent its support. Executive Director Randy Thomasson says, "These homosexual
> clubs will be putting other children under their influence, and it goes
> against what parents want." Thomasson calls Colin "very much a rebel.

This child is not interested in learning. He's simply interested in promoting himself and tearing the school upside down."[33]

These statements illustrate that religious right organizations have been
rather successful at getting media coverage for their morality framing strategy and that larger organizations have been successful at communicating
this strategy to local activist groups, school board members, and parents
who are capable of effectively articulating it to the public and the press.
This is important in spreading the impact of the opposition and, at the same
time, giving it the added legitimacy of local authority. These statements also
strive to de-legitimize student leadership and activism by framing them as
puppets, which suggests that they are merely children who are incapable of
making their own informed decisions. These attacks on the political (or any
other) agency of LGBT students are amplified by parallel statements about
parental rights.

A 2003 story in the *Washington Post*, centered on a local conflict over a
GSA outside of Austin, Texas, put the conflict in a national context:

> In some conservative school districts, school officials and their allies
> continue to resist the efforts of gay students to form organizations,
> saying they violate their communities' values and that discussions of
> homosexuality don't belong on school campuses or among impressionable
> teenagers. Gay rights organizations are "trying to, anywhere they can, come
> out and set their agenda," said Judy Strickland, a Panhandle representative
> for the Texas Eagle Forum, a conservative pro-family organization, and
> a former member of the Texas Board of Education. "The whole society
> is going down because they're trying to make this an acceptable, normal
> lifestyle. And I personally think it should be fought to the nth degree."
> Against the backdrop of that debate, gay students such as Caudillo have
> become lightning rods for controversy in some communities.[34]

As the number of GSAs has risen nationally, the warnings about the gay
agenda have become even more prominent, and the urgency to stop it
more intense. Religious conservatives have continued their success at influencing media framing, as newspapers have continued to make "the gay
agenda" the newsworthy story about as often as a GSA itself is the subject
of the article.

A 2004 article about a controversy over a proposed GSA in New Orleans reported:

> Though the club's intentions sound noble, some parents said they
> worry that the goal is to advance a national homosexual agenda. "They
> accomplish this by gaining a foothold on our nation's schools through
> the establishment of student-led clubs to propagandize legitimacy for the
> homosexual lifestyle," said Scott Lester, one of four parents who spoke
> at Tuesday's meeting.[35]

In this framing of the story, the reader is urged to view this local debate as part of a national phenomenon. The implication is that the outcome will affect both the local community and, more importantly, the nation, by either strengthening or weakening the tide of the gay agenda. As a result, the story takes attention away from the problems faced by LGBT students and the rights guaranteed to them by law. Therefore, the opposition succeeds in its efforts to make this a story about morality rather than civil liberties.

In addition to the warnings about the gay agenda, there are several other common elements in news accounts of the opposition to GSAs. The most common and pronounced of these are morality/values/religion, the vulnerability of minors, and deviant sexual behavior. As was discussed before, the results of twenty-five years of tracking public opinion on homosexuality show a strong and relatively stable trend indicating that the majority of the general public believes that homosexuality is morally "always wrong," a view that focuses primarily on sexual behavior. In opposing GSAs on the national and local level, groups and individuals play to this negative public attitude and its underlying premise that homosexuality is a chosen sexual behavioral deviance. These connections are called up in news stories and letters to the editor often by declaring that GSAs are "sex clubs" that encourage sexual experimentation.

This line of argument was prominently featured in a series of articles reporting the conflict over students' proposal for a GSA at a high school in Lubbock, Texas:

> "I would have denied other clubs whose basis was sex," Jack Clemmons,
> who was the school superintendent in Lubbock at the time, said in
> an affidavit filed in connection with the case. "I would have denied

a Bestiality club. I would have denied a Gigolo Club. I would have denied a Prostitute club. Likewise I would deny any club that has as its basis an illegal act, such as the Marijuana Club, Kids for cocaine, the Drinking Club, etc." ... Lawyers for the school district argue that the Equal Access Act permits schools to override students' free speech rights and forbids clubs if they jeopardize students' well-being. In support of that argument, they cite a little-known section of the Texas Penal code that prohibits gay activity between youths younger than 17. Allowing a Gay–Straight Alliance amounts to giving students license to break the law, said Ann Manning, an attorney for the school district. Because the club's "basis is sex," Manning said, it would also violate the school district's strict policy of promoting abstinence.[36]

Although this is a very strong statement of opposition, and one sure to catch the attention of the reader, its strength is founded not in any truth or evidence, but rather solely on stereotypes and unfounded fear. The entire premise of the opposition rests on the supposed fact that GSAs are clubs established for the discussion and encouragement of sexual behavior. This purposeful misstatement of fact reduces LGBT people to completely sexual beings—assuming that, unlike heterosexuals, the pursuit of sex is their only focus and goal. The absurdity of this statement, not to mention the lack of empirical evidence to support it, is lost on many readers to whom cultural stereotypes, religious doctrine, and media images are the only basis of understanding they have about LGBT people. This is the potential power media has on public opinion that the opposition hopes to tap into by getting their interpretation of events into print as often as possible.

The section of the Texas Penal Code and the district's policy on abstinence-only sex education are facts, but they are completely irrelevant as reasons to oppose a gay–straight alliance club whose actual purpose is to discuss prejudice and discrimination experienced by LGBT people and educate the school in hopes of making it a more tolerant place. The effort to oppose this GSA in Lubbock is a perfect example of how the master strategy of conservatives to perpetuate negative public opinion of homosexuality—by fostering negative sexual stereotypes to emphasize issues of morality and deemphasize any consideration of rights—specifically plays out in debates over GSAs. The strategy works by distracting the public from the stated purpose of the GSA and the legal rights of students by using stereotypes and myths to stir up fear in parents and the community.

The power of this general strategy, which is used in every arena where conservatives oppose gay rights, is amplified in the school arena because the debates involve children. Added to the fear of the deviant sexual behavior of homosexuals is the fear of any issue involving sexuality and minors. This is illustrated in the reporting of a story about a controversial GSA in Louisiana:

> Some parents of Fountainebleau students say talk at meetings probably will veer toward sex, which could cause liability problems for the school system. They said a parent could sue the system if a student who had been questioning his or her sexuality joined the club and then adopted a gay or lesbian lifestyle. They say they also are concerned about the possibility of students contracting sexually transmitted diseases in a gay relationship. They said they worry that straight students could be recruited into a gay or lesbian lifestyle by the club. "I would not want to have an impressionable teenager who is confused about sexual issues be exploited or influenced by a homosexual advocacy group," said Lennie Ditoro, the mother of a Fountainebleau student, at a recent board meeting."[37]

The impressionability of children is used again and again to call up the image that they are viewed by gay rights activists as easy prey, not only to use as puppets to carry out their political agenda, but also to exploit sexually. If they believe these claims, nothing could incite more fear in parents. Another prime example of this framing of the story appeared in a 2003 newspaper article about a GSA in Texas:

> Opponents of such groups say it is inappropriate for schools to promote gay rights and fear the clubs will turn into dating services where kids will talk about sex and seek partners. "Their behavior is risky behavior that results in disease and death," said Kathy Haiger of Houston, executive director of the Texas Eagle Forum, a conservative pro-family organization. "We would be against a high school allowing them to meet together. It'd be like having a smoking club or a drinking club. It's unhealthy behavior. Why would the schools want to promote minors having sexual discussions with each other?"[38]

Interestingly, in this story, as in many others like it, the real issue—the rights of LGBTS students to form a club that discusses and educates about gay rights—is mentioned, but the focus is shifted to elaborate on the gay agenda and sexual behavior.

Local spokespersons have become convinced of the unhealthy and diseased nature of LGBT individuals, not only through strong, long-standing and perpetuated stereotypes, but also through information produced by religious right organizations. On just about every conservative Christian organization's website, there are links to "research studies" that claim to prove that AIDS is a gay disease, that there are higher rates of a plethora of diseases (sexually transmitted and others) among homosexuals, that gay men die at a dramatically younger age than average, and other negative consequences associated with homosexuality. Although the press rarely reports these findings, because they do not meet any of the standards of verified scientific research, some of them occasionally get mentioned. The following excerpt is from an opinion piece objecting to a GSA at Fountain Valley High School that was published in *The Los Angeles Times* in 1994:

> It is a preposterous concept that a school is condoning a chosen life-
> style that is extremely dangerous. Based on a study of obituaries in
> 17 homosexual publications by the Family Research Institute, Inc. of
> Washington, D.C., the median age of death for a homosexual is the
> early 40s. According to information gathered by the Oregon Citizen
> Alliance, a group opposed to minority status based on homosexuality,
> male homosexuals experience a higher rate of disease than the general
> population. It reports that homosexual males are 14 times more apt to
> experience syphilis, at a three times greater risk for genital warts ....
> It is a transgression against the moral principles of our country to tell
> the children of our high schools, who are at an impressionable age, that
> homosexuality is a healthy alternative lifestyle.[39]

These "facts" about the rate of diseases of gay men do not come from legitimate scientific sources such as the Centers for Disease Control or the American Medical Association. They are from two conservative Christian organizations' own "research institutes." Perhaps frustrated that the research conducted by legitimate scientific institutions increasingly discounted the perspective that homosexuals were diseased or mentally ill, religious right organizations began to fund and conduct their own research. The weaknesses of this research, even in terms of the most basic principles of the scientific method based on objectivity, representative sampling, and verification, should be obvious even to the lay audience. However, these groups continue to produce this research, espouse their findings, and manage to convince thousands, if not millions, of their followers to accept it as fact. Much of this convincing is done through the organizations' own publications and Internet sites, which provide these groups with an audience that is already predisposed to view them as experts.

Again, this strongly supports the analysis that opponents know about the spilt in public opinion over morality and civil rights and, therefore, work hard to turn a civil liberties issue into a morality issue. It also reveals that opponents rely on the power of the stereotypes and misconceptions about homosexuality rather than any evidence or reasoned argument to support their position. Statements like these not only rely on old stereotypes of gays and lesbians as immoral and mentally ill and the myth of AIDS as a solely gay male disease, but also ignore the mountains of legitimate scientific research about the sexual behavior and rate of sexual disease transmission and pregnancy among heterosexual adolescents. For example, according to research by the American Social Health Association and the Centers for Disease Control, two-thirds of all STDs occur in people 25 years of age or younger; one in four new STD infections occurs in teenagers; 25% of all new HIV cases occur in those under the age of 21; 10% of kids have sex before turning 13; 16% of high school students have had four or more sexual partners; one quarter of all sexually active teenagers will contract an STD; 20% of sexually active girls age 15 to 19 get pregnant each year; girls age 15 to 19 have a higher rate of gonorrhea than any other age group (much of this of the mouth from performing oral sex on teenage boys); and among those age 13–19 with HIV, 61% are female and 39% are males.[40]

Parents, school boards, school administrators, and community members could have many valid concerns about teenage sexual behavior in terms of the risk it poses to students' physical and emotional health and safety, and cost to the public. However, the vast majority of this risky behavior is heterosexual, and teenage girls are more at risk for negative outcomes of sexual behavior with teenage boys than any other group. All of this is, of course, completely unrelated to the existence of a gay–straight alliance school club. These facts are never pointed out in newspaper coverage of these local conflicts over GSAs.

Newspaper stories about local conflicts over GSAs do, of course, present both sides of the debates and, therefore, seek to explain the reason proponents advocate in favor of GSAs. An analysis of how newspaper reporters frame the rationale behind the establishment of a GSA reveals some measure of the successes and failures of the GSA movement to define the issues that impact its group and to establish organizations that serve as legitimate sources of "expert knowledge" for the media and, therefore, for the public. Overall, an analysis of the newspaper coverage of GSAs reveals that they have been very successful in establishing a firm understanding of the harassment and suicide risks faced by LGBT students, and the research on this is generally cited as expertly established fact. Some of this research is done by the organizations themselves, such as the often cited annual GLSEN "School Climate Report," which brings up some of the same questions of objectivity and sampling that are raised about the research conducted by religious right organizations. However, there are important differences, the most significant being that the results of the research conducted by GSA movement organizations are similar to the findings of research conducted by other groups such as the U.S. Department of Health and Human Services, various states' departments of education, the Harvard School of Public Health, etc. Verification of results by these groups gives greater legitimacy to the research of groups like GLSEN. The research conducted by the religious right has not been verified by outside objective scientific sources.

In addition to research on harassment, risk factors, suicide, and educational outcomes, the GSA movement also draws strength for its perspective from the law. Nearly every article about a local conflict over a GSA also cites and discusses the 1984 Equal Access Law and some of the lawsuits that have been won in favor of students using that federal law. In this way, even a news report that attempts to be balanced in presenting both sides of the debate inadvertently comes out tipped in favor of advocates of GSAs based on empirical evidence. In addition to this, many newspaper stories include personal stories of harassment, suicide attempts, or discrimination reported in the words of LGBTS students that add weight and detail to the advocates' side of the story. This imbalance is particularly evident in longer feature stories about a GSA. In my analysis, this is because the more information a reporter gathers to write a longer more detailed piece—to put the issue in social and historical context, to offer as many perspectives as possible, to include valid and reliable related research—the more the weight of the story leans to the side of those advocating for the rights of LGBT students.

Numerous examples of feature stories that appeared in newspapers from across the country since the late 1990s fit the above analysis. One such example is a feature article that appeared in the *Christian Science Monitor* on February 1, 2000. The headline of the feature was, "High Schools' Gay–Straight Clubs Draw Fire," and it offers an overview of the controversies. "Students join to fight antigay harassment, while critics charge that school isn't the place for such groups. The student groups are intended to create an atmosphere of tolerance. Yet in some school districts, gay–straight alliances have unleashed a storm of dissent from those who say such groups have no business in school halls." The article provides a brief history of the idea and the growth of GSAs, then discusses the conflicts surrounding them. "But their rapid spread has not sprung from the support of school boards. Indeed, numerous school districts have been stalwart in their opposition—and willing to fight over the issue in court. Last week, the Orange County, Calif., school board faced a hearing over a challenge to its effort to shut down a GSA."

According to the article, a disagreement about the purpose of the groups was at the heart of these fights. "The clubs exist 'to end the ignorance and the stereotypes,' insists Patricia Boland, chair of the gay, lesbian, and bisexual issues committee of the National Association of School Psychologists in Bethesda, Maryland. But, in the eyes of many parents, the groups are nothing more than recruiting clubs promoting a homosexual lifestyle. 'They are homosexual propagandists and will recruit these kids into the homosexual lifestyle,' says Evelyn Reilly, executive director of the Christian Coalition of Massachusetts.'" The reporter then notes that, regardless of this disagreement over purpose, "The Equal Access Act offers schools few choices with respect to GSAs. They must either ban all extracurricular clubs, renounce all federal funding, or accept the clubs." After citing the landmark Utah case and several others, the reporter states that the legal right of GSAs is clear, but that there is a broader question of whether schools should do more to prevent harassment among students and looks for evidence to address this question—"There is substantial evidence that—despite increased tolerance of homosexuality by U.S. society at large—young people continue to express hostility toward peers tagged as gay ..."—and goes on to discuss Jamie Nabozny and Matthew Shepard as examples.

After presenting these dramatic examples of horror stories, the reporter cites studies by both the Vermont and the Massachusetts boards of education, which report high rates of harassment suffered by LGBT students and the negative impact this has on student academic performance and on the suicide rate. This empirically grounded argument in favor of schools' addressing the concerns of LGBT students is followed by a look at the opposition's perspective:

> But opponents protest that there's no need to single out prejudice against homosexuals to teach kids, "You don't need to get into homo- sexual behaviors to teach tolerance." Reilly says groups like GSAs may replace one kind of danger with another ... Schools fear lawsuits if they don't permit such clubs, Reilly says, but they ought also to fear lawsuits "from parents whose children end up being ... preyed upon by older homosexuals or seduced into a homosexual lifestyle."

There is no evidence or factual basis of any sort offered to ground the position, fears, and danger offered by those who, like Reilly, oppose GSAs, and no testimony by students who claim they have been "preyed upon." So, although the featured story does give recognition to the opposition's position, presenting it in relation to the empirically, legally, and personally supported argument for GSAs exposes its opaqueness. This occurs over and over again in stories on this topic. No legitimate research or evidence is reported for the opposition's position because no such empirical evidence exists. Therefore, all that is ever offered is unfounded accusations about a gay agenda, kids and sex, or immorality grounded in religion.

This imbalance in evidence and rational argumentation is further revealed when analyzing letters to the editors and op-ed pieces. The translation of the framing strategies from social movement organizations to average citizens is also visible. An analysis of letters to the editor provide one indication of the impact that the framing of the issue, both by national organizations on each side and the media, has on public opinion about GSAs. It is fairly common for letters to the editor that point out the prejudice and lack of evidence apparent in the opposition's position to be written after a story about a local conflict over a GSA is published. For example, these excerpts are taken from a 1998 letter entitled "Why Won't Caton's Group Speak Freely?" published in the *Tampa Tribune* in response to a story about a group protesting a GSA in Pinellas, Florida:

> The opponents claim that [the GSA] "misuses taxpayers' money and tramples students' freedom of speech." Excuse me? How does a group

devoted to open dialogue "trample" students' freedom of speech?
The story never mentions exactly how—because, I suspect, the claim is
completely without merit. The "misuse" of taxpayers' dollars refers to
$550 from a federal program that has been used to pay a school counselor
to facilitate the group, which, after 18 months in operation, has been
linked by school officials with a decreased number of attacks on gay
students. ... What bothers me the most about all of this is the dishon-
esty behind the whole ridiculous protest. Why can't Caton and his flock
just say what they mean? Why do they have to hide behind supposed
"freedom of speech" violations and cries of tax money abuse—a blatant
attempt to rouse people who get vocal when they think their pockets
are being picked by the government? How refreshing it would be just to
hear Caton and his supporters step up and say: "The fact of the matter is
that we don't like homosexuals, we won't approve of their lifestyles and
we certainly don't want any group—particularly one involving young
people—teaching tolerance toward these deviants." At least then I could
respect them for being honest even if I despised their narrow-minded
bigotry. But if they approached it that way, they couldn't hide behind
the smoke and mirrors of wasted taxpayer dollars. People might actually
see them for what they are. ... Now I'm sure that the *Tribune* will receive
letters from people defending their stance against homosexuality—
complete with passages from the bible—who maintain they're not bigots.
That homosexuality is wrong because God says so, and they're just
following his lead. And I hope they do write, because that will prove
my point that this isn't about tax dollars or free speech at all; it's about
control. Controlling the way people live their lives.

This letter, boldly pointing out the lack of support for the opposition's
arguments against the GSA and proposing the real sources of objection, was
directly responded to four days later in a letter from David Caton, president
of the Florida Family Association:

> This letter responds to Nicole Ruday's biased attack on Florida Family
> Association's opposition to Pinellas County schools' funding the Gay
> and Straight Alliance. ... I provided the *Tribune* reporter who wrote
> the April 3 article the factual basis of our opposition to GSA. She never
> reported these facts. Ruday's commentary notion that GSA meetings are

"open dialogue" to help students deal with their homosexual temptations is a gross distortion of the facts. Students attending GSA are required to sign a pledge that they will not tell anyone who attended GSA meetings or what was said. Students secretly attend GSA meetings during school hours to turn in the names of straight students whose speech opposes the homosexual lifestyle. Paid school officials approach these straight students to stop them from making any more negative statements regarding homosexuality. Worst of all, students who are struggling with their sexual identity are told by GSA that it is OK to be gay, so proclaim your sexual preference. How many parents want their children to make a sexual preference decision to be homosexual without their knowledge and to have it paid for by their tax dollars? Government reprogramming of our children's minds and morals should concern every parent and taxpayer. It is outrageous that Pinellas County schools are using our tax dollars to "empower gay students" to secretly meet for the purpose of convincing our youth to commit their lives to the immoral and destructive homosexual lifestyle and depriving straight students of their thoughts, their speech, and their morals.

One can only surmise that, if this letter is a reflection of the "facts" that were supposedly not included in the initial story reporting the debate over the GSA, the reason the reporter did not use the information was because the "information" was a complete fabrication. It is interesting that the letter's author claims foul because his facts were left out of the story, but then offers none. It appears that he thinks if he states he is giving facts no one will notice that none actually follow, confident in the impact of his morality frame and that the audience will read the situation the same way he does. These ominous notions of what happens behind the "closed doors" of GSA meetings are common in publications put out on websites and mailings of national religious conservative organizations.

These allegations of recruitment, conversion, and sex talk are always stated as if they are established fact, but no evidence or first-hand account is ever offered to back these fear-inducing assertions. The distortion of which side has the facts is interesting in the Caton letter. He refers to Ruday's statements about the purpose of the GSA to provide an "open dialogue" as a "commentary notion," when, in reality, her assessment is at least based on the actual mission statement of the group, although she did not actually cite it. Even Caton's reporting of what Ruday said is a distortion of what appeared in black and white three days earlier. She simply said the group was devoted to open dialogue, but Caton reported her comments as follows: "Ruday's commentary notion that GSA meetings are 'open dialogue' to help students deal with their homosexual temptations." He then follows this false statement with the accusation that *she* is distorting the facts. There is no evidence supporting Caton's report of the "facts" about what actually happens at GSA meetings. Although it may be true that, to protect their safety, the group's members are asked to make some sort of pledge to keep the names of its members and private information shared at its meeting confidential, the rest of Caton's story is complete fiction. He takes this idea of secrecy and uses it to weave a frightening tale of what is being hidden that is born out of paranoia and supported by stereotypes not evidence. Even though Ruday's letter exposes Caton's false claims of large amounts of tax dollars being spent on the GSA, he continues to complain about taxpayers' money in his response, and fails to acknowledge or refute her numbers with counter evidence about large sums being spent on this group. He seems to rely on the hope that his position in the Florida Family Association will give him some authority as an expert with some readers and that his framing of the GSA will resonate with those that share his fear of the "gay agenda."

Caton's assertion that it is the conservative Christian students who are being harmed by school policy against anti-gay harassment that deprives them of "their thoughts, their speech, and their morals," is intriguing and a few years ahead of its time. It is now a rather common framing strategy for religious right groups to try to counter LGBT student claims of harassment and denial of free speech by making counter claims that students who are punished for homophobic and verbally abusive taunting of LGBT students are being denied the right to free speech. The more detailed version of this argument is that, although LGBT students might find anti-gay statements offensive and insulting, they are not actually harassing statements, but rather the expression of religious beliefs, which is protected by the First Amendment.[41]

First Amendment rights, of course, are always extended only as long as exercising them does not harm, or incite harm, of another person. The fact of the matter is that all of this is specifically irrelevant to the school having a GSA, which serves as a place for students who wish to belong to freely discuss issues of harassment, acceptance, and tolerance. This alone does not prevent anyone's free speech. Again, an analysis of the types of arguments offered in opposition to GSAs reveals that they are overwhelmingly based on false accusations, stereotypes, fear, and the use of very specific conservative Christian doctrine. They are not based on empirical evidence established by scientific research or the law.

Statements about the religious moral base of conservative Christian opposition to GSAs and the rights of LGBT students is presented in almost every newspaper article on the topic, whether it is a short report on a current conflict or a more lengthy feature story on the subject in general. However, nowhere is the religious position on GSAs more strongly stated and debated than in letters to the editors of newspapers. In these letters, because they are free from journalistic standards of fact checking and objectivity, community members are free to make any claims they wish and passionately express their beliefs. Surprisingly, letters in support of GSAs mention religion more frequently than letters in opposition. My analysis of this phenomenon is that letters to the editor are written in response to an article in which opponents' religious-based objections are quoted. This prompts letters from those who support GSAs that argue against the opposition's use of religion to justify their position. In reaction to these letters, opponents then write letters that, generally, do not defend their use of religion, but rather try to offer other objections to GSAs as a way of countering the idea that their opposition is founded only on a limited religious view and trying to appear to have a more objective stance.

This analysis was illustrated by the exchange of the letters cited earlier. Two even stronger examples of letter writers' using religion in their statements of support came in response to a *St. Petersburg Times* report:

> It seems to me that the opposition voiced at a recent Pinellas County
> School Board meeting to the Gay and Straight Alliance at Largo High
> School actually reinforced the need for some sort of organized plan to help
> these young people. It is bad enough when you go through school, and life
> in general, feeling that you are so different as to be evil in some people's
> eyes. The additional fact that fear-filled (as opposed to love-filled) religious
> and other conservatives would find it necessary to organize against you
> would seem to add weight to the validity of supporting students whose
> safety and well-being are so obviously at risk.[42]

A second letter makes the same point even more strongly.

> Re: Your report on the April 28 School Board meeting. I believe you are
> missing the real story, that a noisy faction is seeking to impose its inter-
> pretation of religion on the entire community. I find it grossly offensive
> that people require me to read their Bible, their way. How dare anyone
> prescribe how God is to connect with any of us? I wish the negative
> clergy members who spoke at the School Board meeting would preach
> often that harassing and beating people up is a sin. If they did, we might
> not need a GSA.[43]

The letter writer's rhetorical strategy of using the opponents'
seemingly strongest argument involving religion and morality, and
turning it around against them as a powerful rationale for supporting
LGBT students, is significant for two reasons. First, it is strong and
effective, especially because it is offered by other Christians critiquing a
conservative's assertion of control over the religious and moral judgment
of homosexuality. Second, the arguments made in these letters to the
editor are quite often much stronger defenses against conservative
Christian opposition to GSAs than is ever offered by GLSEN, Project
10, The GSA Network, or any other organization that is part of the GSA
movement. Why this might be the case is a difficult question to answer
precisely. However, based on my interviews with the heads of these
various organizations, it appears that their strategy for dealing with the
moral and religious opposition, generally, is to ignore it. As was discussed
in chapters four and five, all of these groups see religious conservatives
as a major source of opposition to their efforts. However, when I asked
them what they did to try to counter this, most of them reported that
they did little or nothing. All of those I spoke with gave different specific
reasons for this, but the underlying reason was based on an understanding
of the consistency of opinion polls documenting that the majority of the
public still believes homosexual behavior is morally wrong. Given this,
they have decided to focus their efforts where they can have the most
impact, and that is on framing this issue in terms of the civil liberties
of LGBT students (free speech and equal access) and avoiding a direct
debate over religion and morals. The letters to the editor reveal that not
all members of the general public believe homosexuality is morally wrong.

In addition, they do not feel they need to back down from the mention of, or debate over, religion in order to express their support for the rights of LGBT students.

Another example of a very direct response to religious opposition comes from a letter published in the *Columbus Dispatch* on October 30, 2003:

> I have heard some hurtful things directed toward people involved with a gay–straight alliance, such as, 'You folks need to read your Bibles more,' or, 'You can't just pick the parts of the Bible that you like and leave out the rest; homosexuality is forbidden!' My family couldn't agree more with the statement that all of us need to read our Bibles more. As a matter of fact, my son, who is straight, spent a lot of time in prayer before he joined the gay–straight alliance as an "ally." Of the 613 laws in the Old Testament, 365 of those are in the negative form. Homosexuality is forbidden in one of them. But also, menstruating women need to leave town. If your children sass you, you have the right to kill them. You must not eat shellfish or pork. Slavery is not only OK but should be endorsed and utilized. The people during Jesus' time who were most concerned about making sure that all of the laws were followed were the Pharisees. These were also the people who angered Jesus the most. Jesus was asked which of the laws were most important. He responded that the first law was to love God with all of your heart, mind, body and spirit, and the second law was to love your neighbor as yourself, which we've paraphrased into the Golden Rule. The students in the gay–straight alliance are doing just that. Whether they are gay or straight (allies), they are trying to treat those around them the way that they would want to be treated, with kindness and respect.[44]

Statements of support like this one clearly refuse to back down to, or be intimidated by, conservative Christians' judgment of homosexuality or the moral danger GSAs pose to students. Such arguments also remind the reader that the specific meanings of religious doctrine have always been subject to debate over interpretation and application. The citizens authoring these letters frame the support for, and the work of, GSAs as moral behavior in its own right. The organizers of the GSA movement could take the cue from statements like these and more strongly incorporate moral language into the articulation of their goals of making schools places that teach respect, tolerance, and the principles of equality.

And the Winner Is?

A comparative analysis of the of the empirical grounding and connection to American values of justice and equality used by each side shows that the GSA movement wins hands down if we just look at any rational, reasoned, evidenced, or legal argument. Those working the frontlines of the GSA movement must find attempts by reporters to present the two sides as having anywhere near an equally solid argument very frustrating. Those involved with the GSA movement, confident that they have the support of empirical research and the law for their framing of the issue, are forced, time and time again, to contend with the religious morality frame of the opposition and the power it has over public opinion. Newspapers continue to give this line of argument near equal time, regardless of the lack of empirical backing.

The GSA movement seems to have largely abandoned debating the morality of homosexuality or GSAs with the religious right, partly because they feel it is a battle they cannot win, and partly because such a debate detracts from their focus on civil rights. Also, I believe that entrenched negative stereotypes and public opinion of LGBT people make it extremely difficult for them to gain any legitimacy in the media or public's eyes to speak as experts on morality. However, as the research presented here shows, trends in public opinion of the morality of homosexuality have been steadily, if slowly, becoming more positive since the early 1990s. Perhaps this indicates that it is not a hopeless endeavor. It might be powerful for the GSA movement to articulate the underlying moral stance of its current civil rights-based frames more specifically. Religion is not the only source on which morality is based and, certainly, as some citizens recognized in their letters of support, what GSAs stand for is moral behavior. I would argue that GSAs provide a potentially fruitful arena from which to elaborate on the morality of civil rights, justice, and equality, and to critique the very narrow conservative Christian moral judgment of homosexuality that has, for too long, had a choke hold on public opinion about LGBT individuals.

The ability to influence expert stances on issues, mass media framing of stories, and public opinion is an important marker of the impact the GSA movement is having on social change. The movement is having relatively good success in getting its frame alignment strategies into the public arena in a way that seems to be resonating with at least some portion of the general public. To achieve this success, they have to compete with oppositional frames put forth by religious conservatives, which appear to have relatively less success, but are nonetheless maintaining their position as legitimate arguments on topics related to homosexuality. The success or failure of a social movement's attempts at influencing media and public opinion is, of course, irrelevant to the GSA movement's success if they do not also lead to real changes in the environment, policies, and procedures of schools that improve the lives and experiences of LGBT students. The impact of the GSA movement on the students involved in these clubs and on the schools they attend is explored in the next chapter.

THE BATTLES CONTINUE
Life on the Frontlines in
Schools across the Country

In this chapter I assess the extent of the GSA movement's success based on three factors: the media's assessment of the movement's progress and of student leadership; the number and location of GSAs nationwide; and, most importantly, the impact GSAs have had on the schools and the personal lives of student leaders and faculty advisors, as reported in their own words. I also briefly explore the process of establishing a GSA today in light of all the developments, organizations, media coverage, supports, and opposition. Based on personal interviews with student leaders and faculty advisors, I present "real-life" examples of the impact the national GSA movement had on their local efforts and their personal motivations to start their own GSA.

For all the networking, coordinating, dissemination of information, and legal advocating done by "adult" organizations, the GSA movement, at its core and in its heart, is a youth movement. The vision, voice, courage, and leadership of LGBT and straight ally students started the movement and continue to propel it forward. It is always difficult to accurately measure the full impact of change generated by new social movements while they are still in motion. This is especially true of one like the GSA movement, which is scattered so widely across the country and whose impact is often so localized.

One qualitative measure of the growth and impact of the movement can be derived from examining the media coverage, as

I did in Chapter 6. Another can be gained through an examination of stories that specifically focus on the growth of LGBTS youth activism. In the years since the public began to take notice of LGBT students, the news coverage has gradually shifted from the doom and gloom of high suicide and substance-abuse rates to victims and survivors of harassment, discrimination and abuse, and to LGBTS students as leaders and political activists. The headlines that have appeared in newspapers over the years provide a snapshot of how the GSA movement has empowered these students and impacted communities across the country. Here are some examples:

"Students Rally for Gay/Straight March," *Boston Globe*, 1995[1]

"Diversity Unites: Gay, Straight Students Find Alliance Supportive," *Boston Herald* 1997[2]

"Pride Prom: About 120 Gay and Straight Students Gathered in Lincoln Saturday to Dance the Night Away," *The Omaha World-Herald*, 1998[3]

"Students Hope to Inspire Tolerance," *St. Petersburg Times*, 1998[4]

"Students Stand Up for Their Beliefs, Form Group to Combat Homophobia," *Milwaukee Journal Sentinel*, 1999[5]

"Atherton Student Shows Savvy in Art of Politics; Gay 18-year-old Extends Activism to a Myriad of Social Injustices," *The San Francisco Chronicle*, 2000[6]

"A Safe Place for Gays or Straights: Tacoma Teens Carry Diversity to Another Level," *Seattle Times*, 2000[7]

"High School Clubs, Gay Students Stake Their Ground," *USA Today*, 2000[8]

"Gay–straight Group Bursting with Pride, Ready for Parade," *The Atlanta Journal and Constitution*, 2001[9]

"Gay Students Demand Schools Recognize Law, State's Districts Slow to End Harassment," *The San Francisco Chronicle*, 2001[10]

"Peace Prize: Student Makes Mark on School, Hernandez Honored for Work on Alliance at Riverside," *Milwaukee Journal Sentinel*, 2001[11]

"Rights Group Honors Queer Youth Action Team," *The San Francisco Chronicle*, 2002[12]

"Safety in Numbers: As Gay–Straight Alliances Grow, So Does Acceptance in Schools," *The Boston Herald*, 2003[13]

"Teens Sue in Favor of Gay/Straight Alliance, Springs District
    Forbids Meeting at Palmer High," *The Denver Post*, 2003[14]
"Students Unite Against Harassment of Gays," *St. Louis Post-Dispatch*,
    2003[15]

This sampling of headlines illustrates both the spread of the GSA movement to every region of the country and the importance of youth activism.
These headlines all position youth as empowered social actors and agents of
change. All note their accomplishments and the impact they are having on
schools. Absent from these headlines are mentions of suicide rates, abuse,
or any of the other negative experiences of LGBT students. In the past,
the main thing papers deemed newsworthy about these youths was their
victimization; now their activism and leadership are, more often than not,
the focus of stories about their lives. Although this change is by no means a
decisive measure of the success of the GSA movement, it is one indication
that it is having an impact on public perception of LGBT youth and that
these students are enjoying some successes.

A 1995 story in the *Boston Globe* reflects on the impact the movement
had in Massachusetts only a few years after it began:

As they looked through the crowd of straight and gay high school
students rallying on the State House steps yesterday, many older
gays and lesbians remembered their own school days. Alone,
confused and misinformed they vowed that some day students
wouldn't have to experience the pain and persecution they
suffered years ago. Yesterday, with students from about 100 high
schools around the state in the nation's first Gay/Straight Youth
Pride March, they rallied behind the students, giving them the
support they went without years ago.[16]

This highlights the courage of the new young leaders to do what lesbian
and gay individuals were not able to do in the past. It also speaks to one
of the important alliances in the GSA movement, that between youth and
adults. When LGBT students began to speak out against the oppressive and
dangerous environment of America's schools that lesbian and gay individuals had so long suffered in isolation, many gay adults jumped at the chance

to stand together with them to support a battle they had waited years, even decades, to fight.

The experiences of LGBT students continue to supply the human interest for the newspaper articles, which reflect both their courage and activism, and the excitement and intrigue associated with forming GSAs. Despite claims made by some of those who oppose GSAs, that students are merely the "puppets" of larger gay rights groups, newspaper coverage of the achievements of LGBTS students reveals that they are more than capable of speaking for and leading themselves. As reported in this same *Boston Globe* article, youths in Massachusetts were beginning to get the support they needed in 1995, and they had become empowered enough to make demands of their state's educational system and set goals for their movement:

> The students said they wanted: Gay-straight alliances in every
> high school; visible penalties for anti-gay harassers in school; ac-
> curate information about gay people included in history, literature
> and health classes, an increase in openly gay teachers and staff ...
> "Ours is a youth movement as well as a gay rights movement,"
> says Melissa Carey, a junior at Belmont High School and a co-chair
> of the commission's youth committee. "By emphasizing the
> importance of gay–straight alliances, the march sends the message
> that no one walks alone."[17]

Students like this one were staking claim to a movement before GLSEN or any other formal organization existed. The opportunity to come together and work with the Massachusetts Safe Schools Committee helped to foster this developing sense of unity and will to create social change.

News coverage of this annual Massachusetts event four years later documents the continued growth of youth activism:

> The 140 publicly funded Gay/Straight Alliances in Massachusetts
> high schools have given new life to gay students who are lonely,
> terrified of being found out, and even suicidal, advocates said.
> Yesterday, a handful of student leaders, some of them victims
> of gay bashing who had considered suicide, pumped the already
> soaring spirits of the gay, lesbian, and bisexual students, parents,
> and teachers at the fourth annual Gay & Straight Youth Pride Day

in Boston. Organizers had expected about 2,000 to turn out, but Boston Police estimated the crowd at 7,500.[18]

This story highlights the importance of student activism and the significance of alliances to the progress in Massachusetts. The state's recognition of the problems faced by LGBT students, the willingness of policy makers to take some responsibility for working to rectify this situation through programs and funding, and the support of teachers, parents, and straight students all helped make the change possible. This article included a quote from a straight student that emphasized the importance of the alliance of straight students with their LGBT peers:

> Sarah Halford, 16, of Needham, co-chairwoman of the Youth
> Committee of the Governor's Commission of Gay and Lesbian
> Youth, said GSA chapters are important because they give
> both gay and straight teens a chance to find common ground.
> "The march is really something for everyone and I really want to
> stress that. Everyone who has a gay friend, a gay brother, sister.
> Everyone is a part of this."[19]

Expressions of allegiance from heterosexual students or adults are powerful reminders of the significance of straight allies to the GSA movement. Statements like these make the issues relevant to many readers who might otherwise feel that the problems of LGBT students are of no concern to them.

The movement would have grown much more slowly, made much less of an impact on change, and perhaps even have died out completely before it really got off the ground, if it had relied only on the courage and activism of LGBT students. On the basis of numbers alone, a youth movement that relies solely on gay students would have little chance of making a noticeable impact on America's schools. Other factors also inhibit their chances of creating change on their own. First, the negative stigma associated with being homosexual somewhat limits the amount of sympathy gay youth can foster in the general public. Second, they lack access to most avenues to institutional power. This often includes their parents, who would usually be most students' institutional advocates. These factors, combined with the daily stress and fear endured by many of these students, make it truly remarkable that any change has occurred. The willingness of heterosexual students to rally around and stand up for the rights of their LGBT peers, of teachers to sometimes risk their jobs to advocate for the safety and education of all their students, and of regional and national organizations to use their resources to coordinate and support all of these efforts, bolstered the political impulse of some LGBT youth and made it into a movement.

Although it is crucially important to recognize the "alliance" factor in the successes of the GSA movement, we cannot lose sight of the fact that no movement or change is possible without LGBT youth themselves. As this story from the *San Francisco Chronicle* reminds us, gay students are the visionaries and leaders:

> Matt Wolf prefers to talk about how gay and lesbian youth are shaping a whole new world of progressive politics than about the times he has been harassed for being gay. The 18-year-old senior at the private Menlo School in Atherton is one of the leading figures in the Bay Area Gay–Straight Alliance Network ... Last fall, he was a key player in organizing the alliance's lobbying campaign in Sacramento in behalf of a bill, signed into law by governor Gray Davis, that bans anti-gay harassment of students and teachers in public schools. A number of the estimated 700 high school students from around the state who rallied on the state Capitol steps several days before that bill's passage, or met with legislators to argue in its behalf, had been trained at workshops run by Wolf on how to get their message across ... "It's amazing that young gay people are taking so much power into their own hands and no one is telling us how to do it," says Wolf, who as a sophomore two years ago, organized the gay–straight group at Menlo school.[20]

The courage of LGBT students to "take the power into their own hands," certainly is made stronger now by the models of youth leaders over the years and by the support and information that they know they will receive from groups like GLSEN, the ACLU, Project 10, and the GSA Network. Each student who stands out as a leader serves as a role model for the next student who becomes empowered by this example and is willing to stand together with other LGBT students. The impact of these individual actions is magnified when they are covered by the media, positioning them as role models for the larger public.

The ability of student leadership to connect to a wide range of supports and build on the work accomplished by other LGBTS over the years has made it possible for new student leaders to expand their goals and be more confident in their chances of success. This is illustrated in many articles on youth activism, including this 2004 story from Oregon:

> "Centennial High School's Gay–Straight Alliance seeks an
> addition to the districts rules against discrimination. ... To
> exclude sexual identity, senior Matt Vail said, "amounts to
> implicitly condoning discrimination against gay, lesbian, bisexual
> and transgender youth." Vail, after facing initial resistance from
> administrators, co-founded the school's Gay–Straight Alliance
> two years ago ... He started the club to create a safe space for
> students to discuss their sexual identity and to cut down on
> hallway harassment by fostering a better understanding of gay
> issues among the student body. Amending the district's non-
> discrimination policy is one crucial step toward the club's goals,
> Vail said.[21]

This confidence is now spreading to students in areas beyond the comfort zones of New York, California, and Massachusetts. An examination of this expansion of gay–straight alliance groups in terms of their numbers and geographical reach provides another avenue through which to assess the social impact of the GSA movement and factors that assist or inhibit its growth.

THE SPREAD OF GSAS: WHAT THE TRENDS IN LOCATION INDICATE ABOUT MOVEMENT SUCCESS

The rapid increase in sheer numbers of gay–straight alliance clubs is often touted in the press and in the literature produced by the GSA Network, GLSEN, and ACLU as a sign of the movement's social and political gains. The increase in numbers across the nation over the past five years does give a sense of dramatic and rapid change. The number has just about tripled over this five-year period. This is progress for the movement, but a closer examination of the numbers provides a more realistic picture of the scope and extent of advancement. First, although the number of gay–straight alliance groups has tripled, they are still found in fewer than ten percent of high schools. Second, the locations of GSAs follow some rather strong patterns. For example, forty percent of California's public schools have a GSA, but not a single school in Arkansas has one. Analyzing these patterns illuminates some of the social, political, and institutional factors that influence the emergence of GSAs.

Because there is no exhaustive, or completely accurate, list of every GSA in the country, it is difficult to be completely confident in discussing patterns in the locations of GSAs. However, GLSEN encourages students to register their school's GSA with them, and a list of these groups is accessible on the GLSEN website. More than 2,000 GSAs were included in this list in 2004. Although this list is certainly not complete, it is large enough to reveal some strong trends in locations of GSAs by state. Unfortunately, this registry does not provide detailed information about the schools listed, such as the size, urban, suburban, or rural setting, socioeconomic status of the student body, racial and ethnic composition, public or a private school, etc. This makes it difficult to conduct a detailed analysis. However, even a cursory examination of the lists by state reveals strong patterns in the concentration of GSAs. There are large numbers in traditionally politically liberal states like California (441), New York (154), Massachusetts (158), and Connecticut (86) and none, or very few, in more traditionally conservative states like Arkansas (0), Wyoming (0), West Virginia (2), and Mississippi (2).

Sociologist Tina Fetner recently conducted a preliminary analysis of the social, political, and demographic factors that foster or impede the formation of GSAs in particular locations.[22] Although this is the only study of its kind done so far, it is useful for assessing the social and political impact of the GSA movement and relating its findings to my own qualitative investigation. Fetner's study analyzed data from the National Center for Education Statistics, which provides detailed demographic information on individual public elementary and secondary schools. High schools were selected from this list and coded for the presence or absence of a GSA based on GLSEN's national registry, The GSA Network's registration list for California schools, and Northeast regional registries kept by Out Proud and Project 10 East. This data was then examined at the individual school and state level.

At the individual school level, factors such as school size, region (South, Midwest, Northeast, or West), teacher/student ratio, racial diversity, and socio-economic status of student body[23] were all tested for their influence on the likelihood that a school would have a GSA. On the state level, the researchers measured the relative impact of state- or city-wide anti-discrimination policies that include sexual orientation and the presence of state and local LGBT organizations supporting GSAs[24] (among other factors) on the number of GSAs in each state.

The findings from this data analysis suggest factors that contribute to the likelihood that GSAs will be present in a state or a particular location. One significant, but perhaps not surprising, finding was that there are more GSAs in urban and suburban locations than in rural locations or towns. According to the data used by this study (which included 1,200 GSAs nationwide), 2% of rural schools, 2.3% of schools in towns, 12.1% of schools in the suburbs, and 11.6% of schools in urban settings have GSAs.[25] The researchers were surprised that the percentage was higher in suburban schools than in urban schools, because they presumed that urban locations are more diverse, more tolerant of differences, and have larger LGBT populations to supply resources and support for GSAs than suburban locations. One possible explanation for the higher rate of GSAs in suburban schools could be the greater number of resources generally available in suburban schools. This may, in fact, be more significant in providing support for LGBT students than the diversity factors usually associated with urban schools. Although this might be partially true, I believe there could be a more complex explanation. Urban areas, as a whole, are much more mixed and diverse than suburbs in terms of race, class, ethnicity, and sexual identities, but this citywide diversity is generally segregated by neighborhood and school district. This causes many individual urban schools to be as lacking in diversity as many suburban schools. This dynamic most likely neutralizes much of the positive edge urban areas seem to have in fostering support for GSAs.

The greater financial resources available to suburban schools may play a role, but these resources are also segregated in both urban and suburban areas, which should caution against generalizing about the influence on one area over the other. This same research study did find that, as the percentage of poorer students a school serves[26] increases, the chance that it has a GSA decreases. This provides evidence about the importance of financial resources. To understand the impact of both financial and cultural resources more clearly, each school would have to be examined individually. Mass media is another important variable that might play a role in equalizing the rate of GSAs in urban and suburban locations. Many of the cultural supports for tolerance and diversity once offered exclusively in urban centers through actual life experience can now be gained through television, films, and, particularly, the Internet. Websites for groups like GLSEN, the GSA Network, Safe Schools Coalition, the ACLU, and sites and chat rooms specifically for LGBT youth can provide students with information, role models, and support networks regardless of their location.

This, of course, is not meant to imply that location is irrelevant. The perceived level of tolerance in an LGBT student's community undoubtedly often weighs on the decision about whether to start a GSA. The influence of living in an area where people are more supportive of gay and lesbian rights was reinforced by the research finding that GSAs were strongly concentrated regionally—with 2.3% of schools in the South, 3.8% in the Midwest, 11.4% in the East and 14.5% in the West having a GSA. The researchers looked at this factor more specifically by examining the rate of GSAs in states having statewide anti-discrimination policies that include sexual orientation, and found a positive, but statistically insignificant relationship.[27] The researchers do not provide the number of GSAs in each of these states, but looking at the number of GSAs registered with GLSEN[28] in the fourteen states with inclusive policies provides a sense of this pattern: Wisconsin (47), Massachusetts (158), Connecticut (86), Hawai'i (2), New Jersey (62), Vermont (11), New Hampshire (21), Nevada (8), Maryland (54), New York (154), Minnesota (47), Rhode Island (13), New Mexico (11), and California (441).[29] Examining this list reveals that there are more GSAs in states with inclusive policies than there are in states without. It also shows that not every state with an inclusive non-discrimination policy has large concentrations of GSAs. This suggests that, although such policies can be important tools in advancing the rights of LGBT students, they are not the only determining factor.

An examination of the numbers of GSAs in states without inclusive policies provides some further insight into the social and political factors influencing the success of GSAs. For example, Florida has 67 GSAs registered with GLSEN; Illinois has 80; and Washington State has 50. Florida, traditionally a politically conservative state, appears to be the biggest anomaly to the pattern, but there are some factors that help to explain why the state has a relatively high number of GSAs. Although the state's non-discrimination law does not include sexual orientation, the Florida State Department of Education's policy does. It is interesting to note that this policy protects only students, not school faculty or staff. In addition, eleven major cities or counties in Florida have passed their own nondiscrimination laws that include sexual orientation. All of these factors have an impact on the social and political climate surrounding GSAs and gay student rights that is very similar to that of a statewide policy.

The relatively large number of GSAs in the state of Illinois is, perhaps, largely explained by the concentration of the population living in the city of Chicago, which does have a citywide nondiscrimination law protecting gays and lesbians.[30] Also, as was mentioned in Chapter One, the city of Chicago has a rather large and politically visible LGBT community, which has been actively supportive of youth for over twenty years through groups like Horizons. The number of GSAs in Washington State is best explained by the presence of the Safe Schools Coalition, which has been tirelessly advocating for the needs and rights of LGBT students since 1988. The impact of organizations that advocate for the rights of LGBT and work to network GSAs is further evidenced by the fact that the number of GSAs in the states with these organizations is much higher than in other states. Some examples include: New York State, the headquarters of GLSEN; Massachusetts, with its Safe Schools Program protecting LGBT students and providing funding for GSAs; and California, with the strong student activism coordinated by the GSA Network. This is perhaps the strongest evidence that political climate is an important factor in explaining the presence or absence of GSAs in schools. Still it is not the only factor.

THE SIGNIFICANCE OF INDIVIDUAL MOTIVATIONS TO THE INCREASE OF GSAS

For all the significant sociological factors that potentially influence the likelihood of a GSA forming at a particular school, there are at least an equal number of significant individual psychological factors. The social and political context might make a particular school environment ripe for a GSA to form with relative ease, and yet nothing will materialize if a student (or group of students) is not dedicated or brave enough to take action. Even if a student does step forward to start a group in this environment, the potential will be fully realized only if the faculty is motivated and strong enough to offer support. In the same respect, the social and political atmosphere of a particular school might, in every way, inhibit the foundation of support and acceptance for a GSA, and yet the will and courage of one or a handful of students combined with the support of even a single teacher can make something out of nothing.

Seventy-five GSA student leaders and faculty advisors from seventeen different states shared their experiences with me. What struck me most about their stories was how remarkably similar they were. The basic underlying element influencing most people's desire to get involved with a GSA at their school was an awareness of the needs of LGBT students and a feeling that being involved was the right thing to do. Despite this common element, there were also some interesting patterns in additional motivational factors among faculty advisors and students. The strongest of these patterns related to the sexual orientation and gender of the respondents. My sample was not random enough, or large enough, to make any grand generalizations about this, but it does allow for discussion and hypotheses.

Of those who responded to my widely distributed requests for interviews, eighty-five percent of the faculty advisors and sixty-six percent of students are female. Among these women, sixty-three percent of the student leaders and thirty-five percent of the faculty advisors, identified themselves as lesbian or bisexual. Among the much smaller number of males in the sample, all of the student leaders and three quarters of the faculty advisors identified as gay. Although a much larger sample would be needed to definitively establish a pattern, my findings suggest that both gender and sexual orientation have an impact on a person's willingness to get actively and visibly involved with their school's GSA. This finding correlates with sociological research on homophobia and gender identity. It is possible that the documented higher rates of homophobia combined with negative attitudes about both the morality and civil rights of gays and lesbians held by heterosexual males (discussed in Chapter Six), might cause them to reject the idea of being a GSA faculty advisor. In addition, a straight male teacher may be the least likely candidate for GSA advisor because students perceive that straight male teachers are not sympathetic to LGBT issues.

While research concludes that homophobia is less pronounced among females, it nevertheless exists in a more complex way. Among the female student leaders in my sample, 37% are heterosexual, reflecting, at least partially, less of a social stigma associated with lesbianism among female youth. Interestingly, two thirds of the female faculty advisors identified as heterosexual. The difference in percentage for students and faculty may possibly be attributed to several factors. The most common explanation offered by the faculty advisors was that straight women had what one person referred to as "heterosexual Teflon." Heterosexual women, particularly those who are married with children, are not subject to any suspicion of ulterior motives for their involvement with a gay–straight student club. LGBT faculty members are often subject to, or fear that they will be subject to, accusations of trying to recruit or abuse students, of being part of a larger "gay agenda," or of starting the group out of their own interests rather than the students' interest. The motivations of heterosexual men who might want to serve as a GSA advisor are often subject to similar suspicions due to the increased homophobia directed at males, particularly those who work with children. Heterosexual married women easily dodge all of these suspicions, which decreases the potential for controversy surrounding the GSA. Many of the heterosexual women told me that they were very conscious of these dynamics and felt a sense of obligation to use their status to help their students start a group.

One very strong, but perhaps not surprising, theme in the faculty advisors' responses to my question about what motivated them to get involved in starting a GSA is that they recognized that LGBT students faced serious problems that were being ignored by their school. Some became aware of the issues faced by these students through their observations as teachers, some through workshops on homophobia they attended, and others through news reports. These general statements of being motivated to fill a need varied in the way they were articulated and in relation to other motivating factors. These variations were significantly patterned according to the gender and sexual orientation of the faculty advisor.

For many of the heterosexual teachers, the motivation to get involved came from their view of their responsibilities as educators. The heterosexual males who told me about their experiences were very clear in stating this type of motivation. A teacher from North Carolina simply said, "A former student requested it." A heterosexual faculty advisor from Arizona also reported that the choice to get involved was uncomplicated, "The students asked me to, and I believe in their mission." The responses of these two men are not enough to make any remotely accurate generalized statement about the attitudes of heterosexual men. It would, however, be interesting to test the above hypothesis and see if, for those who do choose to be advisors, the motivation is as straightforward as it was for the two who shared their experience with me. However, because there is no official record of all GSA advisors in the country, there is no easy way to measure the percentage who are heterosexual males or to draw a sample for study.

There were far more female heterosexual GSA advisors, and their motivations also primarily stemmed from a perceived need and sense of obligation as a teacher. Sometimes their responses were as simply stated as the men's were. For example, a teacher in Wisconsin said, "Students felt the need to have a group and that was enough for me." Quite often, the explanation of why they became involved was combined with a statement of admiration for their student. For example, a teacher in California said, "A student asked; a very brave thing to do in an area with neo-nazi activity." These rather direct and brief responses were the exception, not the rule.

The majority of heterosexual female teachers provided more detailed and complex responses than those supplied by their male counterparts. A teacher in California stated, "This organization needed an administrator who backed them in philosophy, ethics, beliefs, and spirit. There was much resistance from the superintendent and students needed someone willing to 'go to bat' for them." A sense of both sympathy and admiration for LGBTS students ran through many of the straight female teachers' explanations for why they were willing to become a faculty advisor. As a teacher in California told me, "It needed doing, and no one else was stepping up. A student was beaten for being gay, which led several openly gay student council representatives to get organized." One of two faculty advisors for a GSA in Wisconsin replied, "We knew nothing about it, absolutely nothing. But, once we found out that these kids actually existed and really needed somebody then we said we would do it together. I don't know that either one of us would have taken it on by ourselves, but we were willing to do it together." All of the women, whether straight, bisexual, or lesbian, reported a very strong sense of obligation to help these students who were so obviously in need. This sense of responsibility, combined with a genuine expression of caring for these students, helped them overcome any hesitancy they may have had about involving themselves with a potentially controversial group.

For some of the heterosexual female teachers, all of these motivating factors coincided with a more personal reason to want to be involved with a GSA. A fair number of the teachers shared with me that a friend or relative was gay or lesbian and that this fact weighed on the decision to be an advisor. This was one of several factors that served as motivation for a Washington teacher, "My parents were both gay, the students asked me to, the students needed a group that would represent them." A teacher in North Carolina stated, "I saw a need for the group with students who were struggling within themselves. Saw lots of intolerance at the school, which was very different from my previous school. I have a close childhood friend who is gay and she struggled a lot in high school." Personal experiences with LGBT loved ones created a greater sense of empathy for LGBT students, and predisposed some teachers to recognize and understand what these kids were going through. For one faculty advisor, the connection to the issue was a familial one. "My brother, who was almost eight years younger than I, lived and died out and proud. ... So, I've always had a high level of consciousness of the situations that gay people, male and female and other genders have faced." This family connection, which brought a lifelong understanding of the discrimination and harassment faced by many LGBT people, prompted this teacher to get involved early on in the GSA movement. In the early 1990s, she became one of the first GSA advisors in the state of Connecticut.

Responses like these from heterosexual faculty advisors demonstrate the power of students to draw in the straight allies who have been so essential to the success of the GSA movement. Whether or not these teachers had a personal adult connection to someone who was LGBT, none had previously been motivated to speak out against homophobia or advocate for gay rights in any formal or organized way. Students were able to change this because the impact of homophobia and discrimination on their lives was visible to these teachers on a daily basis. Seeing this institutionalized discrimination and the students' courage to stand out and fight for change despite their vulnerable social and institutional status, inspired these faculty advisors to stand with their students and use their influence in hopes of increasing the success of the GSA.

This personal connection to LGBT issues was a much larger factor for gay, lesbian, and bisexual teachers. For them, this recognition of need was both rooted in what they witnessed students experiencing in their current educational surroundings, and tied deeply to their own adolescent experiences. Some gay and lesbian faculty advisors described this motivation simply and directly. One teacher from California told me, "I am a lesbian and want to see the climate improve here at my school for GLBTQ [gay, lesbian, bisexual, transgender and questioning] students." Most lesbian or female bisexual teachers offered a more elaborate explanation of their personal motivations and what they hoped might result from their work with GSAs. For a number of these women, their job as faculty advisor advocating for the rights of LGBT students and supporting them as they worked to understand their sexual identity coincided with their own parallel process. This connection was very direct for one lesbian teacher, who said, "I taught for one year in Southern California where I was closeted and miserable. Moving to San Francisco, I was dedicated to being out, and to helping lead a group for GLBT students. After my first year, I found two straight boys who wanted to start the group." For some faculty advisors like this one, the motivation to make the schools in which they are teaching safer and more welcoming to LGBT students than the ones they had attended preceded any actual request from students for help. Lesbian teachers more frequently reported that their personal motivation for becoming a GSA advisor coincided with students' revealing to them an immediate need. A teacher from Massachusetts explained this very succinctly, "It was right; we had self-identified GLB kids; and I was coming out myself and wanted for them what was not available for me." A teacher in Oregon provided a more detailed account of the desire to both meet the immediate needs of students and to work to rectify, in some way, her own difficult experience as a lesbian high school student. "One of our first 'out' gay students was punched out by three boys from his neighborhood. I was coming out as a gay teacher at the same time. He and I hooked up and established one of the strongest and longest-running GSAs in the State. I felt strongly that gay kids should be able to be themselves while still in school. It was not safe for me when I was in high school."

Another significant influence on the decision to become a GSA advisor was expressed best by a bisexual teacher in New Jersey. "Getting tenure! Also, I had a very bright, very accomplished, very sweet student whose shame connected to his (then secret, only partly personally accepted) gay identity was so intense that I was outraged on his behalf and felt a moral obligation to help change the culture, at least in the high school." A response like this brings up the important issue of job security. Although research has documented that LGBT teachers worry about losing their jobs or not receiving tenure if they come out or are discovered (or even rumored) to be other than heterosexual,[31] very few of the teachers who shared their stories with me directly mentioned that a fear for their job caused them to hesitate to become a GSA advisor. Of course, it is important to note that I did not speak with any of the countless LGBT, or straight, teachers out there for whom this fear curtailed their willingness to get involved. I did not ask directly, but the majority of the teachers in my study were old enough to have already achieved tenure before becoming GSA advisors. My small non-random sample included more faculty advisors over the age of forty than below it. I had expected to hear from a greater number of younger faculty advisors—guided by the hypothesis that younger teachers would be more attuned to, knowledgeable about, and receptive of LGBT students. The fact that the majority of my respondents were over the age of forty may or may not be significant. It may relate to the importance of job security and tenure; or to an increased comfort level in dealing with potentially controversial topics; or to a gradual increase in motivation to address the issue, or there might be no relationship, beyond my sample, between a GSA advisor's age and his or her motivation to become involved. More research, with much larger samples, needs to be done before conclusions about the impact of tenure on faculty willingness to become GSA advisors can be confidently drawn.

The responses to questions about personal motivation provided by the few gay men in my sample generally mirror the type of response given by lesbian or bisexual female teachers, with one distinction. The gay men, like the women, reported a very personal connection with the issue and a strong motivating desire to help make the schools they teach in better places to be a LGBT student than the schools they attended as students. However, although the women articulated this motivation in terms of a desire to actively help students change their schools, the men described their motivation in terms of a drive to help better LGBT students' experiences by serving as a role model for them. A male teacher from New York expressed his motivation as a form of activism. "After doing volunteer work with GLBTQ youth in the community through a county funded program, I decided that I could be more helpful—as well as a better role model—by bringing my involvement into the school where I work." A teacher from

New Hampshire expressed a similar motivation. "Well, I'm gay myself, so that is the number one factor, a personal connection .... I went to school in the late 80s and there were no positive role models of openly gay or lesbian people who had healthy wonderful lives ... So, I have said that I don't want high school students to go through that. I'd like them to be able to feel free to talk about what they want to talk about and to deal with these issues and to have positive role models—straight and gay, black and white, you know. The whole gamut."

STUDENT LEADERS' MOTIVATIONS

Unlike some teachers who may have been motivated to become a GSA advisor by the desire to be an adult role model for students, LGBT and straight ally students sought to be their own role models. About half of the student GSA leaders who shared their experiences with me are heterosexual females. Like their faculty counterparts, these young women were partially driven to lead a GSA because they saw the needs of LGBT students and because they had some form of personal connection to the issues through a friend or family member. One student from upstate New York explained it simply this way, "I have several friends that are LGBT and was interested in joining GSA ... Now I'm president and just really committed to continuing to expand education and peace between gay and straight people throughout my school and community." A student from Connecticut expressed a similar motivation, "My friend asked me to help out. I always had an interest in political activism, but no outlet for it. At the time, I didn't know my friend was gay, but that soon became apparent. Soon more and more of my friends started coming out and, after being confronted with homophobia, I became more involved in the organization."

Although some students, like those I just quoted, expressed their desire to create social change in a rather understated way, it was much more common for the young women to state their political intentions more boldly. As one respondent said, "Well, raising a little hell is always fun. ...Plus, homophobia has always been a kinda disturbing and incomprehensible phenomenon to me, and I like to get the wheels turning so that we can roll our culture out of the mud of its own prejudice as soon as possible." This particular GSA student leader, who started a club in a Massachusetts high school in 1995, clearly did not require a personal connection to an LGBT family member or friend to hold the opinion that this was an important issue for her school to address. For many of these female student allies, the view that GSAs address important issues appeared to be almost instinctual and required little explanation. According to a North Carolina student, the decision to get involved could not have been clearer. She said, "The maltreatment of GLBT people is a horrific injustice. To me, the issue is black and white. I see no ambiguity in the poor morality of homophobia and discrimination."

It is important to note that the vast majority of responses from straight ally students about their personal reasons for getting involved were explicitly political. This is in sharp contrast to the stated motivations of the majority of faculty advisors. There are a few possible explanations for this difference. First, the professional position of teachers might prohibit them from assuming overtly political stances on any issue. Second, these teachers' years of experience working in educational institutions probably taught them that most school boards and high school administrators generally strive to avoid political issues in their schools. In this way, these teachers' responses may reflect their socialization into an apolitical educational culture. Finally, the difference in responses might be partially generational. High school students today (the vast majority of students I heard from were in high school in the 2000s) have grown up in a time in which this issue of LGBT students has been visible and clearly been framed as a political one. In contrast, although the teachers I heard from might also understand the recent politicization of the issue, most of them grew up at a time when providing support and services was the most common approach to addressing the problem of LGBT students. Even the lesbian and bisexual teachers who directly expressed some sentiment that they felt this was in some ways a political issue, nonetheless, said that their goals were to help their students rather than promote some broader social change.

Most of the students, particularly the LGBT students, prominently mentioned their political motivation and goals when explaining why they became GSA leaders. Although the connection to a GSA is clearly personal for all LGBT students, the extent to which personal and political factors combined to affect their decisions to become leaders among their peers varied in a variety of ways. There was no discernable patterned difference in the responses of gay male and lesbian students. For some, the decision was more prominently influenced by a direct desire to become a political activist. This was true for a Massachusetts woman who was a high school student in 1993, when the Safe Schools Program was first getting under way. She told me that her primary motivation was, "The need for more diverse voices from among the student body, which was primarily white. I wanted to be an activist for something in my community. I was questioning my queerness; my social group was politically aware of what was going on around the country at that time. There was an increasing amount of supportive faculty. It was time to shake the school up a little." This statement is reflective of the intertwining of personal and political factors in many students' motivation to become GSA leaders.

An unwelcoming, or even dangerous, school environment was part of the motivation for many students to want to become leaders in their schools. One young woman in Wisconsin stated, "Discrimination in our school had gotten unbearable. In a small town like ours, people were very uneducated about GLBT and gender identity issues, and I felt like, if I didn't help the problem, no one else was going to." Sometimes the drive to change the school was precipitated by a specific event. A young woman from Utah stated that the well-publicized Salt Lake City controversy over the East High GSA was the catalyst for her leadership in 1998:

> It was very politically contentious to have a GSA running in a
> Utah public school after a recent political struggle with the school
> district to ban all student clubs in an effort to do away with GSAs.
> I felt that it was a really important resource to have at my high
> school for that reason and to support gay and questioning stu-
> dents. Also, I valued it personally as a place to come, relax and
> meet other queer youth like myself.

For this student, the personal gains that her activism would bring were not her primary motivating factors. Helping other students was her first priority. This was a fairly common pattern, particularly for the female students. A female student from Missouri stated: "I couldn't let myself sit by and let other students be called names and hear 'that's so gay,' 'homo,' and 'fag' all the time. I was sick of hiding in the closet and one small but strong step in the right direction found me several other student leaders; we all wanted to see the school become more tolerant." All movements for social change, large and small, have begun with actions like these. Individuals who have become fed up with accepting the unjust treatment take one strong step to stand out in resistance and find that others are also tired of taking a back seat in life and waiting for someone to stand with and lead them toward the front. The result of these courageous first strong steps is almost always powerful and transformational.

MEASURING SUCCESS: THE IMPACT OF THE GSA MOVEMENT ON SCHOOLS AND STUDENTS

It is clear from the stories students told me about their experiences as GSA leaders that they were strongly motivated by a desire to change their schools and make them places where LGBT students could feel comfortable with themselves and free from fear of harassment and discrimination. However, it is difficult to accurately and succinctly measure the degree to which students in the GSA movement, along with their adult allies, have been successful in fulfilling these goals. As stated earlier, one measure of the growth and reach of the movement is the number and location of GSAs registered with GLSEN and other organizations. These organizations often use these same numbers as evidence of the success the movement, and particularly its student leaders, are having in making schools safer and more tolerant places for all students. Although these organizations, and everyone directly involved with whom I spoke, assert that schools with GSAs are better places for LGBT students than schools without them, any real-life evidence that can be gathered to test that hypothesis is mixed. There is no evidence that schools with GSAs are worse places for LGBT students—as some of those who oppose the groups argued they might be because they call more attention to gay students and greater potential for stigma and harassment.

When discussing success, two questions need to be answered: (1) How much lasting and substantial change in school climate has the movement produced? and (2) What percentage of LGBT students are reached and assisted? Since 1999, GLSEN has conducted its own research into the school experiences of LGBT students. The results of this research are released biannually under the title "The National School Climate Survey: The School Related Experiences of Our Nation's Lesbian, Gay Bisexual and Transgender Youth." They use these results to illustrate the need for more change and advocacy on behalf of these students and, of course, to stress the importance of the work that the organization does.

Analyzing this report for indicators of the movement's impact on the school experiences of LGBT students suggests that there is still a great distance to travel before the goals of the movement are reached. The results of the 2003 survey of 887 LGBT students from across the country[32] largely highlight the persistence of wide-sweeping problems for LGBT students. Findings in the report include the following:

- 84% of LGBT students reported they have been verbally harassed.
- 82.9% stated that teachers or administrators rarely, if ever, intervened when they witnessed homophobic comments.
- 55% of transgender students reported being physically harassed because of their gender identity.
- 41% of lesbian, gay and bisexual students said that they had been physically harassed because of their sexual orientation.
- 64.3% of LGBT students reported that, because of their sexual orientation, they felt unsafe at school.[33]

GLSEN grades every state based on how well they protect and meet the needs of LGBT students. In 2003, forty-two states received a failing grade. These results indicate that, despite over a decade of social change efforts (or over two decades, if Project 10 is used as the historical marker), America's high schools are still largely unpleasant and unsafe places for LGBT students. However, it would be incorrect to conclude, from these statistics alone, that the GSA movement has not made a difference in the lives of students.

This same 2003 report from GLSEN also provides some indications that GSAs do have a positive effect on LGBT students. Researchers at GLSEN summarize these findings this way:

Many schools fail to provide resources or support for their LGBT students. However, when supportive faculty or LGBT-related resources are available, LGBT students do better in school and are much more likely to plan to attend college. Furthermore, there is a definitive relationship between schools and communities having policies and laws regarding violence, bias and harassment against LGBT students and student safety.[34]

Some of the specific data on the impact of GSAs and school nondiscrimination policies on the experiences of LGBT students show that 68.3% of LGBT students in schools without GSAs report feeling unsafe in their schools because of their sexual orientation, compared with 60.9% of LGBT students in schools with GSAs. In addition, 36.5% of LGBT students in schools without a school harassment policy that includes sexual orientation stated that they skipped class recently because they felt unsafe; for LGBT students in schools with an inclusive policy the number is 26.6%.[35] These numbers indicate that GSAs and policies do make a difference, but they also clearly indicate that these things fall far short of solving the negative school experiences of all LGBT students. Although this GLSEN survey provides only one snapshot view of the impact the GSA movement has on the lives of LGBT students, it is currently the only available national quantitative source of data.[36]

In an attempt to add a qualitative, and more in-depth, look at the impact of GSAs that focuses specifically on the first-hand experiences of GSA student leaders and faculty advisors, I queried seventy-five of them. I asked about the impact GSAs have had on their schools, on the lives of LGBT students, and in their own personal lives. In general, the assessments of progress were positive and optimistic; however, they also reported that there is much more work to be done.

When asked to assess the degree and type of impact the GSA had on their school, they gave somewhat mixed responses. They spoke positively about their successes, but also spoke about the frustrations and limitations of the progress. One of the biggest indicators that the GSA movement still has a good deal of work left to do is how many students, and what types of students, are involved in their school's GSA. The vast majority of those I heard from reported that they had relatively low membership, that the membership was generally more straight allies than LGBT students (which in a way might also be a sign of success), membership was more heavily female than male, and was not very racially or ethnically diverse. These factors suggest that, although the number of GSA groups is increasing, the number and range of students actually actively using the group as a positive resource is relatively small.

My research also suggests that GSAs are not reaching working-class LGBT students and students of color as effectively as they are white middle-class teens. This appears to be a twofold issue. First, both my small non-random sample and the much larger more inclusive sample used in the Fetner research reveal that the majority of schools with GSAs are middle- or upper middle-class. Although Fetner's research found there was only a small, and statistically insignificant, relationship between the percentage of the student body that is white and the likelihood of a GSA,[37] the vast majority of faculty and students in my sample worked in or went to schools with little racial or ethnic diversity. Also, most student leaders and advisors in my study reported that the membership of their groups was overwhelmingly white and middle-class. In some cases, they noted that this reflected the composition of the student body and, in others, they reported that the GSA was less diverse than the school as a whole. A few reported that the GSA was more diverse. Of the seventy-five student leaders and advisors who responded to my request for interview, only two teachers and three students were not white. Obviously, this was not a true representative sample, but it still suggests a trend. Clearly, issues of race, ethnicity, and class, as they relate to GSAs, require more research and need to be addressed by the movement and its leading organizations.

Directly addressing race, ethnicity, class, and gender expression along with sexual orientation has been a central mission of the GSA Network's founder and director Carolyn Laub. In 2001, after talking about and struggling with these issues as an organization for a couple of years, the GSA Network received funding to pay an intern to do a qualitative interview-based research project on the issues. From this small interview study of twenty youths of color, they found four main factors that deterred youths of color from involvement in GSAs.[38] The first was that they perceived many GSAs to be single-issue organizations, so that the focus on gay identity issues would force them to ignore issues of race and ethnic identity. The second major factor was one of cultural differences in the degree and intensity of homophobia. Youths of color felt there was a greater social risk for them participating in a GSA than was involved for their white peers. The third finding was that many youths of color felt GSAs ignored the link between homophobia and racism. The final finding was that youths of color who were in the minority of the student body population were more likely to join a GSA than students of color who were in the majority. In other words, Hispanic students in a school with 75% Hispanic students were less likely to join a GSA than students in a school that was 10% Hispanic. The general conclusion from this is that GSAs become a "catch-all" club for students, gay or straight, who feel they do not fit into the mainstream culture of the school. Thus, the outsider status makes students more likely to join, and insider status makes joining more risky to one's social standing in the larger school culture.[39] This last finding seems to match well with the reports of the general composition of most GSAs around the country.

In the past, other organizations and some of its own contingent of student leaders have criticized GLSEN for failing to directly address this pattern of GSA membership and failing to more overtly promote programs that also deal with the very real racial inequality in education, and the racial harassment and discrimination faced by students. GLSEN has responded and, in recent years, has made some efforts to focus on these concerns. In January 2005, GLSEN sponsored its first conference specifically for LGBTS students of color and has devoted resources and specific staff positions to these concerns. Breaking down the barriers that deter students of color from participation in GSAs is crucial if the movement is to fully realize both its potential as a movement based on alliances and its goal of making schools tolerant and respectful of all forms of diversity.

Another factor that needs to be addressed when assessing how effective GSAs are in improving the lives of students is determining how comfortable students feel, within their school environment, about becoming a GSA member. I asked advisors and leaders if they thought most of the LGBT students in their school were involved with the GSA and if not, why not. The sexual orientation of GSA members is difficult to assess accurately because most groups follow an informal policy of not asking about or specifically discussing the sexual identity of club members. Most respondents acknowledged this, but gave their general impressions anyway. The vast majority believed that most of their members were straight ally students and that only a small fraction of the LGBT students in the school came to their group's meetings. Most attributed this to fear of stigmatization or harassment. Those who said the majority of their GSA membership was LGBT were, generally, groups with only five or six members.

When I posed this question about membership numbers to a faculty advisor from a rural Oregon GSA she responded, "Oh no! That is why our straight advocate population is so high. Some of the gay kids in our school are not safe enough within their family and friend structures to be seen at a GSA meeting. I bet we only have 20% of the gay population of our school in attendance." A teacher in an urban school in North Carolina similarly replied:

> I definitely do not. I know there are still a lot of students who perceive the GSA as the gay dating club. They forget the "straight" and "alliance" part. Last year there was a student who was harassed on his way to the meetings. He stopped showing up, and eventually left the school. The students who do attend the meetings don't let the words of others bother them, but many students can't do that.

Although the reports of an unsafe school environment were slightly more common in rural schools and schools in more conservative states, the problem is not exclusive to these locales. As one teacher in a suburban school in Massachusetts replied in response to the same question, "No. The school itself is unsafe because the staff do not want to put the effort into making all students feel safe."

The faculty advisors' analyses about the low rate of LGBT student involvement primarily focused on issues of safety. They expressed a strong understanding that, until schools instituted nondiscrimination and anti-harassment policies that included sexual orientation and gender identity, and then trained and encouraged faculty to enforce such a policy, a clear and present danger would always exist for LGBT students. Fear of this potential harm would always inhibit most LGBT students from getting involved. At the local, state, and national level, groups are starting to respond to this issue by lobbying for the addition of sexual orientation (and sometimes also gender expression) to district or statewide nondiscrimination policies. For example, the GSA Network and Project 10 worked diligently with several other groups for years to get such policy passed in California and are now working hard to make sure the policy is known and enforced by school faculty.

I asked student leaders the same question about group membership. They strongly agreed with the faculty advisors' assessment that far from all LGBT students participated. However, their analysis of the reason for this focused on reluctance based on fear of social stigmatization rather than fear for their physical safety. A student from a suburban North Carolina school explained this analysis directly, "I seriously doubt anyone wanted to run the risk of being identified as GBL or T. It was mainly the seriously brave that took part." A student from suburban New Jersey agreed with this assessment, "No, not every LGBTQ student felt safe participating in the club because we were, obviously, labeled the 'gay' club. Students perceived that only queers, and not allies, could participate. Thus if someone were to join, they would be labeled homosexual. Many people did not want the label." This type of response was given over and over again, indicating that there is still a very strong climate of homophobia in most high schools. It is clear that, for teenagers, the social dangers of ostracization and potential loss of friends and social status are paramount to concerns for their own physical safety.

This is a frustrating situation for student leaders and faculty advisors. They feel that having a strong and active GSA could make their school a more accepting place, but it is very difficult to establish an effective GSA in a school climate where students fear the stigma of the homosexual label and the potential abuse it might bring to them. These GSA leaders find themselves in a double bind. Having a strong and active GSA could have a powerful impact on changing school nondiscrimination policies and dispelling stereotypes and homophobia, and yet building a large and active GSA is challenging without these changes in place.

These statements from GSA leaders strongly inform a conclusion that GSAs, by themselves, are far from an instant cure-all to all of the problems and fears faced by LGBT youth at school. They also indicate that even the majority of schools with GSAs are social institutions that perpetuate, and often condone, heterosexism and the stigmatization and ill treatment of LGBT people, but nothing in the assessments given suggests that GSAs make the school climate worse in any way. Saying that most LGBT kids fear potential negative outcomes for themselves if they become visibly involved in a GSA does not indicate that the GSA itself causes the fear or potential harm. The cause for this is in both the preexisting school climate and the larger cultural climate. It does, perhaps, suggest that GSAs do not result in much change and, therefore, does little to improve the reality of the school experience for the majority of LGBT students.

According to those who shared their experiences and analysis with me, that, too, would be an incorrect conclusion to draw. In the response to my question about the impact the GSA had on their school and on the lives of LGBT students, all faculty and student leaders stated that the evidence indicated it created positive change, although some felt this change was more limited than others did.

The students' assessments of the positive impact of their leadership and alliance work centered on two major factors. First, the majority of students I heard from believed that their hard work had improved the way school faculty and administration dealt with homophobia and anti-gay harassment. Many of these students argued that this improvement came about primarily through their persistence. As a student from suburban Missouri stated, students' refusal to back down from their goals "shows the school that GLBT youth do not have to, and will not, take harassment from other students and faculty. Tolerance has become a policy and will be enforced. [This] shows many young students the power of standing up for what you believe in." A gay male student leader from New Jersey provided this enthusiastic assessment:

> I cannot think of any other single thing that created as much change on such a broad scope as the GSA. It truly brought the school to a new level. Once LGBT students and issues could be considered mainstream nothing was off limits. It genuinely changed how people thought about diversity issues. ...Both allies and LGBT members were more aware of the change they could bring about just by sticking up for their beliefs.

The common analysis of these two students is representative of the connection that many students made between a changed school environment and the empowerment of LGBTS students. A reciprocal relationship forms and this propels the movement forward by accomplishing small steps toward change and inspiring new student leaders to take another step forward.

Many students thought that the greatest repercussion of the GSA was in the lives of the students who participated in the club itself. A student from a rural Wisconsin school explained that "it made GLBT students in our school feel like they had a place in our school. It gave them a purpose. When people would feel like they were on the outside of everything, coming to GSA meetings and support sessions would be the highlight of their week. GLBT students often feel depressed and isolated in high school, and I think that we really helped lessen that feeling." A straight ally student from suburban Connecticut said, "It made us stronger, braver, and more supportive of those around us that need support for ANY reason." It was intriguing to me that so many students spoke about the support the GSA provided as being one of its most important functions. It seems that, although gay–straight alliance groups were initially sought as a way for students to break away from the support group model that had become the response of choice by the schools that had been persuaded to address the needs of LGBT students, in the end, they got a support group anyway. The major difference with a GSA is that it is support of the students' own making and it is support that has produced social action, and not merely personal reflection.

In general, the student leaders' assessment of the amount of change was more positive than that of the faculty advisors. The main reason for this is that faculty advisors do not have the same strong personal connection to the gay–straight alliance. Although every faculty advisor expressed a great deal of pride and professional satisfaction in the work they did with these student groups, they did not experience this as a transforming professional or personal experience. Therefore, the students' evaluation of how the school was changed is intertwined with their feelings of how it changed their personal experiences. In contrast, a faculty advisor's appraisal generally is more of a detached assessment of the school environment. A teacher in Washington thought that the impact of the GSA on her school has been "minimal. We have not been a large or especially active club during the last two years. We have done small things, but more importantly, at least to me, we are visible and teachers know about us. I think it has empowered some students. It has provided community to students who do not otherwise have it." Statements like this one illustrate the faculty advisor's greater skill at separating out the change in the school from the change in the students.

The majority of faculty advisors reported to me that they were amazed by the extent of positive influence GSAs had on group members' lives and, at the same time, were disappointed and frustrated by the more limited change in the school as a whole. A faculty advisor for a GSA in an urban California school noted that the effect the group had on the school has been limited, in a way, by their early successes at empowering students. "I think it is hard. Our administration believes that because we have a GSA and we have a few students who are out, that our campus is safe. It's NOT. These kids have to go to classes with teachers that don't stop hate speech, or don't teach tolerance, that don't keep these kids safe. Not to mention between classes, before and after school, in PE locker rooms, etc....UGH!" Student leaders' view of the GSAs impact on their group members and on the school is limited to four years or less. In contrast, teachers have a more extended view of a wider array of students and faculty and administrators over a longer period of time. When viewed together, both perspectives reflect the same conclusion that all the factors examined in this chapter found: The GSA movement has made significant change, but there is a still a long road ahead.

WHAT GSA MEMBERS GAINED

The most profound indication of the impact of the GSA movement can be measured in students' own assessments of what they gained from their participation. Their own words explain the powerful impact far better than any trained social analyst could, so I close this chapter with their testimony alone.

> I learned about the real level of anger and fear in our community against GLBTQ people, even kids, and I realized what some of the awful consequences of that fear were for people my age. I also learned about the importance of networking in the GLBTQ community and drawing on it for support, especially when I was a teenager. People were so happy to see GLBTQ youth coming out and feeling good about ourselves when they couldn't do that before that they were delighted to help us however they could. I would advise all teens trying to start a GSA, don't try to do it alone.

> I learned that even though our community was small, Christian, and mostly homophobic, we received a lot of support from the community. We had parents and teachers come to us and tell us stories, like, their brother is gay and he had such a hard time in high school, or, their son/daughter is gay, etc. It was very inspirational to go out in the community and ask for support, and see how big of a response you get.

> What you see is only the tip of the iceberg, but once uncovered it will all begin to melt. Nothing is more powerful than a convincingly strong first step to convince people to stand behind you. No one can make you feel inferior without your consent. I am who

I am and I love who I love, nowhere does it say that I am not a human being entitled to the same rights as everyone else.

I learned that there are always many, many sides to an issue. I learned that one of the main problems is not that people are hateful, but that they don't understand. I learned to respect people even if their opinion differs from my own. I learned that activism takes a lot of work, but really comes down to refusing to take no for an answer.

Wow! I learned a lot from my high school experience as leader of GSA. I learned how silence is violence, and that the key goal of homophobia is not interference, but erasure—as long as gay people and issues do not exist, neither do gay people. There is defeat even before there is debate.

I realized there are a lot more gay kids than I thought around here! Also, I really gained some admiration for the straight kids who had the balls to show up at the meetings and show their support … I did try to consider issues on a deeper level. … We've talked about how strongly some Christians feel that homosexuality is a sin, and I've always thought they were awful bigots. But I've realized that they believe that as strongly as I believe that sexual orientation should be embraced, and I'm not so angry at them anymore. They're still wrong, but I feel like I understand where they're coming from now.

I found that when a face is placed on LGBT people, and that face is one of people they know and trust, it is easier to address the damage their homophobia does. While the notion that being gay is "wrong" is difficult to address, as it is so ingrained in society and religion, the notion that others should be accepted for who they are despite their sexual orientation is much easier for others to understand … In terms of rights, I have learned that rights are not just those that can be granted, but that the hardest right to get is the right to emotional safety and respect. Without that it is hard to defend other rights.

EIGHT

HARNESSING THE SOCIAL
AND POLITICAL POWER OF
THE GSA MOVEMENT

I chose to showcase the voices and perspectives of student leaders and their organizational allies in this book because they so often expressed the combined wisdom of dozens of sociologists without the sometimes overly pretentious verbiage of academics. I also wanted to emphasize that social change is almost always driven by the actions of individuals. Individual high school students have been the driving force for change in their schools, starting gay–straight alliance clubs, fighting to add sexual orientation to non-discrimination policies, and running workshops to educate students and faculty about homophobia and the difficulties faced by LGBT students. In the process of doing this, I argue, they started a new social movement. One that is separate from, yet related to, the gay rights movement.

Young people, particularly high school and college students, played a very important role in many social movements, including the civil rights and women's rights movements. In fact, the gay rights movement was the only major movement coming out of the 1960s that was unable to utilize young people in a significant way. This new student-led GSA movement now has the potential to bring the power, energy and creativity of youth—which was used so well by other social movements—to the gay rights movement, potentially propelling it forward and, in the process, making America's schools more tolerant and respectful places where all students are given all the tools they need to reach their full potential.

From early on, fighting for equality in education was a key part of both the civil rights and women's rights movements. Activists involved in these movements understood the importance of the public school in reproducing stereotypes and prejudices through the socialization and segregation of children, and by offering different students unequal access to one of society's most valuable resources available for social advancement. The gay rights movement waited a long time to fight for educational rights, and even now, its members have not fully embraced it as a central issue on which to focus their energies and resources—choosing first to focus on the military and marriage. The fact that they address educational rights at all was forced by the urgency of LGBT youth.

In my conversation with Beth Reis of the Safe Schools Coalition, she spoke about the ability of youth to bring change to schools at a quicker pace than the gay rights movement has been able to bring to other social institutions:

> I think that the fact that it's personal has been part of why it's happened so fast. And in terms of GSAs in particular and not the queer rights movement overall, I think it's because youth activism is very powerful. Administrators don't have a lot of choice in the face of the angry urgency of youth. Every successful human rights movement throughout history has been youth led. There is kind of an urgency and a passion about fairness that youth just have.

What students brought to the civil rights, women's rights and other social movements that was so vital was an intense impatience with injustice. This youthful restlessness, for example, thrust African-American college students into the civil rights movement in large numbers in 1960. Aldon Morris and Cedric Herring point out that:

> By 1960, Black college students were frustrated with the pace of the Civil Rights movement. The students wanted racial segregation overthrown immediately. In February 1960, Black college students stepped directly into the Civil Rights movement, quickening its pace and stiffening its resolve to topple the system of racial segregation.[1]

The sit-in movement that these college students started brought much-needed public attention to the irrationality of racial segregation and the violence with which it was often enforced. It also was able to quickly mobilize large numbers of students to join the cause and eventually start the Student Nonviolent Coordinating Committee (SNCC), which became a significant force in the advancement of the civil rights movement. College students contributed similarly indispensable energy and innovation to anti-war movements, women's liberation movements, and environmental movements, just to name a few.

LGBT and straight ally students took the leadership role in changing schools because they were not willing to wait for the gay rights movement to advocate for change on their behalf. In the late 1980s, they began speaking out against the oppressive homophobic culture of schools. LGBT students asserted that these social institutions, which enforce a culture of normative heterosexuality and homophobia, have a negative impact on LGBT students— making them feel invisible; compelling them to hide their thoughts, feelings and beliefs; persuading them to lie about these things; and forcing them to accept verbal and physical harassment. This process of heterosexual hegemony has a large negative impact on the experiences LGBT, and, in fact, all students have in schools. However, the actions of some LGBT students prove that this hegemonic process in schools has not been fully successful.

Hegemony is a system of oppression that maintains itself with the consent of the oppressed. To work effectively, it requires that the oppressed accept, on some level, that they should be dominated. Hegemonic systems achieve this consent through both cultural and institutional means. Culturally, those in positions of power and influence are able to control and manipulate the definitions and images of oppressed groups in ways that perpetuate the internalization of the belief that these groups are naturally inferior and, therefore, rightfully subordinate. This is achieved by establishing values, beliefs, and norms that all convey the notion that the lesser value, the immorality, and the deviance of subordinate groups is, in fact, based in nature—either genetic/biological predetermination or the predetermination of a higher power. As long as oppressed groups accept these definitions and the evidence used to support them, they will consent to their subordinate status and not resist it (at least not on a regular basis or in an organized way).

The powerful thing about LGBT and straight ally student activism is that it strikes potent blows to both mechanisms of hegemonic domination at once. First, from the beginning, these students have rejected the cultural values, beliefs, and norms that define LGBT people as naturally inferior or pathological, unquestionably immoral, and behaviorally deviant. They refuse to define themselves in these terms, and, perhaps even more importantly, they understand that the terms are constructed by those in power in the interest of power, and not by nature or a higher power in the interest of the common good. Many gay adults eventually come to this understanding, but usually after years of acquiescence. It is notable that some youth never submit to this ideology, so it cannot do the psychological damage it is meant to do, which is to make the oppressed feel that they deserve it. Essentially, LGBT and straight ally student activists are calling their schools out for using their status as neutral conveyers of knowledge to dominate and oppress a group of students.

Every gay and lesbian adult (and most heterosexuals as well) knew the truth in the students' testimonies about harassment and abuse, because they had experienced or witnessed it themselves, but had done nothing to improve things for the generations that would follow them through these institutions. The courage, passion, and urgency of youth eventually persuaded organizations like Lambda Legal, The National Lesbian and Gay Task Force, and the ACLU to take the risk of controversy and put emphasis on schools as a major social institution that needed to be addressed in the struggle for gay rights. It also prompted the formation of groups like Project 10, GLSEN, and the GSA Network to assist youth in their important efforts to change schools.

Student-led GSAs, because they are adolescents, have perhaps a greater potential than other groups to fracture the facade of legitimacy that upholds the oppression of gay and lesbian people, because it is more difficult to rationalize mistreating children than it is adults. Also, because each teen is some adult's child, some teacher or principal's student, they more easily cultivate alliances and support. As a faculty advisor of a GSA in Oregon said:

> The students are compelling when they argue for their rights and protections. The community can't help but to see how beautiful they are. They are not some "special interest group" when they are your neighbor, classmate, or daughter's best friend. GSAs help a community to see that gay people are just people. We play a huge role in working for tolerance for gay rights.

The impact that LGBT youth have had in bringing both alliances and opposition to the GSA movement is analogous, in some ways, to the impact that the AIDS epidemic had on the gay rights movement. News of the AIDS epidemic brought in both straight people with the "gay disease" and family members who might have ignored, been embarrassed by, or denied their child's homosexuality but were motivated to be involved in gay rights to fight for their dying child's life. The tragedy of AIDS caused tremendous losses to gay communities across the country, but it also changed the movement and in some ways made it stronger. The alliances made with heterosexuals in the fight against the disease and with government agencies for providing accurate information, increasing funding for research, and distributing medicines, have been key to this change. However, for all of the alliances and public sympathies that AIDS drew to the gay rights movement, it also fueled, at least initially, a strong backlash against the progress made up to that point. The opposition called AIDS the "gay disease" and claimed it was proof that homosexuality is a deviant lifestyle, a sexual perversion, and a punishment from God.

Over time, the LGBT community won a good deal of sympathy for their cause and brought a more personalized understanding of the harm done by social stigmatization of gay people. The mass media and the entertainment industry paid more attention to the plight of the LGBT community's fight for the rights of those with AIDS and for the civil rights of gay people. This motivated many who may not have been previously willing to advocate just for the rights of LGBT people, but who felt they could rationalize their support now that it was a matter of life and death.

A similar sense of urgency in response to students' stories of abuse and to the reports of suicide and other risk factors ushered in energized and dedicated allies who sped up the progress of the GSA movement. These alliances further break down hegemonic forces by increasing the numbers of heterosexual people who have come to realize that the oppression of LGBT individuals is unjust and to start to understand the power behind the social construction of inequality. A GSA faculty advisor and student leader articulated the impact this way:

> I think tolerance starts in the schools. Without educating students about these types of issues the ignorance will continue. I think that GSAs help bring this taboo subject "out of the closet" and make it okay for students

to support their LGBTQ friends and to be okay with their identity
within this group. I truly believe and hope that twenty years from now
my daughter will think it's crazy that people discriminated against gays
and forbade them to marry.

Educated youths grow up to be educated adults. If one person learns not
to vilify LGBTQ persons, my high school GSA had a powerful effect.
And if every high school produces one person like that, eventually the
LGBT rights movement will cease to be necessary.

A key to social change is that privileged groups come to realize that
their position is unearned, that it is a matter of social definition and established traditions of power, rather than inherent or demonstrated superior-
ity. Once they recognize this, they see that the rights and advantages they
enjoy should be granted to everyone.

The GSA movement has facilitated this process for many of its
straight allies. A straight ally student from Wisconsin reported that she
"will continue to be involved in LGBT issues in the future. I know that
it's something that I am so passionate about that it would be impossible
for me not to. I hope that when I am older I will be able to start my own
organization and continue to educate others around me." The involvement
of straight students with their high school gay–straight alliance had such
powerful impact on their understanding of inequality and discrimination
that the vast majority claimed they were forever dedicated to fighting
for gay rights and against homophobia. For a straight ally student from
Arizona, her plan is stay involved with the GSA movement. "I am going
to continue to be involved in this, and hopefully will be able to be involved
after I graduate college as well. Currently I want to teach high school, so I
would love to eventually be a faculty advisor for a high school GSA." These
statements illustrate the ability of GSAs to bring heterosexual people into
the movement in a lasting way.

LGBT youth have the potential to make great gains in the struggles
for gay rights because of the freshness and creativity they can bring to the
practices and discourse of the movement. They are, in a sense, the "outsider
within." They are part of the gay and lesbian community and the gay rights
movement by virtue of their sexual orientation. At the same time, they are
outside of both, as youth and as students focused on changing their schools.

Because of these things, LGBT students are not as schooled or invested in the "master frames" of these groups, which have become so tightly locked in the polarized culture war with the opposition. Their lives and experiences often also transcend the traditional narrative of "the closet" that is too often used to try to understand and speak about the lives of LGBT people. The ready-made rationales for opposing the rights of gay and lesbian people do not work as well when the subject is teenagers and the arena is public education. As one teacher stated:

> I think young people are necessary to bring the gay rights struggle out
> of this "don't ask, don't tell" phase that we seem to be in. The straight
> community seems to be saying, "OK, we don't think you're evil. But why
> do you want to push it so much? Why do you need marriage? Etc. Young
> people are needed to keep our issues alive and to help people to understand
> that it's not a "boutique" issue important only to a small segment of society
> identified as "those gay activists pushing their radical agenda."

The religious right expected that accusations of a radical homosexual agenda threatening the impressionable minds of children would be the downfall of the GSA movement. They continue to work hard to make this happen by trying to stir up fear in parents, school boards, and communities through the use of old stereotypes, narrow religious doctrine, and false accusations. Although this has fostered controversy and fortified institutional resistance to LGBT and straight ally student's efforts to change their schools, it has not stopped them. Student leaders asserted that they were determine not to be curtailed from their efforts:

> Homophobia is horrifically stupid and I plan to do everything I can do to
> stamp it out by educating people and participating in the political process.

> I think it is very important. We need to educate our peers as youth if we
> expect people to grow up with an awareness of and tolerance for LGBT
> issues. I think that this should continue. I even hope that the realities
> of gay and lesbian relationships begin to be worked into classroom
> lessons. I think that the adult LGBT community needs to acknowledge
> this and make efforts to improve education of LGBT issues in schools.
> Without that, my generation will be fighting the same fights that the

"adult" generation of gays is fighting now with people who are just as uneducated about why LGBT rights should be equal to those of hetero-sexuals—as individuals, couples, and parents.

I have no way to measure the number of students who have been too frightened by the tactics of the opposition to start a GSA in their school, but the growth in numbers of GSAs tell us that thousands have not been intimi-dated. Based on my conversations with youth leaders from around the country over the past decade, I have no doubt that the resistance has, in fact, further motivated hundreds of individuals to dedicate themselves to this cause.

The role of the GSA in high schools is immeasurable. Public schools may be the only true "melting pot" that still exists. There are people from every group and sub-group that you can think of. When an active GSA exists in a high school it may be one of the few opportunities to impact the larger society. Simply our presence and refusal to be intimi-dated makes an impression.

We keep it progressive. We don't settle for compromises at the expense of any part of the queer community. I would like to see student activists move beyond progressive, and make the movement radical.

Students are the ones who put things into perspective for adults when they lose their way. GLBT youth activism is the future of the move-ment, without them the movement will die.

The simplicity with which youth see the issue is not really a lack of sophistication or experience. It is really wisdom—the wisdom to get to the heart of the matter, which really is simple. It is all the political positioning and academic analyzing that has made it complex.

Debates over GSAs serve not only to repeat old established political arguments, but also to help forge new and transcending ones. The role of LGBTS youth in these social movements and the political battles waged in their name is crucial to the short-term and long-range impact they will have on American schools and larger cultural wars. This is the first time in history that there has been a cohort like these LGBT youth activists, and I believe it is their unique and new perspective that has the power to forever change the culture of homophobia in schools and, while doing so, revolutionize gay politics. If their voices are lost and their leadership co-opted by the institutionalization of their cause, I fear the reverberations of their efforts to stand out and stand together will be muted.

The vast majority of student leaders I spoke with plan on continuing their activism well beyond their high school years. One of the GSA movement's most significant achievements is that it produced a new generation of political activists to fight for the civil liberties of LGBT citizens. This is a remarkable accomplishment, especially at a time when there is so much talk about the apathy and civic illiteracy of youth (and the majority of adults, for that matter). Their passion and dedication to continue working for change came through loud and clear when I asked student leaders if they planned to remain involved with the GSA movement.

> Of course! It's my life's passion and duty. My aspiration is to become a
> secondary school English teacher, so I will seek to incorporate GLBT
> authors into the curriculum and explain how they fit into not only the
> GLBT tradition, but also the human tradition. I will continue to exude
> compassion, honesty, and good faith and I will never hesitate to empha-
> size that the GSA is, above all, a human rights group.

> Yes. I am who I am. I want to get married, I want to be treated as a human
> being just like everyone else. No one has been able to convince me that
> I am worth less than everybody else and until someone does I will continue
> to stand tall and be strong, demanding and working for my rights.

> Now it is about taking the skills I learned by being a leader in the LGBT
> community and applying them to school, life, everything and becoming
> the best, most successful, well-adjusted, "normal" person that I can be.
> I certainly wish I had seen more of those as a kid struggling to come out.
> I can't explain how that would have helped me. I just want to be that for
> a kid who is struggling to come out one day.

> Yes. I wish to be a GLBT youth counselor and be a gay activist because
> being equal is very important to me and nothing is going to stop me from
> achieving this goal.

Of course. I am going to be involved until we get the full and uncondi-
tional rights that we've deserved for 2,000 years. Maybe when I'm old
I'll be "that nice old queer down the street" and the kids in my neighborhood will invite me out to play football with them. We'll see.

The GSA movement has the potential to be a major driving force in
helping these students as they continue to work to reach these goals. The
movement's focus on changing schools and building alliances, which was
established by the first student leaders, have provided a foundation for the
future. The question is how will they build upon it? The GSA movement
needs to reach out to those youths who are still suffering in isolation and
silence. There seems to be an assumption that these kids are being helped
by the very presence of a GSA in a school, even if they do not take part.
Although this may be true, I also believe that more could be done to reach
out, support and include them. It is important to realize that the GSA
movement has not been felt at all in many areas of the South and Midwest.
Expansion into these areas could have a huge impact on students who lack
the resources and cultural images available to those on the West Coast and
in the Northeast where the movement is the strongest.

As a straight ally teacher from California states:

Schools in this country are designed to prepare students to live in a
pluralistic society. Unfortunately, this ideal has not been realized with
many segments of our society, including the GLBT ones. Unless we
begin early to address attitudes and rights, we will graduate young
people who perpetuate old stereotypes. GSAs provide a forum for
students to address hate, learn positive ways to change society, and
establish commitment to changing the world one person at a time.

What the continuing social and political impact of all this hard work
and progress will be is largely contingent on how many are willing to stand
out and stand together with these students and follow their lead.

REFERENCES

ACLU, 2003. "Summary of School Harassment Lawsuits." http://www.aclu.org/ LesbianGayRights/LesbianGay rights.cfm?ID=12879&c=106

AFA Journal, May 2001 http://www.afa.net/journal/may/cover.asp

Ainlay, S., Becker, G. and Coleman, L.M. 1986. *The Dilemma of Difference: A Multidisciplinary View of Stigma*. New York: Plenum.

Altman, D. 1982. *The Homosexualization of America*. Boston, MA: Beacon.

Anderson, D.A. 1987. "Family and Peer Relations of Gay Adolescents." *Adolescent Psychiatry* 14:162–178.

Anderson, D.A. 1994. "Lesbian and Gay Adolescents: Social and Developmental Considerations." *High School Journal*, special edition: 13–19.

Beckham, Lauren (1997), "Diversity Unites: Gay, Straight Students Find Alliance Supportive," *Boston Herald*, May 5, 1997, section: News, page 18.

Bell and Weinberg. 1978. *Homosexualities: A Study of Diversity Among Men and Women*. New York: Simon and Schuster.

Bell, A. et al. 1981. *Sexual Preference: Its Development in Men and Women*. Bloomington, IN: University of Indiana Press.

Benford, Robert D. and Snow, David A. (2000) "Framing Processes—39.

Berstein, Mary (1997) *"Celebration and Suppression: The Strategic Uses of Identity by the Lesbian and Gay Movement."* American Journal of Sociology 103: 531–565.

Best, Joel 1987 *"Rhetoric in Claims-Making."* Social Problems 34:101–121.

Best, Joel 1989a "Claims." In Joel Best (Ed.), *Images of Issues*: 1–3. New York: Walter Gruyter.

Best, Joel 1989b "Dark Figures and Child Victims: Statistical Claims About Missing Children." In Joel Best (Ed.), *Images of Issues*: 21–38. New York: Walter Gruyter.

Billings, Dwight B. and Shaunna L. Scott (1994) *"Religion and Political Legitimation."* Annual Review of Sociology 20: 173-201.

Blumer, Herbert 1971 "Social Problems as Collective Behavior." *Social Problems* 18:298–306.

Bravmann, S. 1996. "Postmodern Queer Identities." 333–361 in *Queer Theory/ Sociology*, Steven Seidman (Ed.). Cambridge, MA: Blackwell.

Brown, Sarah H. (1997) "Popular Opinion on Homosexuality: The Shared Moral Language of Opposing Views." *Sociological Inquiry* 70: 446–461.

Brulliard, Karin (2003). "Texas Students Sue to Organize Gay Club at High School." *The Washington Post*, October 21, 2003, section: A, page 3.

Bruske, Ed (1983) "First Amendment Cited; Gays Lose Lawsuit Against GU," *The Washington Post* October 15, 1983, First Section, A1.

Bull, Christopher and John Gallagher (1996) *Perfect Enemies: The Religious Right, the Gay Movement and the Politics of the 1990s*. New York: Crown.

Calhoun, Craig (1994) "Social Theory and the Politics of Identity." In Craig Calhoun (Ed.), *Social Theory and the Politics of Identity*. Cambridge, MA: Blackwell.

Carnoy, Martin (Ed.) (1972) *Schooling in a Corporate Society*. New York: McKay.

Carnoy, Martin and Levine, H.M. 1976 *The Limits of Educational Reform*. New York: McKay.

Carnoy, Martin and Levine, H.M. 1985 *Schooling and Work in the Democratic State*. Stanford, CA: Stanford University Press

Cass, V.C. 1979. "Homosexual Identity Formation: A Theoretical Model." *Journal of Homosexuality* 10:77–84.

Cass, V.C. 1984. "Homosexual Identity: A Concept in Need of Definition." *Journal of Homosexuality*, 9:105–126.

CDC-NCHSTP-Divisions of HIV/AIDDS Prevention, retrieved Januanry 3, 2005 Fact Sheet— Young People at Risk: HIV/AIDS Among America's Youth http://www.cdc.gov/hiv/pubs/facts/youth.htm ASHA Facts and Answers About STDs: STD Statistics, http://www.ashastd.org/stdfaqs/statistics.html

Chandler, K. 1995. *Passages of Pride*. Los Angeles, CA: Alyson Books.

Cianciotto, J., and Cahill, S. (2003). Education policy: Issues affecting lesbian, gay, bisexual, and transgender youth. New York: The National Gay and Lesbian Task Force Policy Institute.

Cohen, J.L. (1994) "Strategy or Identity: New Theoretical Paradigms and Contemporary Social Movements." *Social Research* 52:663–716.

Coltrane, Scott. and N. Hickman 1992 "Rhetoric of Rights and Needs: Moral Discourse in the Reform of Child Custody and Child Support Laws." *Social Problems*, 39.

Cook and Herdt. 1990. "To Tell or Not to Tell: Patterns of Self-Disclosure to Mothers and Fathers Reported by Gay and Lesbian Youth." in *Parent and Child Relations Across the Lifespan*, Pillemer, K. and K. McCartney (Eds.). New York: Oxford University Press.

Cooper, Tony (2002), "Rights Group Honors Queer Youth Action Team," *The San Francisco Chronicle*, July 26, 2002, section: Contra Costa, page 2.

Daly, Gavin (1995) "Students Rally for Gay/Straight March," *The Boston Globe* May 21, 1995, section: Metro/Region, page 34.

Davis, Mark (1998) "Courage of Gay Speakers Was the Real Story," *St. Petersburg Times* (Florida) May 3, 1998, Sunday Section: Neighborhood times; letters; pg. 2

DeBeauvoir, Simone (1952), *The Second Sex*. New York: Knopf.

DeCrescenzo, C., (Ed.) 1994. *Helping Gay and Lesbian Youth: New Policies, New Programs, New Practice*. Binghamton, NY: Harrington Park Press.

Dejowski, Edmund F. (1992). "Public Endorsement of the Restrictions on Three Aspects of Free Expression by Homosexuals." *Journal of Homosexuality* 23:1–18.

D'Emilio, John 1998. *Sexual Politics, Sexual Communities*. Chicago, IL: University of Chicago Press.

D'Emilio, John (2000) "Cycles of Change, Questions of Strategy: The Gay and Lesbian Movement After Fifty Years." In The Politics of Gay Rights, Craig A. Rimmerman, Kenneth D. Wald, and Cylde Wilcox (eds.) Chicago: University of Chicago Press, page 48.

D'Emilio, John (Ed.) 2002a *Creating Change: Sexuality, Public Policy and Civil Rights*. New York, NY: St. Martin's Press.

D'Emilio, John (Ed.) 2002b *As the World Turned: Essays on Gay History, Politics and Culture*. Duke University Press.

D'Emilio, John and Estelle Freedman 1998 *Intimate Matters: A History of Sexuality in America*. Harper Collins Publishers.

Dennis, D.I. and Ruth E.H. 1986. "Gay Youth and the Right to Education." *Yale Law and Policy Review*, 4:445–455.

Dilley, Patrick (2002). *Queer Man On Campus: A History of Non-Heterosexual College Men, 1945–2000*. New York, New York: Routledge.

Due, L. 1995. *Joining the Tribe: Growing Up Gay and Lesbian in the '90s*. New York: Doubleday.

Durby, D.D. 1994. "Gay, Lesbian, and Bisexual Youth." 1–37 In *Helping Gay and Lesbian Youth*, T. DeCrescenso (Ed.). Binghamton, NY: The Haworth Press, Inc.

Durocher, C. 1990. "Heterosexuality: Sexuality or Social System." *Resources for Feminist Research*, 19:13–19.

Edwards, W.J. 1996. "A Sociological Analysis of An Invisible Minority Group: Male Adolescent Homosexuals." *Youth and Society*, 27: 334–355.

Epstein, D. (Ed.) 1994. *Challenging Lesbian and Gay Inequalities in Education*. Philadephia: Open University Press.

Epstein, Steven (1999), "Gay and Lesbian Movements in the United States: Dilemmas of Identity, Diversity, and Political Strategy." 30–90. In *The Global Emergence of Gay and Lesbian Politics*, B.D. Adam et al. (Eds.) Philadelphia: Temple University Press.

Falk, R. (1988), *"Religion and Politics: Verging on the Postmodern."* Alternatives *13:379–394*.

Fetner, Tina and Kristin Kush (2003), "Gay–straight Alliances in High Schools: An Emerging Form of LGBTQ Youth Activism." Unpublished paper presented at the American Sociological Association Annual Meeting, August 2004.

Fey, Marc A. (2003) "Homosexual Agenda in Public Schools Marches Forward." Focus on the Family. http://www.family.org/cforum/fosi/p_friendly.cfm?articleurl=cforum/fosi/education/nac/a0029442.cfm.

Foucault, M. [1976] 1990. *The History of Sexuality Volume 1: An Introduction*. New York: Vintage Books.

Foucault, Michel (1980) Power/Knowledge: Selected Interviews and Other Writings, 1972–1977. *Translated by C. Gordon, L. Marshall, J. Mepham, K. Soper. New York: Pantheon Books.*

FRC FAQ 1997 *"What is FRC's Response to the Homosexual Agenda?" http://www.frc.org/frc/faq/faq12.html.*

FRC FAQ (1997b), "The 'Gay Youth' Campaign and 'Safe Schools.'" http://www.frc.org/frc/podium/pd96g9hs.html.

Gallois, C. and Cox, S. (1996), "Gay and Lesbian Identity Development: A Social Identity Perspective." *Journal of Homosexuality*, 30:1–30.

Gamson, Joshua (1994), "Silence, Death, and the Invisible Enemy: AIDS Activism and Social Movement 'Newness.'" *Social Problems* 36:351–367.

Gamson, Joshua (1996), "Must Identity Movements Self-Destruct? A Queer Dilemma." In Steven Seidman (Ed.), *Queer Theory/Sociology:* 395–420. Cambridge, MA: Blackwell.

Gamson, William A., David Croteau, William Hoynes, Theodore Sasson (1992), "Media Images and the Social Construction of Reality." *Annual Review of Sociology* 18: 373–393.

Gamson, William A. and Meyer, David S. (1994) "Framing Political Opportunity." In Doug McAdam, John D. McCarthy, and Mayer N. Zald (Eds.), *Comparative Perspectives on Social Movements*. New York, N.Y.: Cambridge University Press.

Gay, Lesbian and Straight Education Network & National Center for Lesbian Rights. (2003). Fifteen expensive reasons why safe schools legislation is in your state's best interest. Unpublished report.

Gerhards, Jugen (1995) "Framing Dimensions and Framing Strategies: Contrasting Ideal and Real-Type Frames." *Social Science Information* 34:225–248.

Gibson, Paul (1989). "Gay Male and Lesbian Youth Suicide." In U.S. Department of Health and Human Services, Report of the Secretary's Task Force on Youth Suicide. Washington, DC: U.S. Government Printing Office, vol. 3 pp. 110–142.

Giugni, Marco (1998), "Was It Worth the Effort? The Outcomes and Consequences of Social Movements." *Annual Review of Sociology* 24: 371–393.

GLSEN. (1996) *Leadership Institute 1997 Manual. New York: Gay, Lesbian, and Straight Education Network. http//www.glsen.org.*

GLSEN (2003a) *http://www.glsen.org/cgi-bin/iowa/all/about/profile/index.html.*

GLSEN (2003b), "The 2003 National School Climate Survey," http://www.glsen.org.

Goffman, E. 1963. *Stigma: Notes on the Management of a Spoiled Identity*. New York: Simon & Schuster Inc.

Goodman, J. 1996. "Lesbian, Gay, and Bisexual Issues in Education: A Personal View." 9–16. In *Open Lives, Safe Schools: Addressing Gay and Lesbian /Issues in Education*, D.R. Walling (Ed.), Bloomington, IN: Phi Delta Kappa Educational Foundation.

Haider-Markel, Donald P. and Meier, Kenneth J. (1996) "The Politics of Gay and Lesbian Rights: Expanding the Scope of the Conflict." *The Journal of Politics* 58: 332–349.

Harbeck, K. 1994. "Invisible No More: Addressing the Needs of Gay, Lesbian, and Bisexual Youth and Their Advocates." *High School Journal*, special edition: 170–180.

Harvey, Linda (2004) "How We Got Here" http://www.truthatschool.org/how_we_got_here.htm.

Hayes, W. (1991), "To Be Young and Gay and Living in the '90s." *Utne Reader*, March/April, pp. 94–100.

Hechinger, Grace and Fred Hechinger (1978), "Homosexuality on Campus," *New York Times*, March 12, 1978.

Herdt, G. (Ed.) (1989a), *Gay and Lesbian Youth*. New York: Harrington Park Press.

Herdt, G. (1989b), "Gay and Lesbian Youth, Emergent Identities and Cultural Scenes at Home and Abroad." *Journal of Homosexuality*, 17:1–41.

Herdt, Gilbert and Andrew Boxer (1993), *Children of Horizons: How Gay and Lesbian Teens Are Leading a New Way Out of the Closet*. Boston, MA: Beacon Press.

Herek, Gregory M. (1988), "Heterosexuals' Attitudes toward Lesbians and Gay Men." *The Journal of Sex Research* 25: 451–77.

Heredia, Christopher (2001), "Gay Students Demand Schools Recognize Law, State's Districts Slow to End Harassment," *The San Francisco Chronicle*, June 3, 2001, section: News, page A24.

Herman, Didi (1994), Rights of Passage: Struggles for Lesbian and Gay Legal Equality. *Toronto: University of Toronto Press*.

Herman, Didi (1997), *The Antigay Agenda: Orthodox Vision and the Christian Right*. Chicago, IL: University of Chicago Press.Hetrick and Martin (1987). "Developmental Issues and Their Resolution for Gay and Lesbian Adolescents." *Journal of Homosexuality*, 14: 25–43.

Hetrick Martin Institute (2002), "The Hetrick-Martin Institute: The Past, Present and Future." http://www.hmi.org/GeneralInfoAndDonations/AboutHMIAndHMHS/default.aspx.

Hetrick Martin Institute (2002) http://www.hmi.org/Youth/FAQs/default.aspx.

Hilgartner, Stephen and Bosk, Charles (1988) *"The Rise and Fall of Social Problems: A Public Arenas Model,"* American Journal of Sociology *94: 53–78*.

Hughes, Jim (2003), "Teens Sue in Favor of Gay/Straight Alliance, Springs District Forbids Meeting at Palmer High," *The Denver Post*, December 14, 2003, section: A Section, page A-29.

Hunter, J.D. (1991) *Culture Wars: The Struggle to Define America*. New York: Basic Books.

Hunter, J. and Schaecher, R. 1987. "Stresses on Lesbian and Gay Adolescents in Schools." *Social Work in Education*, 9 (3):180–190.

Iles, Trey (2004) "Gay/Straight Club Disturbs Parents; School Board Urged to Scrap New Group." *The Times-Picayune*, New Orleans, March 11, 2004, section: Metro, page 1

Irving, J. [1994] 1996. "A Place in the Rainbow: Theorizing Gay and Lesbian Culture." 213–240 in *Queer Theory/Sociology*, Steven Seidman (Ed.), Cambridge, MA: Blackwell.

Jan, Tracy (2004), "Students Want 'Sexual Identity' in Policy," *The Oregonian*, February 11, 2004, section: East zoner, page D2.

Jenness, Valerie (1994) "Social Movements Growth, Domain Expansion, and Framing Process: The Gay/Lesbian Movement and Violence Against Gays and Lesbians as a Social Problem." *Social Problems* 42:145–170.

Jennings, Kevin (1994), *One Teacher in Ten: Gay and Lesbian Educators Tell Their Stories*. Alyson Publishers.

Johnson, Susan (1992), *"On the Fire Brigade: Why Liberalism Won't Stop the Anti-Gay Campaigning of the Right."* Critical Sociology *20: 3–19.*

Jonsson, Greg (2003), "Students Unite Against Harassment of Gays," *St. Louis Post-Dispatch,* February 27, 2003, section: Metro, page B1.

Kandermans, Bert and Oegema, Dirk (1987) *"Potential Networks, Motivations, and Barriers: Steps Toward Participation in Social Movements."* American Sociological Review *52: 519–531.*

Karp, S. (1995), "Trouble Over the Rainbow." Pp. 23–35 In *Rethinking Schools: An Agenda for Change,* D. Levine et al. (Eds.), New York: The New Press.

Kaufman, Michael, "Homosexuals Organize at Universities," *New York Times,* January 28, 1973.

Kim, Ahan (2001), "Gay–straight Group Bursting with Pride, Ready for Parade," *The Atlanta Journal and Constitution,* June 21, 2001, section: DeKalb Extra, page 13A.

Kinsey, Alfred [1948] (1998), *Sexual Behavior and the Human Male.* Indiana: Indiana University Press.

Kinsey, Alfred [1953] (1998), *Sexual Behavior and the Human Female.* Indiana: Indiana University Press.

Kissen, Rita M. (1996), *The Last Closet: The Real Lives of Lesbian and Gay Teachers.* Heinemann Publishers.

Kite, Mary E. and Bernard E. Whitley (1996), "Sex Differences in Attitudes toward Homosexual Persons, Behaviors, and Civil Rights; A Meta-Analysis." *Personality and Social Psychology Bulletin* 22: 336–53.

Kournay, R.F.C. "Suicide Among Homosexual Adolescents," *Journal of Homosexuality* 13 (4):111–117.

Kriesi, Hanspeter (1994) *"The Organizational Structure of New Social Movements in Political Context." In Doug McAdam, John D. McCarthy, and Mayer N. Zald (Eds.),* Comparative Perspectives on Social Movements: *152–184. New York, N.Y.: Cambridge University Press.*

LaMar, Lisa and Mary Kite (1998). "Sex Differences in Attitudes toward Gay Men and Lesbians: A Multidimensional Perspective." *Journal of Sex Research* 35:189–96.

Lambda News and Views (1997) "Near $1 Million Settlement Raises Standard for Protection of Gay Youth. http://www.lambdalegal.org/cgibin/pages/documents/record?record=56.

Linneman, Thomas, J. (2003), *Weathering Change: Gays and Lesbians, Christian Conservatives, and Everyday Hostilities.* NY: University of New York Press.

Lipkin, Arthur (1999), *Understanding Homosexuality, Changing Schools.* Boulder, CO: Westview Press.

Lo, Clarence Y.H. (1982) "Countermovements and Conservative Movements in the Contemporary U.S." *Annual Review of Sociology* 8:107–134.

Loftus, Jeni (2001), "America's Liberalization in Attitudes toward Homosexuality, 1973 to 1998." *American Sociological Review* 66, no. 5: 762–782.

Lugg, Catherine A. (2002), "Reading, Writing, and Reconstructionism: The Christian Right and the Politics of Public Education." *Educational Policy* 14: 622-637.

Macgillivray, Ian K. (2004), *Sexual Orientation and School Policy: A Practical Guide For Teachers, Administrators, and Community Activists.* New York, NY: Rowman and Littlefield Publishers.

Margruder, B. and Wider-Haugrud, L.K. (1996), "Homosexual Identity Expression Among Lesbian and Gay Adolescents: An Analysis of Perceived Structural Associations." *Youth and Society,* 27:313–333.

Martin and Hetrick (1988), "The Stigmatization of the Gay and Lesbian Adolescent." *Journal of Homosexuality,* 16:163–183.

Martin, A.D. (1982), "Learning to Hide: The Socialization of the Gay Adolescent." *Adolescent Psychiatry,* 10:52–65.

Martin, William (1996), *With God On Our Side: The Rise of the Religious Right in America.* New York: Broadway Books.

236 REFERENCES

McAdam, Doug, McCarthy, John D., and Zald, Mayer N. (1996) "Opportunties, Mobilizing Structures, and Framing Processes—Toward a Synthetic Comparative Perspective on Social Movements." In Doug McAdam, John D. McCarthy, and Mayer N. Zald (Eds.), *Comparative Perspectives on Social Movements*: 1–20. New York: Cambridge University Press.

McDonald, G.J. (1982), "Individual Differences in the Coming Out Process for Gay Men: Implications for Theoretical Models." *Journal of Homosexuality*, 8:47–60.

McIntosh, M. [1968] 1996. "The Homosexual Role" 33–40. In *Queer Theory/Sociology*, Steven Seidman (Ed.), Cambridge, MA: Blackwell.

Meyer, David S. and Staggenborg, Suzanne (1996), *Movements, Countermovements, and the Structure of Political Opportunity.*" American Journal of Sociology *101: 628–660.*

Miceli, Melinda S. (1998), "Recognizing All the Differences: Gay Youth and Public Education in America." State University of New York at Albany. Unpublished Dissertation.

Miceli, Melinda S. (2002a) "Gay, Lesbian, and Bisexual Youth." In Diane Richardson and Steven Seidman (Eds.), *The Handbook on Lesbian and Gay Studies*. London, UK: Sage Publications.

Miceli, Melinda S. (2002b) "Gay, Lesbian, and Bisexual Students: The Impact of School on Sexual Identity Development," In *Sexual Lives: Theories and Realities of Human Sexualities*, Robert Heasley and Betsy Crane (Eds.), McGraw-Hill.

Millett, K. (1984), "Beyond Politics? Children and Sexuality." In *Pleasure and Danger*, C.S. Vance (Ed.), New York: Routledge.

Mills, C. Wright (1956), *The Power Elite*. New York: Oxford University Press.

Mission America 2004 http//:www.missionamerica.com.

Morris, Aldon and Cedric Herring (1996), "The Civil Rights Movement: A Social and Political Watershed." In Pedraza, Silvia and Ruben Rumbaut (Eds.) *Origins and Destinies: Immigration, Race, and Ethnicity in America*. Belmont, CA: Wadsworth.

Mottl, Tahi (1980), "The Analysis of Counter Movements." *Social Problems* 27: 620–635.

Nissman, Cara (2003), "Safety in Numbers: As Gay–Straight Alliances Grow, So Does Acceptance in Schools," *The Boston Herald*, April 7, 2003, section: Arts and Life, page 30.

O'Sullivan, Eileen (1998), Courage of Gay Speakers Was the Real Story" *St. Petersburg Times* (Florida) May 3, 1998, Sunday Section: Neighborhood times; letters; pg. 2

Owens, Robert E. (1998), *Queer Kids: The Challenges and Promise for Lesbian, Gay and Bisexual Youth*. New York: Harrington Park Press.

Pace, Eric, "Parley Urges College Facilities For Counseling of Homosexuals," *New York Times*, December 15, 1971.

Page, L. (1994), "The Potential Effects on Education, Curricula, and Policy of Homosexual 'Marriage.' http://www.frc.org/frc/podium/pd967hs.html.

Patton, Cindy (1995), "Refiguring Social Space." In Steven Seidman and Linda Nicholson (Eds.), *Social Postmodernism: Beyond Identity Politics*: 216–249. Cambridge, UK: Cambridge University Press.

Pemberton-Butler, Lisa (2000), "A Safe Place for Gays or Straights: Tacoma Teens Carry Diversity to Another Level," *Seattle Times*, October 16 2000, section: South, page B1.

Perrotti, Jeff (2002), When the Drama Club is Not Enough: Lessons From the Safe Schools Program for Lesbian and Gay Students. Boston, MA: Beacon.

Peterson, Iver, "Homosexuals Gain Support on Campus," *New York Times*, June 5, 1974.

P.E.R.S.O.N Project 1995 D. Marshall, R. Kaplan, and J. Greenman. The P.E.R.S.O.N Organizing Manual. http://www.youth.org/loco/PERSON Project/

Plummer, K. 1975. *Sexual Stigma: An Interactionist Account*. New York: Routledge.

Plummer, K. 1990. "Understanding childhood sexualities." *Journal of Homosexuality*, 20 (1/2):231–249.

Prate, Trish (1993), "A Comparative Study of Attitudes toward Homosexuality: 1986 and 1991." *Journal of Homosexuality* 26–77–83.

Project 10 Handbook 2003.Addressing Lesbian and Gay Issues in Our Schools: A Resource Directory for Teachers, Guidance Counselors, Parents and School Based Adolescent Care Providers. Los Angeles, CA: Friends of Project 10, Inc.

Project 10 (2004) http://www.project10.org.

Raymond, D. (1994), "Homophobia, Identity, and the Meaning of Desire: Reflections on the Cultural Construction of Gay and Lesbian Adolescent Sexuality." Pp. 115-150 In *Sexual Cultures and the Construction of Adolescent Identities*, J.M. Irvine (Ed.), Philadelphia: Temple University Press.

Reinhold, Robert (1971) "Campus Homosexuals Organize To Win Community Acceptance." *New York Times*, December 15, 1971.

Remafedi, G. 1987. "Homosexual Youth: A Challenge to Contemporary Society." *JAMA*, July 10, 258.

Rich, A. 1983. "Compulsory Heterosexuality and Lesbian Existence." In *Powers of Desire*, A.Snitow et al. (Ed.), New York: Monthly Review Press.

Richardson, Diane (2000), Rethinking Sexuality. *London, UK: Sage Publications.*

Ritter, John (2000a), "High School Clubs, Gay Students Stake Their Ground," *USA Today*, January 18, 2000, section: News, page 1A.

Ritter, John (2000b), "Judge Lets Club Meet at School." *USA Today*, February 7, 2000, section: News, page 4A.

Robertson, R. (1987), "Young Gays." In *The Theory and Practice of Homosexuality*, Hart and Richardson (Eds.), London, U.K.: Routledge and Kegan Paul.

Rofes, E. (1989), "Opening Up the Classroom Closet: Responding to the Educational Needs of Gay and Lesbian Youth." *Harvard Educational Review*, 59:444–453.

Rohde, Marie (1999), "Students Stand Up for Their Beliefs, Form Group to Combat Homophobia," *Milwaukee Journal Sentinel*, April 14,1999, section: News North, page 7.

Roiphe, Anne, "The Trouble at Sarah Lawrence," *New York Times*, March 20, 1977.

Rummler, Gary (2001), "Peace Prize: Student Makes Mark on School, Hernandez Honored for Work on Alliance at Riverside," *Milwaukee Journal Sentinel*, June 27, 2001, section: News, page 6B.

Savin-Williams, R.C. (1989), "Coming Out to Parents and Self-Esteem of Gay and Lesbian Youth." *Journal of Homosexuality*, 18:1–35.

Savin-Williams, R.C. (1990), *Gay and Lesbian Youth: Expressions of Identity*. New York: Hemisphere.

Schneider, Joseph W. (1985), "Social Problems Theory: The Constructionist View." *Annual Review of Sociology* 11: 209–229.

Schneider, M. (1989), "Sappho was a Right On Adolescent: Growing Up Lesbian." *Journal of Homosexuality*, 17:111–130.

Sears, J.T. (1992), *Sexuality and the Curriculum: The Politics and Practices of Sex Education*. New York: Teachers College Press.

Seidman, Steven (1991), *Romantic Longings*. New York, New York: Routledge.

Seidman, Steven (1992), *Embattled Eros*. New York, New York: Routledge.

Seidman, S. (1995), "Deconstructing Queer Theory or the Under-Theorization of the Social and the Ethical." 116–140 in *Social Postmodernism: Beyond Identity Politics*, Steven Seidman and Linda Nicholson (Eds.) Cambridge, UK: Cambridge University Press.

Seidman, S. 1996. "Introduction." 1–29 in *Queer Theory/Sociology*, Steven Seidman (Ed.), Cambridge, MA: Blackwell.

Seidman, Steven (2002) *Beyond the Closet: The Transformation of Gay and Lesbian Life*. New York,: Routledge.

Seltzer, Richard (1993), "AIDS. Homosexuality. Public Opinion and Changing Correlates Over Time." *Journal of Homosexuality* 26:85–97.

Simonds, R. (1996), "President's Report July 1997." National Association of Christian Educators/ Citizens for Excellence in Education. Box 3200, Costa Mesa, CA 92628.

Sizer, T.R. 1997 "The Meanings of 'Public Education'." In J.I. Goodlad and T.J. McMannon (Eds.), *The Public Purpose of Education and Schooling*: 33–40. San Francisco: Jossey-Bass Publishers.

Snow, D.A. and R.D. Benford (1988), "Ideology, Frame Resonance, and Participant Mobilization." *International Social Movements Research* 1:197–217.

Snow, D.A. and R.D. Benford (1992), "Master Frames and Cycles of Protest." In A. Morris and C. McClurg Mueller (Eds.) *Frontiers in Social Movement Theory*: 133–155. New Haven, CT: Yale University Press.

Sprigg, Peter (2004), "Testimony in opposition to HB 345, 'An act concerning education-prevention of harassment and intimidation in public schools." Family Research Council. http://www.frc.org/get.cfm?I=TS03C1&v

Sullivan, T. and M. Schneider. (1987), Developmental and Identity Issues in Adolescent Homosexuals. *Child and Adolescent Social Work*, 4:13–23.

Tarrow, Sidney G. (1994), *Power in Movement: Social Movements, Collective Action, and Mass Politics in the Modern State*. Cambridge: Cambridge University Press.

Troiden, R.R. (1979), "Becoming Homosexual: A Model of Gay Identity Acquisition. *Psychiatry*, 42:362–373.

Troiden, R.R. (1988), *Gay and Lesbian Identity: A Sociological Analysis*. New York: General Hall.

Troiden, R.R. (1989), The Formation of Homosexual Identities. *Journal of Homosexuality*, 17:43–73.

Tubbs, Sharon (1998), "Students Hope to Inspire Tolerance," *St. Petersburg Times*, February 8, 1998, section: Seminole Times, page 1.

Unks, G. (1993), "Thinking About the Homosexual Adolescent." *High School Journal*, special edition: 1–6.

Unks, G. (Ed.) (1995), *The Gay Teen: Educational Practice and Theory for Lesbian, Gay, and Bisexual Adolescents*. New York: Routledge.

Uribe, V. (1994), "Project 10: A School-Based Outreach to Gay and Lesbian Youth." *High School Journal*, special edition:109–113.

Uribe, Virginia (1995), "Project 10: A School-based Outreach to Gay and Lesbian Youth." In Geral Unks (Ed.) *The Gay Teen*. Routledge, New York: 203–210.

Vaid, U. (1995), *Virtual Equality: The Mainstreaming of Gay and Lesbian Liberation*. New York: Doubleday.

Valocchi, Steve (1999), "Riding the Crest of a Protest Wave? Collective Action Frames in the Gay Liberation Movement 1969–1973." *Mobilization: An International Journal* 4: 59–73.

Wald, Kenneth D., Butler, James W., and Rienzo, Barbara A. (1996), "The Politics of Gay Rights in American Communities: Explaining Anti-Discrimination Ordinances and Policies." *American Journal of Political Science* 40: 1152–1178.

Wall, Lucas (2003), "Students fight to open doors for gay clubs in area schools; Equal Access law puts districts in all-or-none bind." *The Houston Chronicle*, January 5, 2003, section: A, page 29.

Walling, D.R. (Ed.) (1996), *Open Lives, Safe Schools: Addressing Gay and Lesbian Issues in Education*. Bloomington. In Phi Delta Kappa Educational Foundation.

Ward Biederman, Patricia (1988), "Views Clash on Homosexual Students Program," *Los Angeles Times*, Los Angeles, CA June 24, 1988. Metro Section page 2.

Warner, M. (1991), "Fear of a Queer Planet." *Social Text*, 9 (14): 1–17.

Williams, Rhys H. (1994), "Constructing the Public Good: Social Movements and Cultural Resources." *Social Problems* 42: 124–144.

Woog, D. (1995), *School's Out: The Impact of Gay and Lesbian Issues on America's Schools*. Boston, MA: Alyson.

Workman, Bill (2000), "Atherton Student Shows Savvy in Art of Politics; Gay 18-year-old Extends Activism to a Myriad of Social Injustices," *The San Francisco Chronicle*, May 18, 2000, section: News, page A19.

Wright, Kristi (1998), "Pride Prom: About 120 Gay and Straight Students Gathered in Lincoln Saturday to Dance the Night Away," *The Omaha World-Herald*, May 19, 1998, section: Youth, page 35.

Wuthnow, R. (1988), *The Restructuring of American Religion: Society and Faith Since World War II*. Princeton, NJ: Princeton University Press.

Yang, Alan S. (1997), "Trends in Attitudes toward Homosexuality." *Public Opinion Quarterly* 61, no. 3: 477–507.

Yang, Alan S. (2001), "Lesbian and Gays and the Politics of Knowledge: Rethinking General Models of Mass Opinion Change." In *Sexual Identities, Queer Politics*, Mark Blasius (Ed.), Princeton, NJ: Princeton University Press.

Zald, Mayer N. 1996 "Culture, Ideology, and Strategic Framing." In Doug McAdam, John D. McCarthy, and Mayer N. Zald (Eds.), *Comparative Perspectives on Social Movements*: 261-274. New York: Cambridge University Press.

Zera, D. (1992), "Coming of Age in a Heterosexist World: The Development of Gay and Lesbian Adolescents." *Adolescence*, 27:848–854.

"Among Youths, the Word Is Out," *The Boston Globe*, May 18, 1995, section: editorial page, page 14.

"Homosexuals Allowed Own Columbia Lounge," *New York Times*, September 19, 1972.

Anonymous (1994) "Moral Outrage Fuels Anti-Gay School Protest," *The Los Angeles Times*, Los Angeles, CA. January 9m 1994, View section, part E, pg. 3.

NOTES

INTRODUCTION

1. I refer to this as the GSA movement, as do most of those involved, but the activities and goals of the movement entail more than just establishing these clubs. The movement also strives to prosecute and prevent cases of harassment and abuse, educate schools and communities about the damage done by homophobia, and to get districts and states to include sexual orientation and gender expression to their nondiscrimination policies.
2. Calhoun 1994.
3. Cohen 1982.
4. Melucci 1980.
5. Vaid 1995; Harris 1997.
6. While this very significantly put gay rights groups visibly at the political table, the Clinton administration nonetheless handed many disappointments to them—the disaster of the military's "don't ask don't tell policy" and the passage of the "defense of marriage act."
7. D'Emilio, John (2000) "Cycles of Change, Questions of Strategy: The Gay and Lesbian Movement After Fifty Years." In The Politics of Gay Rights, Craig A. Rimmerman, Kenneth D. Wald, and Cylde Wilcox (eds.) Chicago: University of Chicago Press, page 48.
8. Seidman, Steven (2002) *Beyond the Closet: The Transformation of Gay and Lesbian Life.* New York, NY: Routledge.

CHAPTER ONE

1. I qualify this by noting that this is my account of selected events and my assessment of the significance of these events from the viewpoint of a social researcher. Others may make equally valid, yet different, assessments of the significant historical events in the growth of a GSA social movement.
2. There was, of course, an LGB college student population and presence before this date, but not an overtly visible and political one. Dilley, Patrick (2002). *Queer Man On Campus: A History of Non-Heterosexual College Men,* 1945-2000. New York, New York: Routledge.
3. Detailed and rich historical documentation and analysis of these pioneering LGB rights groups can be found in a variety of texts (i.e. Seidman 1992, D'Emilio 1998, Epstein 1999)

4. Many researchers in a variety of academic field have published books that document and analyze the history of the gay rights movement. Some excellent examples include, D'Emilio 2000, 2002a, 2002b, Seidman 1992, Epstein 1999, Bernstein 1997, Valocchi 1999.

5. Reinhold, Robert (1971) "Campus Homosexuals Organize To Win Community Acceptance." *New York Times*, December 15, 1971.

6. Some examples of these articles: Pace, Eric, "Parley Urges College Facilities For Counseling of Homosexuals," *New York Times*, December 15, 1971. "Homosexuals Allowed Own Columbia Lounge," *New York Times*, September 19, 1972. Kaufman, Michael, "Homosexuals Organize at Universities," *New York Times*, January 28, 1973. Peterson, Iver, "Homosexuals Gain Support on Campus," *New York Times*, June 5, 1974. Roiphe, Anne, "The Trouble at Sarah Lawrence," *New York Times*, March 20, 1977. Hechinger, Grace and Fred Hechinger, "Homosexuality on Campus," *New York Times*, March 12, 1978.

7. Bruske, Ed (1983) "First Amendment Cited; Gays Lose Lawsuit Against GU," *The Washington Post* October 15, 1983, First Section, A1.

8. Hetrick Martin Institute (2002), "The Hetrick-Martin Institute: The Past, Present and Future."http://www.hmi.org/GeneralInfoAndDonations/AboutHMIAndHMHS/default.aspx

9. Hetrick Martin Institute (2002) http://www.hmi.org/Youth/FAQs/default.aspx

10. Martin, A.D. 1982. "Learning to Hide: The Socialization of the Gay Adolescent." *Adolescent Psychiatry*, 10: 52-65. Martin and Hetrick (1988). "The Stigmatization of the Gay and Lesbian Adolescent." *Journal of Homosexuality*, 16: 163-183. Hetrick and Martin (1987). "Developmental Issues and Their Resolution for Gay and Lesbian Adolescents." *Journal of Homosexuality*, 14: 25-43.

11. Project 10 (2004) http://www.project10.org. Uribe, Virginia (1995), "Project 10: A School-based Outreach to Gay and Lesbian Youth." In Geral Unks (Ed.) *The Gay Teen*. Routledge, NY: NY, pp. 203-210.

12. Personal interview with Dr. Virginia Uribe 2004

13. Personal interview with Dr. Virginia Uribe 2004.

14. Herdt, Gilbert and Andrew Boxer (1993). *Children of Horizons: How Gay and Lesbian Teens Are Leading a New Way Out of the Closet*. Boston, MA: Beacon Press.

15. Herdt and Boxer (1993), pp. 77-78.

16. Several books providing journalistic accounts of the strength and courage of LGB youth in the face of stigmatization followed. Due 1995, Hayes 1991, Owens 1998, Chandler 1995, Woog 1995

17. Gibson, Paul (1989). "Gay Male and Lesbian Youth Suicide." In U.S. Department of Health and Human Services, Report of the Secretary's Task Force on Youth Suicide. Washington, DC: U.S. Government Printing Office.

18. Kinsey, Alfred (1948, 1953).

19. Not surprisingly, because of the powerful impact of this report, those who oppose GSAs and LGBT inclusions in public schools dispute the USDHHS report. This will be discussed in greater detail in Chapter 5.

20. Personal Interview with Kevin Jennings, August 2003.

21. Personal interview with Kevin Jennings, August 2003.

22. Personal interview with Priscilla Bonney-Smith, by e-mail, January 2005.

23. I want to thank S. Bear Bergman, one of the founding members of the Concord GSA, for this particularly useful insight about these schools.

24. Perrotti, Jeff and Kim Westheimer (2001). *When the Drama Club is Not Enough: Lessons from the Safe Schools Program for Gay and Lesbian Students.* Boston, MA: Beacon Press.
25. Perrotti, Jeff and Kim Westheimer (2001). *When the Drama Club is Not Enough: Lessons from the Safe Schools Program for Gay and Lesbian Students.* Boston, MA: Beacon Press.
26. http://www.glsen.org/cgi-bin/iowa/all/about/history/index.html
27. Personal interview with Kevin Jennings August 2003. http://www.glsen.org/cgi-bin/iowa/all/about/history/index.html
28. Personal interview with Kevin Jennings August 2003.
29. http://www.safeschoolscoalition.org/about_us.html#OurHistory
30. Personal interview with Beth Reis of the Safe Schools Coalition, 2004
31. Personal interview with Caroyn Laub, executive director of the GSA Network, 2004
32. http://gsanetwork.org/about/index.html
33. Nabozny v. Podlesny 1996; Wagner v. Fayetteville Public Schools 1998; Iverson v. Kent 1998; Vance v. Spencer County Public School District 2000; Lovins v. Pleasant Hill Public School District 2000; O.H. v. Oakland Unified School District, Ray v. Antioch Unified School District 2000; Montgomery v. Independent School District 2000; Putman v. Board of Education of Somerset 2000; Snelling v. Fall Mountain Regional School District 2001; Dahle v. Titusville Area School District 2001; Gay/Straight Alliance Network California v. Visalia Unified School District 2002; Henkle v. Gregory 2002
34. Gay, Lesbian and Straight Education Network & National Center for Lesbian Rights. (2003). Fifteen expensive reasons why safe schools legislation is in your state's best interest. Unpublished report.
35. Cianciotto, J., & Cahill, S. (2003). Education policy: Issues affecting lesbian, gay, bisexual, and transgender youth. New York: The National Gay and Lesbian Task Force Policy Institute.
36. Nabozny v. Podlesney, 92 F.3d 446 (7th Cir. 1996).

CHAPTER TWO

1. e.g., Dennis and Ruth 1986; Hetrick and Martin 1987; Hunter and Schaecher 1987; Martin and Hetrick 1988; Remafedi 1987.
2. e.g., Herdt 1989a; Harbeck 1992, 1994; Cook and Herdt 1991; Herdt and Boxer 1993; DeCresenzo 1994.
3. e.g., Due 1995; Woog 1995; Chandler 1995; Hayes 1991.
4. e.g., Cass 1979, 1984; Lee 1977; Ponse 1978; Schafer 1976; Troiden 1979, 1988, 1989; Weinberg 1978.
5. e.g.,Foucault 1976, 1980, Seidman 1995, 1996, 2002, Bravmann 1996, Irving 1994, Warner 1991.
6. e.g., Hetrick and Martin 1987, Herdt and Boxer 1993, DeCresenzo 1994, Harris 1997, Walling 1996.
7. ibid v.
8. ibid i, ibid ii.
9. Of course, because my sample was non-random, no generalization can be made as to the age range of "sensitization" for the LGBT population as a whole.

10. All names have been changed to protect the anonymity of those I interviewed. I use the sexual identity label that each respondent prefer to use in describing themselves.
11. Seidman (2003) Beyond the Closet. New York: Routledge.
12. e.g., Foucault (1976), Butler 1993; McIntosh 1968; Namaste 1996; Seidman 1994; Gamson 1996; Weeks 1981, 1985.

CHAPTER THREE

1. These are not the actual names of the groups or the high school. All names of people, places, and groups have been changed to protect the anonymity of all participants in this study.
2. The names of the high schools that served as case studies have been changed as have all of the individuals interviewed and quoted throughout the chapter.
3. e.g., Harbeck 1992; Kissen 1997; Jennings 1994; Khatatt 1992.
4. Goodman 1996:13.
5. At the early stages of my research, I had a few brief phone conversations with the superintendent and assistant superintendent of Westville schools. I contacted them in hopes of gaining permission to conduct some observational and interview research at the high school. This request was denied. The reason they gave for disallowing my request was that there were no policies or procedures in place to guide them in granting access to researchers. After refusing my request on these grounds, the assistant to the superintendent made a very strong point of telling me that Pride was not now, and never had been, an officially recognized or sanctioned school club.
6. Mr. Wilson never mentioned the two years he spent dealing with one of my interviewee's complaints of anti-gay abuse and harassment. It seems that his handling of Mike's case was largely informed by these understandings of homosexuality.
7. This is an interesting statement from Mr.Wilson given his knowledge of the severe abuse Mike reported experiencing at Green Valley. I was unable to question Mr.Wilson about this as I had a responsibility to protect Mike's anonymity.
8. This motivation was an important part of Mr. Wilson's support of the group and, later, for his support of adding "sexual orientation" to the sexual harassment policy of the school. Although these actions by principal Wilson were supportive of LGBT students' right to be protected at school, they, in fact, do very little to change the heteronormative culture of the school. As he stated, it does not work to end a heteronormative environment, but rather merely to punish those students who use verbal or physical harassment to enforce it.

CHAPTER FOUR

1. Personal interview with Virginia Uribe, October, 2004.
2. Personal interview with Virginia Uribe, October, 2004.
3. Personal interview with Virginia Uribe, October, 2004.
4. As was illustrated though the case studies presented in Chapter 3, and time and again through my interviews with student leaders and faculty advisors of GSAs a receptive and supportive principal and school board can have a tremendous impact on defusing potential conflict. As will be discussed in more detail later, getting this support from these administrative and public officials has been made easier as the

result of victories in lawsuits brought by students represented by the ACLU and Lambda Legal defense fund. These legal victories set the precedent that it can be costly to not include and protect LGBT students.

5. Personal interview with Virginia Uribe, October 2004
6. Personal interview with Virginia Uribe October 2004
7. Personal interview with Virginia Uribe, October 2004
8. Personal interview with Virginia Uribe, October 2004
9. http://www.project10.org
10. Personal interview with Gail Rolf, October 2004
11. Personal interview with Virginia Uribe, October 2004.
12. Personal Interview with Elizabeth Reis, November 2004.
13. Personal Interview with Elizabeth Reis, November 2004.
14. As was discussed in the previous section, Project 10 had been running support counseling groups for LGBT students in schools in the LA area since 1984, however, these were not student run and lead activity oriented clubs.
15. Personal interview with Kevin Jennings August 2003.
16. Personal interview with Kevin Jennings August 2003.
17. Personal interview with Kevin Jennings August 2003.
18. http://www.glsen.org/cgi-bin/iowa/all/about/history/index.html
19. There is no way of knowing how close this number represents the actual number of GSA clubs in existence at that time, but GLSEN's registry of GSAs was then, and continues to be, the only source available for a count of GSAs.
20. DeBeauvoir, Simone (1952), *The Second Sex*. New York: Knopf.
21. Personal interview with Kevin Jennings, August 2003.
22. I was unable to substantiate this figure or to find an accurate account of the religious leanings of school board members.
23. I chose to focus on the ACLU's Lesbian and Gay Rights project's role in the legal victories for LGBT students, however, Lambda Legal Defense Fund and the National Lesbian Task Force have also played large roles in major lawsuits as well as in educating the public about the legal rights of LGBT students. The choice to cover only one in detail was simply one of space and not wanting to be repetitive.
24. ACLU, 2003. "Summary of School Harassment Lawsuits." http://www.aclu.org/LesbianGayRights/LesbianGay rights.cfm?ID=12879&c=106
25. http://www.aclu.org/getequal/aboutus.html
26. http://www.aclu.org/getequal/scho/alliance.html
27. http://www.aclu.org/getequal/scho/alliance2.html
28. Personal interview with Ken Choes, staff attorney for the ACLU Lesbian and Gay Rights Project, September 2004.
29. Personal interview with Ken Choes, staff attorney for the ACLU Lesbian and Gay Rights Project, September 2004.
30. Personal interview with Ken Choes, staff attorney for the ACLU Lesbian and Gay Rights Project, September 2004.
31. These factors, along with race, ethnicity and socioeconomic factors will be explored in detail in chapter 7.
32. Personal interview with Carolyn Laub, founder and executive director of the Gay–Straight Alliance Network, October 2004.
33. Personal interview with Carolyn Laub, October 2004.
34. Personal interview with Carolyn Laub, October 2004.
35. Personal interview with Carolyn Laub October 2004.
36. Personal interview with Carolyn Laub, October 2004.

CHAPTER 5

1. Linda Harvey (2004) "How We Got Here" http://www.missionamerica.com
2. http//:www.missionamerica.com
3. Blumer, Herbert. 1971. "Social Problems as Collective Behavior." *Social Problems*, 18:298–306.
4. Haines 1979.
5. Tarrow 1994, Mottl 1980, Lo 1982.
6. Meyer and Staggenborg (1996)
7. Tarrow (1994)
8. Billings and Scott 1994: 178.
9. Some good examples of this research: Bromley and Shupe 1984, Bruce 1994, Diamond 1989, 1995, Hunter 1991, Jorstad 1987, Leibman and Wuthnow 1983, Lienesch 1993, Moen 1992, 1994, Rozell and Wilcox 1996, Wald 1991, Wilcox 1992, 1996, Martin 1996
10. Herman, Didi, 1997, 2000, Lugg 2000
11. Herman, Didi 1997, 2000
12. Meyer and Staggenborg, 1996, 1632.
13. For some good examples of this research: Herman, Didi 1997, Hunter 1991, Gallager, John and Chris Bull 1996, Linneman, Thomas 2003, McGillivary, Ian 2004
14. Personal interview with Beth Reis co-chair of Safe Schools Coalition, October 2004.
15. McAdam, McCarthy, and Zald 1996: 6.
16. Zald 1996,Williams 1995.
17. Snow and Benford 1992.
18. Gamson 1988.
19. Zald 1996: 267.
20. Tarrow 1992.
21. Benford and Snow 2000: 617.
22. Snow and Benford 1992, Tarrow 1992, Williams 1995, and Meyer and Staggenborg 1996.
23. Meyer and Staggenborg, 1996: 1639.
24. GLSEN 1997: 352.
25. Coltrane and Hickman 1992.
26. Best 1987, 1989; Johnson 1989.
27. (Jenness 1995) Coltrane and Hickman (1992)
28. AFA Journal, May 2001 http://www.afa.net/journal/may/cover.asp
29. Fey 2003, 1.
30. Sprigg 2004: 2.
31. Page 1996: 4.
32. P.E.R.S.O.N. Project, http://www.personproject.org
33. Calhoun 1994, Wiley 1994, Cohen 1982, Melucci 1980.
34. Goffman, Erving 1963
35. Project 10 handbook: vi.
36. Project 10 handbook: 6.
37. GLSEN 1997:321.
38. Sprigg 2004: 2.
39. Patton 1995: 217.
40. Patton 1995: 233.
41. GLSEN 1997.

42. In their study on the politics of gay rights, Haider-Markel and Meir (1996) found that, "morality politics issues are highly salient with little need to acquire any information (technical or otherwise) to participate in the debate. Everyone is an expert on morality. The combination of high salience and low information structures the nature of the politics involved" (P. 333).
43. Martin 1996: 347.
44. Martin 1996: 347.
45. FRC FAQ 1997.

CHAPTER SIX

1. Mann, Judy (2000) "Where Homophobia Does the Most Harm," *The Washington Post*, Washington, D.C.: March 1, 2000. Pg. C 15
2. The "day of silence" is a day in which students and faculty who wish to participate restrict themselves for speaking to illustrate how LGBT people are often silenced by having to be in the closet. GLSEN, the ACLU, PFLAG, the GSA Network, and other groups have produced literature and helped students coordinate their efforts to use the day of silence to successfully educate their schools.
3. Ordona, Michael (2004) "Gay and straight students aim to make hallways safer" *Los Angeles Times*, Los Angeles, CA: August 3, 2004. Pg. E.1.
4. Foucault (1976), 1980 Yang (2001), Seidman, 1992, Epstein 1999, D'Emilio 2002b, Valocchi 1999
5. Yang (2001)
6. Mills, C. Wright (1956). *The Power Elite*. New York: Oxford University Press.
7. Yang (2001)
8. Gamson, et al. 1992, page 373.
9. Gamson, et al. 1992, page 373.
10. Yang (2001)
11. Connolly 1993.
12. Yang (2001) notes that once the APA changed its position on homosexuality in 1973, the media changed the way it framed stories—from deviance and disease to civil rights. This underscores just how dependent the media is on subject-matter specialists and experts in framing and reporting the news. Gay activists had been making this change and argument before, but it wasn't until they managed to influence the experts, convince them to reconsider their official stance that the media took notice and gave credibility to their position.
13. Loftus (2001), Burstein (1998), Farley (1997)
14. Connolly (1993), Gamson (1992), Yang (2001), Zaller (1992)
15. Importantly, this national public opinion research does not include examination of opinion about bisexual or transgender individuals
16. Yang (1997), Loftus (2001), Brooks (2000), Kite and Bernard (1996), Herek (1988), LaMar and Kite (1998), Pratte (1993), Seltzer (1993), Dejowski (1992)
17. Yang (1997), Yang (2001), Epstein (1999), Loftus (2001), Brooks (2000), Kite and Bernard (1996), Herek (1988), LaMar and Kite (1998), Pratte (1993), Seltzer (1993), Dejowski (1992)
18. According to Loftus' (2001) examination of GSS data, in 1972 13% of the population believed that homosexuality was "not wrong at all," while 71% stated that they believed homosexuality was "always wrong." In 1987 the percentage that believed it

was not wrong at all remained the same, but the negative opinion that it was "always wrong" increased to its highest point of 75%. By 1998, the opinion about the morality of homosexuality had become decidedly more favorable, although the majority of people still feel that it is morally wrong—56% reporting that they believed it was "always wrong" and 31% stating that they felt it was "not wrong at all."

19. For example, in Loftus' (2001) study, the trend in attitude change about the civil rights of gay and lesbian people becomes increasingly positive steadily from 1973 to 1998 and each year more people were against the restriction of civil liberties for homosexuals than in favor of it (with a slight dip in this upward trend 1985 to 1988). In 1973, 30% of Americans favored restricting the civil liberties of homosexuals while 39% were opposed to such restrictions, by 1998 the numbers were 12% in favor of restrictions and 65% opposed.

20. Brooks (2000)

21. Loftus 2001,764

22. Loftus 2001

23. The General Social Survey is the instrument most researchers use to study national trends in opinion about homosexuality because it is the only national survey that has consistently asked the same questions to solicit opinion on the topic.

24. Loftus 2001: 778

25. Herek and Capitanio 1995

26. Gamson et al. (1992) summarize the situation this way: A cultural level analysis tells us that our political world is framed, that reported events are pre-organized and do not come to us in raw form. But we are active processors and however encoded our received reality we may decode it in different ways. The very vulnerability of the framing process makes it a locus of potential struggle, not a leaden reality to which we all inevitably must yield (384).

27. As Gamson et al. (1992) argue, social movements "read their success or failure by how well their preferred meanings and interpretation are doing in various media arenas. Prominence in these arenas is taken as an outcome measure in its own right, independent of evidence on the degree to which the messages are being read by the public." (385).

28. Yang 2001: 346

29. Yang 2001:355

30. Ward Biederman, Patricia (1988) "Views Clash on Homosexual Students Program," *Los Angeles Times*, Los Angeles, CA June 24, 1988. Metro Section page 2.

31. Davis, Mark (1998) "Courage of gay speakers was the real story" Times Publishing Company St. Pertersburg Times (Florida) May 3, 1998, Sunday Section: Neighborhood times; letters; pg. 2

32. Ritter, John (2000) "Judge Lets Club Meet at School." USA Today, February 7, 2000, section: News, page 4A.

33. Ritter, John (2000) "High School Clubs: Gay Students Stake Their Ground." USA Today, January 18, 2000, section: News, page 1A.

34. Brulliard, Karin (2003). "Texas Students Sue to Organize Gay Club at High School." The Washington Post, October 21, 2003, section: A, page 3.

35. Iles, Trey (2004) "Gay/Straight club disturbs parents; School Board urged to scrap new group." The Times-Picayune, New Orleans, March 11, 2004, section: Metro, page 1

36. Brulliard, Karin (2003). "Texas Students Sue to Organize Gay Club at High School." The Washington Post, October 21, 2003, section: A, page 3.

37. Iles, Trey (2004) School Club Sparks Dispute: Gay Students Meet Opposition." The Times Picayune, New Orleans, March 28, 2004, section: Metro, page 1.

38. Wall, Lucas (2003) "Students fight to open doors for gay clubs in area schools; Equal Access law puts districts in all-or-none bind." The Houston Chronicle, January 5, 2003, section: A, page 29.

39. Anonymous (1994) "Moral Outrage Fuels Anti-Gay School Protest," *The Los Angeles Times*, Los Angeles, CA. January 9m 1994, View section, part E, pg. 3.

40. CDC-NCHSTP-Divisions of HIV/AIDDS Prevention, retrieved January 3, 2005 Fact Sheet—Young People at Risk: HIV/AIDS Among America's Youth http://www.cdc.gov/hiv/pubs/facts/youth.htm ASHA Facts and Answers About STDs: STD Statistics, http://www.ashastd.org/stdfaqs/statistics.html

41. This type of argument has only once been tested in a court of law. In 2001 a federal appeals court in Philadelphia ruled that the anti-harassment policy of the State College Area School district was too broad and punished students severely for name calling and teasing that did not rise to the level of harassment. Even the ACLU consented that this one specific school district policy was overly restrictive of students' free speech. The ACLU advises that such anti-harassment policies "must draw the distinction between harassment and student expression that is protected by law. Harassment is conduct that substantially interferes with the education or physical or mental health of a student, or that threatens or intimidates a student. By punishing only these types of conduct, a school strikes the proper balance between two equally important and entirely compatible constitutional rights" (http://www.aclu.org/LesbianGayRights/LesbianGayRights.cfm?ID=12901&c=106). No other case has even found a school's anti-harassment policy to be in violation of the right to free speech. However, as discussed elsewhere, multiple lawsuits have been filed and won against schools for failure to protect LGBT students from harassment.

42. Davis, Mark (1998) "Courage of Gay Speakers Was the Real Story" Times Publishing Company *St. Pertersburg Times* (Florida) May 3, 1998, Sunday Section: Neighborhood Times; letters; pg. 2

43. O'Sullivan, Eileen (1998) Courage of Gay Speakers Was the Real Story" Times Publishing Company *St. Petersburg Times* (Florida) May 3, 1998, Sunday Section: Neighborhood Times; letters; pg. 2

44. Kelley, Lizbeth (2003) "Gay-Straight Alliance Follows Golden Rule," *The Columbus Dispatch*, October 30, 2003. Home Final Edition, Editorial and Comment; Letters to the Editor, pg. 08A.

CHAPTER SEVEN

1. Daly, Gavin (1995) "Students Rally for Gay/Straight March," The Boston Globe May 21, 1995, section: Metro/Region, page 34.

2. Beckham, Lauren (1997), "Diversity Unites: Gay, Straight Students Find Alliance Supportive," Boston Herald, May 5, 1997, section: News, page 18.

3. Wright, Kristi (1998), "Pride Prom: About 120 Gay and Straight Students Gathered in Lincoln Saturday to Dance the Night Away," The Omaha World-Herald, May 19, 1998, section: Youth, page 35.

4. Tubbs, Sharon (1998), "Students Hope to Inspire Tolerance," St. Petersburg Times, February 8, 1998, section: Seminole Times, page 1.

5. Rohde, Marie (1999), "Students Stand Up for Their Beliefs, Form Group to Combat Homophobia," Milwaukee Journal Sentinel, April 14,1999, section: News North, page 7.
6. Workman, Bill (2000), "Atherton Student Shows Savvy in Art of Politics; Gay 18-year-old Extends Activism to a Myriad of Social Injustices," The San Francisco Chronicle, May 18, 2000, section: News, page A19.
7. Pemberton-Butler, Lisa (2000), "A Safe Place for Gays or Straights: Tacoma Teens Carry Diversity to Another Level," Seattle Times, October 16 2000, section: South, page B1.
8. Ritter, John (2000), "High School Clubs, Gay Students Stake Their Ground," USA Today, January 18, 2000, section: News, page 1A.
9. "Kim, Ahan (2001), Gay–straight Group Bursting with Pride, Ready for Parade," The Atlanta Journal and Constitution, June 21, 2001, section: DeKalb Extra, page 13A.
10. Heredia, Christopher (2001), "Gay Students Demand Schools Recognize Law, State's Districts Slow to End Harassment," The San Francisco Chronicle, June 3, 2001, section: News, page A24.
11. Rummler, Gary (2001), "Peace Prize: Student Makes Mark on School, Hernandez Honored for Work on Alliance at Riverside," Milwaukee Journal Sentinel, June 27, 2001, section: News, page 6B.
12. Cooper, Tony (2002), "Rights Group Honors Queer Youth Action Team," The San Francisco Chronicle, July 26, 2002, section: Contra Costa, page 2.
13. Nissman, Cara (2003), "Safety in Numbers: As Gay–Straight Alliances Grow, So Does Acceptance in Schools," The Boston Herald, April 7, 2003, section: Arts and Life, page 30.
14. Hughes, Jim (2003), "Teens Sue in Favor of Gay/Straight Alliance, Springs District Forbids Meeting at Palmer High," The Denver Post, December 14, 2003, section: A Section, page A-29.
15. Jonsson, Greg (2003), "Students Unite Against Harassment of Gays," St. Louis Post-Dispatch, February 27, 2003, section: Metro, page B1.
16. Daly, Gavin (1995) "Students Rally for Gay/Straight March," The Boston Globe May 21, 1995, section: Metro/Region, page 34.
17. "Among youths, the word is out," The Boston Globe, May 18, 1995, section: editorial page, page 14.
18. Beckham, Lauren (1997), "Diversity Unites: Gay, Straight Students Find Alliance Supportive," Boston Herald, May 5, 1997, section: News, page 18.
19. Beckham, Lauren (1997), "Diversity Unites: Gay, Straight Students Find Alliance Supportive," Boston Herald, May 5, 1997, section: News, page 18.
20. Workman, Bill (2000), "Atherton Student Shows Savvy in Art of Politics; Gay 18-year-old Extends Activism to a Myriad of Social Injustices," The San Francisco Chronicle, May 18, 2000, section: News, page A19.
21. Jan, Tracy (2004), "Students Want 'Sexual Identity' in Policy," The Oregonian, February 11, 2004, section: East zoner, page D2.
22. Fetner, Tina and Kristin Kush (2003), "Gay–straight Alliances in High Schools: An Emerging Form of LGBTQ Youth Activism." Unpublished paper presented at the American Sociological Association Annual Meeting, August 2004.
23. This variable was measured by the percent of the student body receiving free or reduced lunch.

24. This variable was measured by a school's location in an urban, suburban, town, or rural setting, with urban being closest to LGBT organizational supports and rural being the least.
25. Fetner and Kush (2003) page 11.
26 This variable was measured by the percent of the student body receiving free or reduced lunch, because budget information is not available in the data set.
27. Fetner and Kush (2003) page 15-16.
28. These numbers were gathered in July of 2004.
29. This count was acquired from the GSA network of California in January of 2005.
30. The state of Illinois passed a statewide nondiscrimination policy that includes sexual orientation in January of 2005. While this policy change was made after these rates of GSAs were measured, it is certainly significant to note that the political environment that fostered the passage of this state policy in 2005 very well may have influenced the relatively large number of GSAs prior to that date. It will be interesting to see if the passage of this policy will correspond with an marked increase in the number of GSAs in the state in the coming years.
31. Jennings (1994), Rofes (1989). Harbeck (1994), Kissen (1996)
32. Getting a representative sample of this group of students is incredibly difficult as there is no listing of all the LGBT students is a single school, let alone the entire country. The only real way to access groups of these youth is to go through various LGBT community or political organizations, which causes samples to seriously over-represent out and politically active youth. GLSEN tries to partially address this sampling problem by making its survey available on line for any students to access themselves, removed from a connection to a physical LGBT group. Of course, the students who would know about this Internet survey are still more likely to be connected in some way to a LGBT organization. The researchers at GLSEN acknowledge this sampling concern in the methodology section of the report itself, however it is not discussed explicitly in press releases they send out to news organizations.
33. GLSEN (2003), "The 2003 National School Climate Survey," http://www.glsen.org
34. GLSEN (2003), "The 2003 National School Climate Survey," page 4. http://www.glsen.org
35. GLSEN (2003), "The 2003 National School Climate Survey," page 5. http://www.glsen.org
36. The only other studies that exist are small ethnographic studies one or a few schools with a GSA. Most of these were written as a master's thesis in education or social work, and a few as doctoral dissertations in sociology. None have been published as books or refereed academic journals.
37. Fetner, Tina and Kristin Kush (2003), "Gay–straight Alliances in High Schools: An Emerging Form of LGBTQ Youth Activism." Unpublished paper presented at the American Sociological Association Annual Meeting, August 2004.
38. Personal interview with Carolyn Laub, October 2004
39. Personal interview with Calolyn Laub, October 2004.

CHAPTER EIGHT

1. Morris, Aldon and Cedric Morris (1996).

INDEX